Voltaire's Bastards — the Dictatorship of
reason in the West
John Ralston Saul Penguin

The Scottish 100 — history's most
influential Scots Duncan A Bruce
Carroll + Graf

A DISTANT FEAST

CW00685195

A DISTANT FEAST

THE ORIGINS OF
NEW ZEALAND'S CUISINE

Tony Simpson

GODWIT

To Derek and the others, who have fed me for longer, more regularly, and to a consistently higher standard, than anyone except myself.

A GODWIT BOOK
published by
Random House New Zealand
18 Poland Road, Glenfield, Auckland, New Zealand

First published 1999

ISBN 1 86962 037 2

Design: Christine Hansen
Illustrations: Christine Ross
Cover illustration: 'Picnic at Woodhaugh', date and artist unknown,
reproduced courtesy of the Otago Settlers' Museum
Printed in Hong Kong

CONTENTS

INTRODUCTION

ABOUT 20 YEARS AGO two important things happened in my life which have largely determined its pattern since, although I was almost completely oblivious of this at the time. In 1980 I returned to Wellington from living for some years in England. And that same year, after 14 years of marriage, I became sole housekeeper for myself and my 10-year-old son. From these two beginnings I can trace an interest in food and cooking which has grown to be central to my daily concerns.

Living in England and travelling in Europe had introduced me to a cultural tradition, particularly that of France and Italy, which located the social activities associated with eating at the centre of life. To those used to the notoriously bad cooking of England this may seem curious, but there has always existed a tradition of fine eating in Britain alongside the habit of eating overboiled cabbage and rubbery fish to which English suburban domestic and institutional living seems regrettably prone. In the post-war and rationing periods this alternative tradition found expression initially, and interestingly, in a movement on the political left,[1] and was ever after associated with the food writing of Elizabeth David and Raymond Postgate. This sought to improve both the diet and the daily eating habits of the English. To Elizabeth David we owe not only an acknowledgement of the existence and the desirability of emulating the great food traditions of France and Italy, but also the rescue from popular oblivion of an English food tradition as rich and varied as its European comparitors. To Postgate, although less well known, we owe both the annual publication from 1951 to the present of *The Good Food Guide*, a register of restaurants which serve food worth eating (and emulated since in many countries), and much other writing on the desirability of everyone eating well, not just the wealthy.[2] As far as Postgate was concerned, fine eating had been the prerogative of the English ruling class for too long. Nowhere was it written that to be working class meant to eat like a pig, and he made it his business to change English eating habits within a generation.

It is the mark of the success of both Postgate and David that, while they may not have changed the predilection of many of their fellow citizens for dreadful food, nor stemmed the tide running strongly towards industrially based mass catering and fast-food chains, they contributed to the creation of a lively food culture of excellence and good eating not only in the home but also in the restaurants and pubs, the enjoyment of which has become one of the central features of my regular visits to Britain.

The French and Italians, to the extent that they were aware of these developments, and who had known all along about the desirability of such a cultural tradition, no doubt shrugged off once more the impossibility of understanding the cold and hypocritical English, and their incomprehensible liking for England and its impossible weather, and went about the business of enjoying their daily living as usual.

For myself, I grew used to eating out regularly and well, and faced my imminent return to culinary New Zealand with dread and foreboding. Prior to my departure for Europe, New Zealand had not been a mecca for gourmets. My experience of the return home, in that regard at least, immediately confounded me. In the space of a few short years, New Zealand had ceased to be the virtually restaurant-less food wilderness of my recollection, and we had become instead a nation of diners-out. Since that time, it has become possible to eat well in even the remotest places. I am sure that the good citizens of Hokitika will forgive me my lack of faith if I say that about six years ago I had occasion to visit their city and to stay overnight. With fear and trembling I enquired of my hosts where it was proposed we should eat. To my astonishment I was taken to one of the best restaurants in which it has ever been my pleasure to dine.

Of course, we too have not escaped from that parallel phenomenon, the fast-food chain, inseparable cultural harbinger of the globalised economy. But our awareness of the availability of an alternative tradition fits us well to deal with its nastier manifestations and ramifications. In a land almost literally flowing with milk and honey, and in which the ingredients of a potentially great cuisine are freshly ready to hand, we have no excuse for not developing one. This much my sojourn in England had taught me.

The question of living with a 10-year-old son was rather more prosaic, less grand and more problematic. Growing boys (as well as their fathers) need feeding. Not only that but they grow bigger every day until, as adolescents, they eat everything in sight. Feeding the brute became an imperative daily task. This was, in theory, not a problem. Of course I could cook. What male of my generation ever thought otherwise, particularly those who were called upon to do so seldom or never? But in my case it was true. My granny, who lived with us off and on for extended periods when I was a child, had seen to that, and I had picked up the rudiments almost unawares. This was unusual in young men of my generation. (It also had unexpected consequences, not the least of which was to make those of us who could cook popular as student flatmates among males who could not. It also meant we did *all* the cooking, so often decamped to live as the only male in a flat of women. This suited both parties. It scared off wandering and unwanted males, and obliged us to cook only once or twice a week instead of every day.)

But those skills were long behind me, and I had to begin again. I therefore did what any sensible person would do in those circumstances. I purchased copies of *Food for Flatters* (the indispensable guide for young people living alone for the first time on how to cook simply, cheaply and well), and the *Edmonds Cookery Book*, and began.[3] So far, so good. My son, the main object of this exercise, ate what I prepared, sometimes more enthusiastically than others, flourished and grew larger. I must, I decided, be doing something right.

But it had not escaped my attention that the works of Elizabeth David, and of a host of other food writers of whom I then knew nothing, were also available in the food section of my bookshop. On the principle that if one is going to do something properly one had better be well informed, I began to purchase and read these books. I was instantly hooked by the discovery that English food had a rich social history. As a putative social historian, that was right up my alley. Not only that, but this was a tradition that we had presumably inherited from the English immigrants who had made their home here. Thinking back to the food of my childhood I could see that was true in some ways, but not in others. I filed this thought away for future reference.

As I read on, I made a further interesting discovery. All over the world people were doing what I was doing and exploring their available gastronomic options. Some of this activity was esoteric indeed. It led me, for instance, to a culture of journals and magazines, and particularly to *Petits Propos Culinaires*, possibly one of the most curious and delightful of all food publications.[4] It also introduced me to the scholarly world of the international food symposia and their published proceedings, the most famous of which is conducted annually under the auspices of Oxford University, and which flourish in many and diverse places, including Australia and now to some extent in this country. All over the world, scholars were puzzling over the problems associated with the relationship between food and culture.

This was not a new phenomenon, nor was its investigation a new development. These explorations had been going on since the decade immediately after the Second World War as serious scholars and commentators on social change became aware of what was happening in their wider world. Thus David Riesman wrote in 1950:

> Earlier there had existed a small coterie of gourmets; fastidious enjoyment of food was one hobby, among others, that inner-directed people might choose. Today in wide circles many people are and many more feel that they must be gourmets. The abundance of America in the phase of incipient population decline is perhaps the most important factor in this development; it has made the good foods available to nearly everybody; the seasonal and geographic limitations that in the earlier period narrowed food variations for all but the very rich have now been largely done away with by the network of distribution and the techniques of preserving food — both being legacies from the phase of transitional population growth. The consumer's choice among foods need, therefore, no longer be made on the basis either of tradition or of Malthusian limits.[5]

And one of the subjects which has perennially interested this growing army of scholars of food and its relationship to culture has been the changes which have occurred to food traditions as they have spread across the world and, conversely, as new ingredients (the most famous European examples are the tomato and the potato) have made their mark on those traditions which knew nothing of them previously.[6] Cultural change happens in the world of food both in the short and the longer term, and the reasons why can be fascinating.

As usually occurs when scholars get their hands on things, a number of theories have grown up about what these changes amount to. Much of the interest centres on colonial societies, and for obvious reasons was initially focused on the eastern seaboard of the United States. When food historians began exploring the origins of the traditional dishes of that region, their work at first amounted to little more than miscellaneous collections of recipes with tentative observations included. But as they grew in confidence they began to draw firmer and broader conclusions. Some of these were more directly technical, and dealt with such matters as the development of food preparation and cooking techniques and their technologies. But other writers explored the cultural implications of change in food habits more generally, increasingly on the basis of contemporary manuscript sources.[7] They also began to cast their net wider. Explorations of the colonial cuisines of the West Indies, of South and Central America, of Asia[8] and of Australia[9] began to put in an appearance. Eventually this fed back into the metropolitan society itself as British scholars explored the other end of the food chain, that is, the effects of this on the cuisine of the colonisers.[10] The Italians and French were hard at work exploring similar territory in tandem with their British counterparts.

As this trickle of scholarship turned into a stream and then a flood, a broad consensus began to develop. There have been three distinct phases in this process. In the wake of Columbus, European expansion was accompanied by increasing exchanges of populations and foods. Then, with the industrial revolution, and the increased opportunities this brought for both colonial and trade expansion, the globalised world food economy immensely accelerated and concentrated this process. Finally, after the Second World War, and as the colonial empires crumbled, reverse waves of immigration to the metropolitan societies brought new influences to bear on the cuisines of those cultures.[11] The upshot has been what one food sociologist has called 'a world cuisine'.[12]

Within this broad framework there has been a continuing debate about the meaning and significance of this development. Has it, for instance, been an enrichment or an impoverishment of the food habits of ordinary people? Has it destroyed more than it has created? Or has it meant the opening of new chapters and vistas in the eating patterns of humankind? These questions have taken on new urgency with the development of international industrialised mass cuisines, and the growing possibility of applying the techniques of genetic engineering to the things we daily put in our mouths.[13]

Notwithstanding, it is important to remark that most of those affected by these developments have continued to eat their way through two and three meals a day entirely oblivious to the debate, pleased only that the variety, abundance and quality of what they eat now is much better than it was in the past, and certainly much better than the food available to their ancestors. If they have thought about it at all, they probably ask: why the fuss; what does it matter?

In point of fact it matters a great deal to the sense of identity which is at the core of human autonomy. Food is important to this sense. When people move from place to place they take that identity with them, and they adapt both the food they eat, and through that, the identity itself, to their new circumstances. The Swedish food ethnologist Beatriz Borda expresses this thought very elegantly in the following passage:

> The place of food in everyday life is both taken for granted and imbued with cultural, social, and personal significance. Everyone must eat, usually several times a day, and this situation leads to highly patterned and regularised behaviour. Indeed, most human life is similarly patterned and repetitive, otherwise everyday life would be lost in details. But the biological need for food and the social act of eating combine to give food patterns a particular meaning, a kind of cultural power . . . It has often been contended that food preferences depend on what is accessible in the environment or what is possible in the technological and economic circumstances, but [studies show] that the way we eat depends as much on what the culture permits and on what the culture insists is appropriate. In this context the concept of culture as a tool for identity maintenance and classification of the social world raises many interesting questions.[14]

And so I found it. My developing awareness of the cultural and intellectual debates around changing food and eating patterns reminded me of the question which I had put away for future reference. Where does New Zealand, an immigrant society *par excellence*, stand in relation to these cultural explorations? This question was particularly focused by some work I was doing which entailed reading the numerous first-hand accounts of emigrants (largely from Britain) to New Zealand in the nineteenth century.[15] These accounts were full of talk about food and drink, interwoven with recipes. The subject seems almost to have been an obsession with our forebears; certainly it was central to their concerns. We have not stopped publishing cookery and recipe books since. What, I wondered, did this tell us about the society and culture which developed from this experience?

But when I turned to the bibliographies to track the relevant cultural analyses, I found very little. Some interesting original work had been done by Helen Leach and her colleagues, some of it under the auspices of Otago University, long the intellectual centre of nutritional and domestic studies in New Zealand.[16] There was one extant attempt that I could find which set out to discover a pattern in our culinary history.[17] And that was all.

Obviously here was an important gap waiting to be filled, and what follows is an attempt to kick-start the process of exploring the origins of New Zealand's food culture. Those origins are to be found, of course, in the long tradition of European, and particularly English and Scottish, food which our forebears brought here with them, and which culminated in the rural kitchens of the eighteenth century, one of the important transition periods of the English culinary tradition. This was the cuisine which our forebears attempted to recreate when they came to New Zealand in the last century, although it took a particular form. But the eighteenth century was also a time of significant famine and want, and it was the responses to this crisis which drove literally millions of emigrants from Britain to all the corners of the earth during the century which followed. This same crisis also stimulated the technical innovations and the global agricultural economy which have had such a formative influence on the development of our food tradition.

The social circumstances from which our ancestors largely came were likewise significant influences. Particularly in rural Britain, the contrasts of plenty and want could barely have been more extreme, with some people living exceptionally well and others, living almost cheek by jowl with them, living badly to the point of starvation and from time to time beyond it. For many people, the experience of adequate eating began on the emigrant ship. For those in the steerage, this was often their first chance to see at close quarters the contrast between what they were given to eat — adequate but basic or even rough fare — and what the first-class passengers had to eat in the cabin. Many steerage passengers appear to have drawn an important conclusion from this. In their new country one of the things which was going to be different was that they were going to eat better.

But when they arrived they had first to accustom themselves to the existence of another culture with its own quite distinct food traditions and techniques. They had also to adapt to a topsy-turvy world in which the seasons were all widdershins, the climate was much milder (at least in the north of the country), Christmas was in summer, the harvest was in March, and their traditional calendar of festivals, hallowed by centuries of European agricultural life, was meaningless as a result. Nor were many of the ingredients which they took for granted readily to hand. Where was the Michaelmas goose? And what was the point of an autumn harvest celebration in what was now spring?

As if this was not enough, important culinary innovations were coming thick and fast. These included the cookbook as we now know it, the coal-burning stove, and a host of new foods, additives and preserving techniques. These all had to be incorporated into a social life which likewise had to be invented for a new country, and which made food and entertaining one of its central features. Faced with such a daunting task, it is no wonder that so many turned to the demon rum, and spawned not only one of the world's most vigorous prohibition movements but also some of the first vineyards outside Europe.

Somehow, the invention of a new way of life, including new food ways, was achieved. We are the people we are today as a result. In the chapters that follow, this process will be traced from a number of roots. From the tradition in food and cooking produced by two millennia of European and particularly British culture, and its culmination in one of the world's great cuisines in eighteenth-century England; from the nineteenth-century experience of poverty and plenty, and the impetus that provided to emigrate; from the experience of emigration itself, and survival in the new land; through the new technologies of the kitchen and hearth, and, by the way, the internationalisation of food production and supply. The journey is a strange one but will, I hope, deliver to you the same sense of discovery which it gave to me. It is certainly a journey worth making, especially as the path is so little explored — surprisingly, in a field so central to all that we are, have become as a people, and partake in every day of our lives.

1

THE LONG TRADITION

THE NINETEENTH CENTURY was the great age of European transition. In almost nothing is this so much the case as in the matter of food. Someone from the later twentieth century suddenly set down in the Europe of the Roman Empire would find very little familiar in the food they were offered. But while someone from the eighteenth century might not feel entirely at home at a Roman table, they would recognise a great deal.

This is not quite as odd as it seems. From the dawn of human civilisation (if not before), human beings had lived in a symbiosis with nature, characterised above all else by an annual agricultural cycle: the preparation of the soil, planting and sowing, watering and tending, reaping and storage. Parallel to this agricultural round was an animal husbandry with its origins similarly buried in the mists of time. Cycles of birth, growth, pasturage and slaughter were also among the primary realities of those of our forebears who lived rural lives, and most of them did. The relationship this creates between food and the seasons is so obvious as almost to go without saying. This did not stop people from not just saying but celebrating it from the earliest times as well. Thus the best known of all classical European culinary bibliographers, Athenaeus, citing the earlier Ananius:

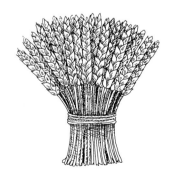

> In spring the meagre [fresh, new-sprouting vegetables] is best; the *anthias* [fish, species unknown] in winter, but the best of all the fine dishes is shrimp in a fig leaf. It is sweet to eat the nanny-goat's meat in the autumn, and the porker when harvesters turn and tread; then is the season for dogs and hares and foxes. Mutton's season is when it is summer and the crickets

Baian Seafood Stew

The Romans used a number of sauces and other ingredients for which we have no precise equivalents, but substitutes are available: kombu, for example, for something called 'sea nettles'. This recipe is from Apicius, *The Roman Art of Cookery* (possibly the most famous cookery book of all classical antiquity), but adapted by Michelle Berriedale-Johnson for her *British Museum Cookbook*. It is notable among Roman recipes for containing neither defructum (wine boiled with honey) nor liquamen (a strong fish sauce rather like anchovy sauce, as far as one can tell). Baia was a luxury seaside resort near Naples.

2 tbsp olive oil
a stick of young celery, chopped
½ tsp ground cumin and 1 tbsp fresh
  coriander
10 g kombu, chopped small
a sprig of fresh rue
300 ml white wine
1 kg fresh mussels
2 dozen scallops
500 g firm white fish, cut into morsels
25 g pine nuts
water, salt and pepper

Heat the oil and fry the celery gently with the cumin, coriander and kombu, then add the rue and wine and a few grindings of pepper. Simmer for a few minutes and add the white fish, mussels and scallops with about 500 ml of water. Add salt to taste and the pine nuts and serve before the shellfish toughen (no more than a couple of minutes).

chirp, and there is tunny from the sea, no bad food, but excelling all other fish when served in *myttotos* [a sauce of garlic, leeks, cheese, olive oil, honey and possibly eggs]. The fatted ox I think is good to eat at midnight and in the day time.[1]

Our putative eighteenth-century visitors' familiarity with the food of the Roman Empire would solely and simply reflect the fact that over two millennia the great majority of the people of Europe lived in a form of subsistence agricultural community which did not change much in its essence.

BETWEEN SICKLE AND SCYTHE

This created a culture in which the seasons, the work, the religion and the celebrations were fused in a single whole. In the seventeenth century a Yorkshire farmer, Henry Best, wrote up and reviewed his year's work.[2] Everything he did he measured by the festivals of his church. Ideally, lambs should be conceived at about Michaelmas so that they were born before Candlemas; he should aim to finish his ploughing before Andrewmas; his hay fields should not be grazed for more than a fortnight following Lady Day, which was also the day on which annual ground rents were paid. According to the sixteenth-century writer Thomas Tusser, lambs were best weaned between St Phillip and St James, and all wheat should be sown before Hallowmas Eve. These writers, and their readers, knew without having to be told what times of the year and what periods these festivals betokened. This pattern had been noted centuries before. As long ago as classical antiquity, Aristotle remarked upon the fact that all of the great Greek festivals occurred after the harvest, when there was most leisure.

The relationship between Easter and spring needs no explication for those who have lived through a northern hemisphere winter and know the countryside at that season. Feasting at Christmas when the winter weather has driven the whole populace indoors near the fire also makes sense. Thomas Tusser goes on to say: 'At Hallowmas (1 November) slaughter time soon cometh in/ And then doth the husbandman's feasting begin/ From that time to Candlemas (2 February) weekly kill some/ Their offal for household the better shall come.'[3]

Magic ceremonies grew up alongside this agriculture, and persisted well into the eighteenth century to ensure that all of the circumstances beyond the control of the farmer — the fertility of land, the weather, the protection of major capital investment such as farm animals from murrains — were the subject of precautions. These make little sense to us, but in ages which believed in sympathetic magic they were pre-eminently sensible. As one major historian of such practices remarks:

> There were all the traditional fertility rites and seasonal observances: Plough Monday to ensure the growth of corn; wassailing to bless the apple trees; Rogation processions and Midsummer fires for the crops; corn dollies at harvest time . . . In the absence of weed killers, there were charms to keep weeds out of the corn, and in place of insecticide and rat-killers, magical formulae to keep away pests. There were charms to increase the land's fertility . . . to make horses work harder, to protect cows from witchcraft, to procure healthy stock, and even to influence the sex of future calves. Bee-keeping and chicken-raising had their semi-magical precautions. So did the making of bread, beer, yeast, and butter — spheres in which witchcraft was particularly feared. Ritual precautions surrounded other household operations: no menstruating women, for example, could ever pickle beef or salt bacon. Similar prescriptions related to hunting and fishing, both speculative activities; in the fishing trade the fear of witchcraft lingered until the nineteenth century. [4]

We do well not to sneer at these activities as superstitions. Our ancestors ran very close to the wind. All it required was a bad year, and many people starved. Taking all known precautions was a perfectly reasonable response to a world in which the agricultural techniques meant that most animals had to be slaughtered at the onset of winter because there was insufficient fodder for them to survive the cold months. So did eating the annual surpluses this created as winter progressed; it is a moot point as to whether religion created Christmas, or Christmas created religion. The dearth which followed explains Lenten fasts and the brief carnivals which preceded them. 'Carnival', indeed, means 'farewell to meat' in the Latin languages.

The relief at the arrival of spring and the offerings to the gods of lamb and other newborn creatures which this encouraged must have had a universal palpability. In rural or island Greece at Easter even today one catches an echo of this sense. Important changes to eating habits

Mawmenye: Lamb with Lentils

This medieval lamb dish is from M.P. Cosman's *Fabulous Feasts: Medieval Cookery and Ceremony*. It's at least humble enough to have been eaten beyond the banqueting hall.

600 g diced lamb
60 g butter
1 cup chicken broth
1 cup brown lentils
4 cups dark beer
½ tsp both cinnamon and basil
1 cup diced turnip
1 cup currants
1 cup diced dried figs
salt and pepper
a handful of dandelion flowers

Brown the lamb in the butter, then add the broth and simmer until tender, about 45 minutes. Meanwhile cook the lentils in the beer until tender. Mix the cinnamon, salt and pepper and basil well into the turnips, and add to the lentils, with the figs and currants, cooking for about another 10 minutes or until the turnip is cooked. Strain the lamb and serve mixed with the lentils, garnished with a sprinkling of dandelion flowers. Medieval Europe liked colour in its dishes, and used hedgerow items much more than we do, thus the dandelions.

Stuffed Hare Roman Style

You might have trouble getting a hare. If you have a friend who shoots rabbits fall upon their charity, and ignore their inevitable scorn.

1 whole hare with its giblets
200 g pine kernels
100 g almonds
100 g other mixed nuts
20 g peppercorns
2 beaten eggs
½ tsp each rue, pepper and savory
1 small onion, chopped
100 g stoned dates
1 tbsp anchovy essence
2 tbsp white wine

Mix together the kernels, the almonds and other nuts, the peppercorns and the chopped giblets. Bind this with the egg, and stuff the hare. If it seems a bit meagre, mix in some fresh breadcrumbs to taste. Sprinkle with salt and pepper and roast in foil at 190°C for about an hour and a half, or until the hare is tender. Serve with a sauce made by combining the rue, savory, pepper, chopped onion, dates, anchovy, wine and the pan juices. Let this boil until it thickens a little, then pour it over the hare.

did occur, as they were bound to, over the two millennia, but this annual agricultural round was the fundamental basis upon which all Europeans, even the wealthiest and most powerful, enjoyed their daily bread throughout the centuries, from Agricola to George, the prince regent. So what did ordinary people, and particularly the people of Britain, eat 2000 years ago?

We know quite a lot about the diet of an ordinary Roman citizen at the height of the empire in Britain. This knowledge comes to us increasingly from archaeology, but also from some literary sources and from depictions on the walls and floor mosaics of villas and other domestic sites. Some of this evidence has been summarised in Hunter Davies' illuminating account of Hadrian's Wall. Other available evidence has recently come to hand from the translation and publication of the letters and other records fortuitously preserved at the wall fort at Vindolanda, on Hadrian's Wall.[5] This material deals mainly with the eating habits of the military and their near settlements, but is probably quite evocative of the more general pattern of eating.

Soldiers were not of particularly high social status, so what they ate every day would have been typical of the food the poorer classes lived on. This included corn meal baked into hard biscuits; something rather like porridge; and something else rather like pasta. They also ate vegetables, but of a limited variety — mainly beans and an earlier form of cabbage. But they did eat a lot of meat too. The legionary fortresses along Hadrian's Wall have large rubbish tips of bones from a wide variety of animals including beef, mutton, venison, chicken and small game.[6] The appearance of small game should not surprise; the Romans appear to have deliberately introduced rabbits into Britain, where they were raised in special enclosures. They also introduced dormice and the large variety of edible snail still eaten in France.[7] The number of animal bones is, however, far exceeded by the number of oyster shells. If the Roman soldiery did not exactly eat oysters every day they probably ate them often enough to complain about it, as soldiers do, when they were served. The soldiery also appear to have drunk wine. This marked them off from the local population who drank beer, a Celtic speciality also widely drunk in France at the time. This drink was unpopular with southern Europeans even then; the fourth-century emperor Julian who tried it in Paris thought it smelled like goats.

In the non-military settlements of Romanised Britain most households made their own bread, both leavened and unleavened, from a range of grains including wheat, barley, oats and rye, and sometimes flavoured with honey or cheese. Mustard, vinegar, rosemary, thyme and garlic were in regular use, and olive oil and the ubiquitous fish sauce, *garum*, were imported in quantity as cooking and flavouring media. Staple fruits were apples and pears. The local ruling class quickly adopted Roman eating habits. This meant three meals a day: a light breakfast at dawn, probably of bread and fruit; a light lunch at midday, comprising fish or eggs or vegetables; and a main meal commencing about three in the afternoon. These dinners could be simple family repasts, or quite elaborate banquets in the Roman style with guests reclining on couches and as many as seven or eight courses. The first-century writer Tacitus (whose father-in-law Agricola was governor for a period) describes such banquets in his *Britannia*; it is clear that they differed little from their counterpart entertainments in Rome itself.[8] Cooking was done over charcoal, using a bricked hearth with metal pots with round bottoms (not unlike the Chinese *wok*) placed over holes in the top, or on hearths in the embers. These techniques were still in relatively widespread use in the south of Italy just a few decades ago.[9]

This pattern of domestic eating in Roman Britain changed very little during the four centuries during which Britannia was a Roman province. It is very difficult to establish what replaced it during the several centuries of political chaos which then ensued, but it is also very likely that the diet of ordinary people changed little, although that of the rulers of the society came closer to it. It was certainly much the same when it emerged into the light of history again during the early medieval period. It was shortly thereafter to be affected by two important agricultural revolutions, both of which had their effects on eating habits.

Stuffed Easter Lamb

This recipe illustrates one of the problems encountered by nineteenth-century immigrants to New Zealand. Easter was not in spring but in autumn, and so it didn't relate. This recipe is from the Dodecanese. To get the offal you will have to order it in advance. Ask your butcher for 'a pluck'.

    1 whole young lamb
    60 g butter
    600 g mince
    the offal (heart, liver, lungs, etc.)
    300 g cooked rice
    2 large onions, chopped
    3 large lemons
    2 tbsp fresh mint
    piece of cinnamon
    salt and pepper

Rub the lamb inside and out with salt and pepper and the juice of the lemons. Trim and chop the offal and mix with the mince, and sauté in a dry pan or with a little butter for about 5 minutes. Mix with the rice, onions, cinnamon and mint, and more salt and pepper. Partially sew up the lamb, stuff it with the mixture, and complete the sewing. Put it in a roasting pan with 2 or 3 cups of water and cover well with foil. Roast at 150°C for about 2 hours and then remove the foil to brown the meat for a further half hour.

Barley Bread

Barley bread was one of the staples of the Roman diet. We know about the ingredients of this bread because incinerated loaves from Pompeii have been analysed for their content.

    150 g barley flour
    450 g plain flour
    2 tbsp gluten
    20 g creamed yeast

Combine the flours, gluten, creamed yeast and enough water to make a pliable dough. Leave to rise for about an hour, then knead well and transfer to a greased tin. Let rise again, then bake at 220°C and then 200°C for 15 minutes each, before turning out and baking for a further 20 minutes at 180°C. The Roman soldiery would have eaten lots of raw onion and cheese with this bread.

THE AGRICULTURAL REVOLUTIONS

The source of both of these revolutions was a change in the European climate. From about the beginning of the eighth century and for the next 500 years, Europe became a warmer and drier place than it had been at any time since 4000 BC. This meant that land which could not previously be brought into cultivation because of its height or latitude was now available for cropping. But before this land could be used three further developments were required.[10]

The first of these was the invention of the horse collar, which was introduced into Europe from the steppe lands of central Asia some time around the beginning of the ninth century. The importance of this advance is hard to overemphasise. Previously draught horses were harnessed in a manner which pressed on their wind pipe, which suffocated them and made them very inefficient. Heavy work had to be done with teams of oxen which were extremely slow and cumbersome. Estimates are that the introduction of the horse collar increased the pulling and lifting power of the much more flexible single horse perhaps tenfold.

The second development was the use of iron shoes nailed to the hooves of horses, again an invention of the horse-riding nomads of Asia but one quickly adopted by the Byzantine armies, and then in western Europe. By the eleventh century they were in common use. This increased both the traction of plough horses and the length of time they could be used, especially on stony ground.

The third development was the invention of the wheeled plough equipped with a blade that cut at an angle. This could turn a much heavier and deeper sod than the vertical ploughs previously in use. These were also widely in use by the end of the tenth century.

These three developments, taken in conjunction with the wider availability of cultivable land with heavier and richer soil, brought significant increases in grain yield (from 2.5 to about 4 kilograms per hectare). Whether the crop was rye, or barley, or wheat, this meant that it was now economic to base the food of the population at large on ground, baked grains. Europe became primarily a bread-eating, rather than a porridge-eating culture (although the habit of eating porridge persisted among the very poor, and among those who lived on the poorer agricultural fringes of Europe).

Manchet Bread

Bread was the great European staple of the middle ages and later. The best people ate manchet bread, a fine white loaf made of the best flour, and sometimes with butter and eggs. There are quite a number of extant recipes. In her *English Bread and Yeast Cookery*, Elizabeth David gives the following variation on two recipes from variously *The Good Huswife's Handmaide for the Kitchen* of 1594 and Gervase Markham's *The English Hus-wife* of 1615. Ms David says the loaves can be reheated, but they've never lasted long enough for me to make the experiment. There is much about medieval breads in Gillian Goodwin, *Manchet & Trencher*, published for the Museum of London by Gelofer Press.

300 g wholemeal
300 g New Zealand plain flour
2 tbsp of gluten
15 g creamed yeast
salt
30 g softened butter
milk and cream

Add the creamed yeast to the dry ingredients and mix with enough cream and milk mixture to make a springy dough. Work in the softened butter. Let it rise for about an hour, then knead and break down into four. Mould into rounded buns and give them about a 30-minute second rising on a baking sheet. Bake at 220°C for about 30 minutes. Light olive oil can be used instead of butter.

Two subsidiary developments also had an effect on the cuisine. These were the introduction of the three-field rotation system rather than the two-field system used by the Romans, and the widespread growth of sheep herding. The first of these meant that fields were available in spring for the mass production of a much wider range of vegetables than before. The sheep, for their part, were valued for their efficiency as producers of the natural fertiliser which the three-field system demanded, and for the wool they produced. But it also meant the widespread availability of mutton and cheese (a very efficient way to preserve sheep milk surpluses).

Despite some ups and downs attributable to local social and physical circumstances, extant accounts of the diet of the poor show that during this medieval period they ate quite well. As early as the twelfth century, in one set of records of a leper colony in Champagne, the inmates were receiving not only bread, oil, salt and onions daily, but also meat three days a week, and fish and eggs on the others.[11] Many other documentary sources show the same. For example, in 1338 the religious order of Hospitallers in Provence decided to undertake an audit. This covered, among other expenses, their budget for food, and shows that even the lowly cowherds got 20 percent of their diet in the form of fish, meat, eggs and vegetables (about two-thirds was bread, and the balance wine). Similar diets can be found throughout Europe over this period. Some have been analysed for their nutritional value, and apart from small deficiencies in vitamins A and C and some trace minerals, they appear to have been well balanced and nourishing.[12]

But none of this would have been of as nearly great effect had it not been for the development of hydraulic power. Medieval Europeans did not invent water mills; that honour belongs to the Romans. But they improved their gearing and vastly increased their use. By the eleventh century, for instance, the Domesday Book identifies 5624 water mills in use just in those parts of Britain surveyed. They were used for all sorts of industrial processes, but for our purposes the most important use was in the production of flour, for grinding and for sieving. Essentially, they industrialised the production of bread in a manner which persisted until new methods of both flour production and baking were invented in the nineteenth century. Without this innovation it would have been impossible for Europe to become so comprehensively a bread-eating culture.

Vegetable Gruel

The medieval poor ate a great deal of grain in much more varied forms and in a far wider range of dishes than we do. Buckwheat is, strictly speaking, not a wheat at all but a form of dock. This would have been a feast-day dish in medieval times. People then were much less concerned than we are about putting sweet and savoury flavours together.

2 cups buckwheat groats (or wheatgerm if you can't get the buckwheat)
2 tbsp butter
4 cups milk
1 cup carrots, diced in rounds
½ cup parsnip, diced
1 cup raisins
10 pitted prunes
½ tsp each dried ginger, cinnamon and basil
6 tbsp honey
3 tbsp plum jam
salt

Toss the groats in the butter over heat for 2 or 3 minutes. Mix in the other ingredients except the spices, basil, honey and jam, and let simmer for about 20 minutes. Serve warm with a little jam and honey and the dried items sprinkled on top.

Khoresh

There many variations on this dish. Margaret Shaida lists 19 in her *Legendary Cuisine of Persia* and Claudia Roden a more modest five in her *Book of Middle Eastern Food*. This recipe is from the latter and is very simple. Others are much more elaborate, with a greater variety of spices and fruits, including peaches and rhubarb. Spinach is also sometimes used.

    1 onion, finely chopped
    4 tbsp butter
    600 g lean lamb, diced
    1 tsp cinnamon
    3 cooking apples, peeled, cored and
      diced
    juice of a lemon
    salt and pepper
    some yellow split peas (optional),
      cooked

Soften the onion in the butter, then add and brown the meat. Season and add the cinnamon. Cover with water and simmer very gently for 2 hours. Also soften the apple in butter and squeeze the lemon juice over. This should be added to the meat about 20 minutes before the end of cooking. This dish is best served with rice. The peas serve to thicken it and should be mashed and added at the same time as the apple.

In addition, this same period saw a significant development not only in the variety and availability of foodstuffs but also in the refinement of the food eaten by the ruling class. Great state banquets, as might be expected, were grand affairs. There is a record of the food served at the coronation banquet of Henry IV in 1399 which astonishes the present-day reader of Froissart's chronicle. There were three courses, of variously 11, 13 and 19 dishes. These included a boar's head, swans, a sturgeon, venison in frumenty and an eagle. Further down the social scale, the funeral banquet for the bishop of Bath and Wells in 1424 was, if anything, even more sumptuous: four courses totalling 52 main dishes.[13] But even among the developing town merchant class, a much more luxurious form of eating was becoming habitual. This elaboration of the diet was built upon a medieval activity which added significant features to the cuisine, some of which are still with us. This was the Crusades, which ensured an Arab influence on the developing European civilisation.

THE INFLUENCE OF ARAB CIVILISATION

The crusading European knights who, after some false starts, recaptured the Holy Land for Christendom, and who settled down to rule parts of the south-eastern shores of the Mediterranean for a century or so, expected that they would be dealing with barbarians and heathens. They were astonished to find a people far more civilised than they, knowledgeable in the Greek classics, and with a highly developed poetry and art. But above all they encountered the cuisine of Persia, which was and still is one of the glories of human civilisation.[14]

It was bound to influence the cooking of Europe, and so it did as the crusaders carried it back to their homelands, where it settled and became acclimatised, incorporated into the European tradition long after the crusaders themselves had been driven from their little kingdoms in the Middle East. Clear present-day traces of it are to be found, for obvious reasons, in the cooking of Spain, Portugal and Southern Italy (the *agrodolce* dishes of Apulia are one of the best-known instances). Some of its direct lineal descendants linger in the special regional dishes of France, such as the *Tarte d'epinards au sucre* of Provence. But its major and largely unheralded contribution to the European cuisine is in the use of sugar and other sweetenings, and fruit, especially dried fruit, in dishes of meat.

The most famous survivor of these in the general European cuisine is duck stuffed or cooked with orange or apricots.

These are descendants of the *khoresh*, one of the archetypal dishes of Persian cuisine. They have now largely disappeared from the British kitchen (most having barely survived into the eighteenth century), but they have made one important contribution to the New Zealand tradition in food: the festival foods of Christmas which incorporate large quantities of dried fruit and nuts in the sweet dishes still widely eaten at the time of year — cakes, puddings and mince pies.

This influence is much more obvious closer to the source, as the available food manuscripts of medieval England make clear. The most interesting of these is probably the *Forme of Curye*, a collection of nearly 200 recipes written down at the order of Richard II in about 1390.[15] There is much which is unfamiliar to the modern taste in this book; a cook is unlikely to encounter a recipe in the present day which begins 'take a peacock, break his neck, cut his throat, and flay him'. As well as indicating that the range of foods eaten (including peacocks and many other birds such as cranes and gulls, and items of offal which now make us shudder, such as cows' udders) was wider than we would now consider appropriate, the *Forme of Curye* also incorporates a range of dishes in which the distinction made in more recent European cuisine between sweet and savoury is not apparent — a clear legacy from the Crusades. These dishes include a number that we would now regard as far more typical of the Middle East or even Asia proper, such as a sweet and sour sauce for rabbit, and others combining unusual but distinctly Persian flavours, such as a fruit and salmon pie, and tripe cooked in a gingered broth.

We would probably also be surprised by the amount of salt used and fish eaten. The former relates to the need to preserve surpluses in the absence of refrigeration (although the technique of the ice house was known). Any large carcass worth preserving was said to be 'worth its salt' — an expensive commodity and not one to be wasted on inconsiderable bits or trifles. It is hard to overestimate the significance of salt in European cooking. We are now used to it being a cheap and standard commodity available everywhere, but access to a source was as good as owning a gold mine in the medieval period, so central was it to the whole process of housekeeping. London salt from the great 'wicks' or

Rabbit in Syrup

This is from *The Forme of Curye*, from the kitchen of the ill-fated Richard II, dating from about 1390. It has been translated into modern English, although is quite comprehensible in the original, and adapted for the modern kitchen by Lorna Sass for the New York Metropolitan Museum. This dish has its lineal descendants in the *agrodolce* or sweet and sour dishes of Southern Italy and Sicily.

Getting the rabbit might be problematic, but you could also use a chicken at a pinch, or a game bird of some kind (a pheasant perhaps).

about 1 kg rabbit joints
½ cup flour seasoned with salt and pepper
3 tbsp oil
3 cups Muscat or dessert sherry
4 tbsp cider vinegar
½ cup raisins
½ tsp cinnamon
1 tbsp freshly minced ginger
10 black peppercorns, 5 cloves, and 10 allspice, ground together

Shake the rabbit pieces in the flour in a plastic bag to cover well, and brown in oil. Combine the other ingredients and simmer until well blended. Pour over the rabbit and cook for about 45 minutes.

Baccala

This dish is common to most of the
northern Mediterranean coast and is best
made with a smallish stockfish called a
ragno. Getting any sort of stockfish (salted
and dried as hard as a board) might be
difficult in New Zealand. The Italian fish
shops of Wellington's Courtenay Place
usually had it hanging in their windows but
I haven't seen it since they were replaced by
trendy cafés. This particular version is from
Vicenza, north of Venice.

In Venice they consider the use of milk
sacrilege but sometimes use cream and
lemon juice. It's sold there as a 'take out'.
Unbelievably the northern hemisphere cod
fishery which once fed much of Europe has
been virtually fished out in the space of
40 years, there being no limit, it seems, to
human stupidity and greed. Get your *baccala*
while you still can.

1 kg stockfish
400 ml olive oil
500 ml milk
1 large onion, chopped
1 clove of garlic, crushed
6 anchovy fillets, chopped (a small tin
 — keep the oil and mix it in)
chopped parsley
salt and white pepper

Break up the stockfish (you may need a steak
hammer), soak it for 2 days, drain and bring
to the boil, and simmer for about 20 minutes.
Drain again, pick out the skin and bones, and
chop into small pieces. Fry the onion in a
little of the oil until golden and then add the
garlic and anchovies. Put in the fish, mix
well, and then very gradually feed in the oil
and milk, beating as if making mashed
potatoes. Add the salt, pepper and parsley,
transfer to an oven dish and bake for 15
minutes at 200°C.

pans of Lincolnshire had its own market area like most commodities,
and here salt could be bought in a variety of grades, colours and textures
for different culinary tasks.[16] A single major enterprise at Droitwich was
producing 1600 tonnes per annum by 1500. Both Venice and Genoa
dominated the medieval salt trade at one time or another; indeed it was
the salt subsidy paid by the Venetian state to its merchants for bringing
home salt which formed the basis for the development of the broader
spice trade on which Venice ultimately throve. But the London Company
of Salters founded in 1180 also played a major role in the European salt
trade.

Most large medieval kitchens included a salting vat which was in
continuous use. This may explain the practice of double cooking many
larger items, first by parboiling (presumably to remove the large amounts
of salt), and then by roasting or by a second seething in a flavoured
broth. This in any event is the advice given by the Goodman of Paris in
the medieval equivalent of Mrs Beeton, the *Ménagier de Paris*, a book of
household advice by a wealthy and elderly professional husband to his
newly-wed young wife:

> The haunch which is salted ought to be cooked first in water and wine to
> get rid of the salt, and then throw away the water and wine and afterwards
> set it to cook slowly in meat broth and turnips, and serve it in strips with
> water in a dish.[17]

Salted or otherwise, the fish eaten in medieval times included not only
the usual fresh and saltwater species, but some curiosities unknown in
culinary use today, such as lampreys and porpoise. Their apparent
popularity is a tribute to the practice of fasting rather than to a love of
fish as such, although salted fish of one sort or another could be tasty
enough and was preserved in large quantities for this reason. It was also
a mass food for the poor. The *Northumberland Household Book*, a medieval
book of accounts belonging to the Percy family, records that in 1512
more than 2000 salmon were salted to last the Lenten fast. [18]

The poor enjoyed no such profusion, of course, and had to make do
with salt herring or dried stockfish. This was not a very refined food and
was unpopular with its enforced consumers, who ate anything but if they
could avoid it. Stockfish in particular must have been virtually inedible,
requiring, in at least one account, an hour of beating and two hours of

soaking in hot water before it was anywhere near ready for cooking. It is understandable in such circumstances that fish had a negative reputation with the poorer classes, although the European lineal descendants of these dishes — such as the Venetian *baccala* — can be quite pleasant. The poorest of the poor could not afford even the roughest breads either, and continued to eat porridge dishes known variously as frumenty or firminty. These too have their lineal descendants — although, oddly, as sweetened festival dishes of the traditional rural cuisine eaten at Christmas. This penchant for sweet dishes was also an outgrowth of the experience of the Crusades.

THE SPICE TRADE

The influence of Islamic culture is most noticeable in the use of spices and flavourings. There were, of course, a number of spices available in Europe prior to the thirteenth century. The Romans made some use of pepper, for example, but they preferred their fish sauce, *garum*. This was partly because spices were rare and expensive items which had to be brought great distances. But by the time of the Crusades the Arabs had begun to grow many of these spices on the southern shores of the Mediterranean, and they suddenly erupted into use in the European cuisine in great profusion shortly after the establishment of the Christian kingdoms of Jerusalem and Acre. They remained expensive, however, and their regular use continued to be confined at the very least to the well-off. Most medieval account books of large households contain references to their annual purchase. In 1419 Alice de Bryene is recorded to have paid over two shillings a pound for pepper (although this was a high price for a quality London product); understandably, like most female heads of households, she kept it with her other spices, securely locked in a special cupboard and doled out only on her authority.[19]

Along with the more readily available pepper, ginger and sugar (this last regarded as much a medicinal item as a food flavouring), there now appeared in quantity for the first time cinnamon, saffron, cardamom, nutmegs, mace and cloves, along with some other spices no longer in use such as grains of paradise, zedoary, galingale and cubebs. That the use of these spices was a direct consequence of the Crusades is clear from a comparison between two existing recipe books from respectively the

Farsed Chicken

One of the middle-class culinary beneficiaries of the developing urban politesse was Francesco Datini, better known to posterity as 'the merchant of Prato'. Datini was a Tuscan contemporary of Chaucer whose many surviving letters teem with references to food. He also ran his own country estate, where he raised the pork which he loved to have made into varieties of sausage and pies, and his own mortadella cheeses. He was particularly fond of poultry — chicken and pheasant, and, rather less usually to our taste, peacocks and turtle doves. This is how he might have served a chicken.

> 1 large roasting chicken
> ½ cup brown lentils
> 1½ cups red wine
> 1 cup chicken stock
> 200 g cherries (try and get tart-
>   flavoured ones)
> 200 g cottage cheese
> ½ cup rolled oats
> ½ tsp basil
> 60 g butter, melted
> 1 cup white wine
> six slices bread, crumbed
> salt

Soak the lentils in the wine and stock overnight, then cook them in it until tender. Drain, reserving about a cup of the liquid afterwards. Chop the cherries, and mix these with the lentils, rolled oats, cheese and basil. Add salt to taste. Stuff the bird with this, sew up, drizzle the skin with the melted butter, and roast for 2 hours at 180°C. Make a sauce to pour over the bird by combining the reserved wine and stock liquid from the lentils with the wine and crumbs, and simmering this gently for 10 minutes or so. A pheasant can also be done this way.

thirteenth and fourteenth centuries and both, rather unusually, by named cooks. The first stands in the name of Muhammed ibn al-Hassam al-Karim, a court cook of Baghdad, and dates from 1226. The second is the *Vivandier* of Guilliame Tirel, a Parisian court cook who began his career as a kitchenboy in 1326, and who was later to become chief cook to Charles V, a position he held for many years as we know from the household accounts which record the purchase of two new knives for him nearly 60 years later. Separated by nearly a hundred years and thousands of kilometres, there are remarkable similarities between the spicings and flavourings used by the two cooks, although these flavourings rarely appear in the European cuisine before Tirel. One of his recipes — a *tailles*, or meat sauce incorporating figs, raisins, almond milk, breadcrumbs, sugar and saffron — is astonishing for being an almost complete copy of an Arabic equivalent.[20]

These Arabic spicing techniques, although used more heavily than we would now find comfortable or even edible, persisted as a basic characteristic of the European cuisine until the end of the eighteenth century or later, and continued to appear in the rural English cuisine until the mid nineteenth century. This was to have some small influence on some forms of New Zealand food. But beyond that it was the hunt for alternative sources of spices which ultimately brought our European forebears to the antipodes.

The merchants of Venice and Genoa grew wealthy on their monopolies of the spice trade, creating an economic surplus which formed the basis for the expansion of commercial and cultural activity that we have come to characterise as the Renaissance. In combination with the wool trade of England, northern France and Spain, to which allusion has already been made, this created a burgeoning urban culture and a developing merchant class who ate much better than those who remained working directly on the land — although still not as well as the large landowners and higher dignitaries of the church.[21]

But the Italian merchants guarded their spice route monopolies ruthlessly. For example, Robert Sturmey, an English merchant who attempted to breach this monopoly in 1458 by developing a direct route between the Levant and Bristol, and who planned to plant suitable spices in England itself, had his vessels intercepted near Malta and his cargo flung overboard. It was this sort of action which stimulated the navigators of initially Portugal and Spain to seek alternative routes to the spice Indies and which led indirectly to the European discovery of the Americas. This in turn gave rise to further discoveries which led to fundamental changes in the European cuisine.

New world: new foods

Until the discovery of the new world of the American continent, vegetables, although a constant, had not been accorded a very significant place in the European cuisine. People ate them as an accompaniment, or if they could get nothing better. More to the point, their variety was rather limited. The principal available vegetables in medieval times appear to have been cabbages, onions, garlic and leeks, with some variation provided by turnips, peas, beans and carrots. Wild vegetables and potherbs were widely collected (as they are still in some parts of Europe), and included rapes, parsnips, sorrel, samphire and orach.

From later medieval times a greater variety of fruits began to supplement the ubiquitous apples and pears. These were mainly imported citruses of one sort or another, and were luxury items. Raw fruit had long been regarded as poisonous, as had raw vegetables, and the latter were used mainly as flavourings in stews and soups — although there is a green salad recorded from 1393, some of the ingredients of which sound rather odd to us: 'Take parsley, sage, garlic, onions, leek, mints, borage, fennel and garden cresses, rue, rosemary, and purslane; lave and wash them well, pluck them small with thine hand, and mingle them well with raw oil. Lay on vinegar and serve it forth.'[22] What oil is referred to here is not clear.

From the sixteenth century this pattern began to change as exotic horticulture began to be fashionable among the wealthy, and market gardening around London and other towns became economic. But still the imports (mainly from Europe, but eventually including curiosities such as pineapples) continued to be in the form of fruits rather than vegetables. These included many newly developed varieties of apples and other tree fruits (the horticulturist John Parkinson denominated 57 apple varieties, 52 pears, 35 cherries and 22 peaches in 1629) as well as gooseberries and apricots, and a great profusion of plum varieties. Quinces had always been relatively common.

John Evelyn's Tart of Herbs

The strict distinction which we make between fruit and vegetables was not nearly so hard and fast in earlier centuries. In his *Acetaria*, John Evelyn recommends a tart of 'herbs', by which he means green vegetables, combined with what we would think a wholly inappropriate egg custard, although a similar dish lives on in Greek cuisine. Jane Grigson gives something close to this version in her *Food with the Famous*.

1 kg spinach (or spinach, chard and chervil if you can get it)
300 ml cream
100 g macaroons (plain coconut finger biscuits)
60 g butter
4 egg yolks and 2 whites
2 or 3 tbsp caster sugar
60 g currants and candied peel, mixed
grated nutmeg
puff pastry

Cook the trimmed spinach in boiling water with salt. Drain, cool and chop. Bring the cream to the boil and add the spinach, then crumble in the macaroons, and add the butter, eggs, dried fruit, and caster sugar. Grate over the nutmeg. Crumble in more macaroon if the mixture looks a bit thin. Line a 25 cm tart tin with the pastry, pour in the mixture, and bake at 220°C for about 15 minutes, then lower to 180°C for about another 45 minutes.

By the Elizabethan period, spinach, chard, beetroot, pumpkins, asparagus and cauliflowers had made their appearance. But vegetable eating was a meagre pastime, even despite the efforts of John Evelyn (1620–1706) and others in the seventeenth century.[23] Evelyn attempted to popularise globe artichokes, cardoons and broccoli, and produced a salad calendar in his book of vegetables, the *Acetaria* of 1699, so that people could eat salads all year if they had a mind to do so. It took the food discoveries of the New World and their progressive adoption from the eighteenth century to change, at least in some degree, the English aversion to vegetables. Pre-eminent in this change were the potato and the tomato.

The Spanish conquerors were, indeed, astonished at the variety of green vegetables available among the peoples they encountered. An anonymous soldier with the force which invaded Mexico remarked: 'They cultivate a great diversity of plants and garden truck of which they are very fond, and these they eat raw as well as in various cooked dishes. They have one — like a pepper — as a condiment which they call chili, and they never eat anything without it.'[24] But it was the potato, both sweet and otherwise, which made the greatest and most significant initial impact. This native of Chile and the Peruvian Andes grew in profusion and great variety in the land of the Incas, who both ate it and worshipped it as a god.[25]

There is some debate over who brought the potato to Europe. It may have been Columbus, or it may have been the Spanish explorer Gonzalo Jiménez de Quesada in 1536. Certainly it was being grown in Europe some time before Walter Raleigh brought it from Cartagena to Ireland (not Virginia as is popularly supposed) 50 years later.[26] Recent developments in industrial horticulture have reduced the several hundred varieties which once grew in England to a handful, although Jane Grigson lists over 30 varieties for different purposes in her potato entry in her

Vegetable Book.[27] For various reasons to be canvassed later, the potato encountered resistance from the poor as an item of diet, but by 1744 the cookery manual *Adam's Luxury and Eve's Cookery* listed recipes for mashed and boiled potatoes, and potatoes made into stuffing, sausages, cakes, puddings and fritters.[28] By the time of the colonisation of New Zealand, the potato was a staple of the English diet.

The tomato (named from the Aztec *tomatl*) has had almost as dramatic an effect on the European cuisine, whole sections of which would now be impossible to conceive without it. The profusion of the tomato also astonished the Spanish. Bernardino Sahagun, a Spanish priest who wrote a very interesting and full account of the conquest of the Aztecs of Mexico, remarked of the tomato markets he encountered: 'The tomato seller sells large tomatoes, small tomatoes, leaf tomatoes, thin tomatoes, sweet tomatoes, serpent tomatoes, those which are yellow, red, bright red, and rosy dawn coloured.'[29] Interestingly, the original tomatoes brought to Europe were yellow and not red, and were initially shunned in some quarters as poisonous, or used only as a base for pickle.

To these two main items should be added maize, pulse beans, avocados, the chilli pepper already mentioned, and the sweet peppers or capsicums. Some of these have only very recently been incorporated in the ordinary diet, but others such as maize almost at once became to southern Europe what the potato became to the north — a dietary standard. The same applied to dried beans, which, because of their storage capacity, ease of transport and ready reconstitution simply by soaking, also became standard items. The influence of American horticulture on European diet was therefore profound.

By the eighteenth century a highly characteristic English diet had developed. It was based on bread, meats and dairy products (especially cheese and butter), supplemented by a wide range of vegetables and fruits. It was also a diet thoroughly conversant with the use of herbs and spices in its cooked dishes. Foreign visitors commented that even the most lowly in England ate meat every day. The Frenchman François Misson, travelling in Britain in 1690, had already commented on it. 'I had always heard that they were great flesh-eaters,' he remarked, 'and I found it true. Among the middling sort of people they have ten or twelve sorts of common meats which infallibly take their turns at their tables, and two dishes are their dinners: a pudding, for instance, and a piece of roast beef.'[30] His words were echoed by the Swede, Per Kalm, in 1748:

> Roast meat is the Englishman's *delice* and principal dish. All English meat, whether it is of ox, calf, sheep or swine, has a fatness and a delicious taste, either because of the excellent pasture, which consists of such nourishing and sweet scented kinds of hay as there are in this country, where the cultivation of meadows has been brought to such high perfection, or some way of fattening the cattle known to the butchers alone . . . I do not believe that any Englishman who is his own master has ever eaten a dinner without meat.[31]

Kalm's qualification is an important one: there were plenty who were not their own masters and who ate very little meat. But these views are worth remarking because they indicate how the English diet appeared to foreigners. They also indicate a pattern of expectation which is probably important to the development of the nineteenth-century New Zealand cuisine, as shall be seen. In the meantime it should be sufficient to remark that the habits of eating which came to New Zealand in the nineteenth century largely derive from those of the late eighteenth, and it is worth exploring these in a little more detail.

JANE AUSTEN'S KITCHEN

It may come as a surprise to the many readers of Jane Austen to discover that had she not made her reputation as a novelist she might as easily have ranked today beside her lesser-known near contemporaries Hannah Glasse and Elizabeth Raffald as a forerunner to Mrs Isabella Beeton. It comes as less of a surprise to those familiar with both Jane's family and personal circumstances, and the domestic economy of rural eighteenth-century England.

Jane Austen grew up in the large family of a rural parson in the middle eighteenth century. At that time it was customary for such livings to include a smallholding or glebe from which the occupant was expected to feed his household. The Austens never lived in the country proper but in small towns, initially in Steventon in Hampshire. There the family glebe supplied pork, mutton and poultry for the table. Mrs. Austen also managed a small dairy herd, and there was a large kitchen garden for vegetables and fruits, including grapes. Rather unusually, the Austens grew potatoes before they were generally cultivated.[32] Later the family lived in Bath and then in Southampton.

In Southampton they were joined by Martha Lloyd, a family relative by marriage who made a collection of 135 favourite recipes almost certainly in daily use in the Austen household, and still extant. She shared some of the housekeeping with Jane who, as a single daughter, had been managing the household under the general eye of her mother for some years. From this recipe book, from Jane's letters to her sister Cassandra, and from the novels themselves, we can get a very good idea of the sorts of foods a comfortable family of the professional classes might have eaten in the late eighteenth century. The novels are also an important source of information concerning the food of the wealthier land-owning class with which Jane was also familiar.

The diet of the well-off in England at this time was a varied and interesting one. In one of her letters Jane describes a dinner, eaten as was the custom at 3.30 in the afternoon. This included boiled chicken, a ragout of veal, a haricot of mutton, some fresh pork, ox-cheek with small dumplings, pea soup, and a cold and lightly pickled brawn. During the later period at Southampton there is a description of a small and relatively informal supper to which outsiders were invited and which commenced at the increasingly fashionable and later hour of 7 pm. It included a duck paté, preserved ginger, and an apple and butter pulp as a sweetmeat. With these dishes we are no longer in the land of the exotic; these are dishes familiar to us.

In addition to what we can learn about the eighteenth-century cuisine from writers like Jane Austen or the diary of her relative Fanny Burney (whose brother sailed with Cook), we can also look to the contents of the increasingly common published books of recipes. Some of these, such as Hannah Glasse's *The Art of Cookery Made Plain and Easy* of 1747, or

A Haricot of Mutton

A haricot is today what we would call a casserole. This recipe, a standard in the Austen household, is from Martha Lloyd's manuscript cookbook in its printed edition, edited by Maggie Black and Diedre Le Faye as *The Jane Austen Cookbook*.

6 or 8 lamb frying chops, depending on size
2 tbsp seasoned flour in a plastic bag
60 g clarified butter or oil, and a further 30 g butter for the sauce
600 ml good strong lamb stock
2 tbsp mushroom ketchup
3 medium-sized turnips, parsnips or a small swede (or a combination), cut into smallish pieces
2 carrots, sliced into rounds
salt and pepper

Shake the trimmed chops in the plastic bag to dust them. Keep the flour. Fry the chops in the butter or oil. Melt the sauce butter in an iron casserole, shake in the flour and cook for 5 minutes over a medium heat. While doing this, heat the stock and then stir it into the cooked flour with the ketchup. Add the chops and vegetables, season to taste, cover well, and simmer gently for about an hour.

Elizabeth Raffald's Orange Custards

Elizabeth Raffald and Hannah Glasse wrote the two best-known eighteenth-century English cookbooks. Raffald's *Experienced English Housekeeper* (1769), from which this recipe comes, was written in the intervals between running several commercial food establishments including two inns in Manchester and a domestic servants' employment agency, running two newspapers, organising a feckless husband and bearing 15 daughters. Surprising she found the time really.

juice of 1 orange and 1 lemon, and the zest of both
125 g sugar
2 tbsp orange liqueur
6 large egg yolks
600 ml cream
a few drops of orange flower water

Blend the juices, zest, sugar and egg yolks in a processor with the liqueur. Heat the cream, and stir in the orange, lemon and egg mixture. Add the orange flower water but be sparing: it has a very pervasive flavour. Pour into a soufflé dish, or individual dishes, and bake in an oven, preferably in a *bain marie*, at 160°C for about 45 minutes. This can be served hot or cold.

Elizabeth Raffald's *Experienced English Housekeeper* of 1769, have become classics of their genre, although it should be noted that these were not cookbooks as we would understand them but rather, as Raffald's title suggests, for the already highly knowledgeable. In a strange reversal of our contemporary expectations, English books about cooking were translated into French and widely admired for their rustic charm on the other side of the Channel.

Dishes such as potted fish replace the fish pies of previous centuries, and the food becomes lighter and less sweet, although the quantities of fat used can still astonish. People stopped eating a range of meats such as goat, and items such as cow udders (although they still enjoyed such delicacies as pigs' ears),[33] and tended to stick to beef, pork and mutton, especially as selective breeding of stock lines became more systematised and the quality of meat became more dependable. Boiled meat was now almost invariably served with dumplings. Hannah Glasse gives an interesting recipe made from a flour and water paste, and including a handful of dried currants, to be boiled with a piece of beef.

Eggs and dairy produce moved to the centre of cooking both as thickening and as lightening agents. The meringue entered the English cuisine, as did the regular use of whipped cream.[34] Country housewives continued to make their own curd cheeses much as they had done for generations, but in the eighteenth century they began to toast it and to sprinkle it over cooked vegetables on a regular basis. This was also the age of the first vinegar-based sauces and chutneys, the latter obviously a tribute to the influence of the developing relationship with India. References to piccalilli begin to abound in the collections of recipes of the period. But these new sauces also included some we now think of as English standards such as mint sauce for mutton, or ketchup sauces made in particular from the newfangled tomato.

Strong broths previously used as flavourings in serving meat became sauces as the use of liaisons of butter and flour became first fashionable, then widespread in use. The extravagances of the rich in preparing these cut little ice with Hannah Glasse, however: 'so much is the blind folly of this age, that they would rather be imposed on by a French booby, than give encouragement to a good English cook.'[35] The same period also developed the bouillon cube, invented the sandwich, and learned to combine meat with fish in the typical dishes of the time — mussels with chicken, lamb with crab, oysters with beef, and anchovies with pork.

For the new practice of taking tea, a snack of muffins and pikelets became commonplace. For festival occasions there arose the pudding boiled in a cloth which, cut up, contained a bean or other small vanity or coin to identify the king and queen of the revels. At some time in the early eighteenth century these survivors from the great meat and fruit pies of medieval times lost their meat component and became confections of dried fruit, flour and suet only, often prepared well in advance and primed to mature with lashings of brandy or one of the fortified wines now becoming increasingly popular.

If much of this sounds familiar then that is almost certainly because it is. The eighteenth century was characterised by a culture of politesse, and Austen's novels both reflect this and satirise its social excesses. But the century was also marked by a domestic richness that expressed itself very well in the things which people ate. One of the leading social historians of European cuisine notes of this development:

> Eighteenth century dining tables were dominated by a new ratio convivialis (way of setting up a feast); a geometrical order and a mathematical reason: the multiplicity of the dishes presupposed the lightness of the substances on offer and variety of tastes was bodied forth in their shimmering colours. The eye, by dethroning the nose, had enhanced the colourfulness of the parade, the brilliance of the cup's minuet, and the victual's dance. Polychromy and miniaturization fuse in the meal's well tempered concert as in the elegant musical phrase.[36]

There was much to satirise in the pretensions of the Enlightenment, but much to admire also. In 1809 Jane Austen returned to Hampshire where she made her home until her death in 1817. The garden of Chawton Cottage where the now widowed Mrs Austen lived with her two daughters and Martha Lloyd was planted with fruit trees — plums, greengages, apricots and mulberries — and potatoes, peas, strawberries, currants and gooseberries. In July 1814 Mrs Austen wrote to her granddaughter Anna: 'We have a very good crop of small fruit, even your gooseberry tree does better than heretofore, when the gooseberries are ripe I shall sit upon my bench, eat them and think of you . . .'[37] Although now in relatively straitened circumstances, the widow Austen and her family continued to eat well. Meals consisting of beef pudding, neck of mutton, duck and

Pepperpot Soup

This dish combines the eighteenth-century flavours of lamb and crab, and probably came to the west of England, to which it can be traced, with the slave trade. It certainly has a very West Indian flavour, and shares some characteristics with another dish, Philadelphia Pepperpot, which comes from the New England end of the same trade but mingles tripe and veal.

1 kg lamb leg, trimmed and diced
6 slices of rindless bacon, chopped
3 onions, peeled and chopped
1 green pepper, seeded and chopped
a sprig of thyme, chopped
½ tsp cayenne
1 tbsp paprika (Hungarian is preferable to Spanish for this dish)
12 peppercorns
salt
½ a young cabbage, shredded
1 small lettuce, shredded
a few heads of spinach, chopped
a little chopped sorrel if you can get it
200 g of crabmeat
120 g shelled prawns
the juice of 2 limes

The lamb, bacon, onions, green pepper, thyme and spices should be simmered in about 3 litres of water for about an hour. Add the green vegetables and cook for a further 20 minutes, then add the shellfish and lime juice and heat through for about 5 minutes.

The dish is also improved by the addition of dumplings after putting in the vegetables. These can be made from 200 g self-raising flour, a little salt, and 75 g suet mixed with enough water to make a springy dough. This should be kneaded and rolled into balls before popping into the soup.

White Soup

No account mentioning the food enjoyed by
the Austen family would be complete
without a recipe for white soup, the dish
upon which the Netherfield ball depended,
according to Mr Bingley in *Pride and
Prejudice*. This recipe is given by Jane
Grigson in her section on Jane Austen in
Food With the Famous.

1 small bacon hock
1 veal knuckle with some meat on it,
  cut in 3
1 onion and 1 carrot, both quartered
4 large celery stalks, sliced
1 tsp peppercorns
½ tsp ground mace
60 g blanched almonds crumbed with 2
  or 3 slices of white bread
1 egg yolk
300 ml cream
lemon juice, a little cayenne and salt

Make a veal stock with the bacon and veal
bone in about 2 litres of water, boiled and
skimmed and then simmered with the
vegetables, peppercorns, mace and a little salt
for about 4 hours. This should be strained,
cooled and skimmed, then boiled to reduce to
about 1½ litres. Into this should go the bread
and almonds, and the cream with the egg
beaten into it. Let it rest, test for taste, and
add more salt if necessary, then gently reheat
it with the lemon juice and a sprinkling of
cayenne. In Austen's day, boiled vermicelli
was sometimes added, but we would find that
odd.

green peas, apple pies and Stilton cheese appear in the family letters,
and Mrs Austen gratefully acknowledged gifts of fresh pork, ham,
cucumbers and sea kale from her son James, now in his turn rector at
Steventon.

It would be quite wrong to suggest that everyone in England ate well
and lived in symbiotic harmony at this time. Patently they did not, as
the contemporary record and much subsequently written social history
makes clear.[38] But the resonances we hear in the letters of Jane Austen
occur because this is essentially the cuisine and domestic economy which
came to New Zealand with the immigrant settlers of the later nineteenth
century. Because of the events of the intervening seven or so decades in
between, they came to New Zealand in a peculiarly attenuated form,
sometimes purely as memory. To understand what became of that cuisine
before it arrived here, it is important to be aware of the basis of that
process.

2

PLENTY AND WANT[1]

I F THE EIGHTEENTH CENTURY was one of the high points in the history of English cuisine, it hardly needs to be said that its most lavish manifestations were rarely if ever available to the English labouring classes. Their lot was, much more typically, the trauma of regular famine and near starvation. The 100 years to 1840 were, throughout Europe, one of successive and serious famine — indeed, the Italian social historian Massimo Montanari has characterised the period as 'the century of hunger'.[2] Its culmination was known to following generations as 'the hungry forties', encompassing among other horrors the Irish potato famine. But it was much wider in scope than that disaster alone.

CROPS AND PEOPLE

There were two reasons why this period of hunger happened. The first was a significant population spurt. As far as can be known from existing population figures and projections, between 1700 and 1800 the population of Europe grew from about 125 million to nearly 200 million.[3] This, understandably, put immense pressure on the food supply. But this was also a period of successive crop failures. In the century to 1840 hardly a year went by without there being a severe failure of the harvest somewhere in Europe. As students of the French revolution will be aware, there was a particularly severe harvest failure in 1789.[4] Perhaps even more disastrously, the famines which resulted tended to cover whole regions rather than particular localities, and to extend over several seasons.

These crop failures were probably caused by changing weather patterns. They can be tracked readily enough by following the price of grain, for which there is excellent and comprehensive data.[5] Fluctuations in the price of grain measure its availability very accurately, and if the price goes up and stays up this usually indicates a significant shortage. Such contemporary weather descriptions as exist usually confirm these analyses. Characteristically, the spells of bad weather entailed wet summers, long winters and short harvests. In 1816, for instance, there was no summer at all. The weather changes were abrupt and harsh, and the consequences for working families significant. Between 1726 and 1791 the proportion of an English labourer's income devoted to feeding his family rose from 50 percent to 88 percent. It stayed at that level more or less until 1830, although there were fluctuations from year to year.[6]

There is, of course, nothing specific to the eighteenth century about periodic famines. Horrible as it sounds, they have been one of the dynamos of European civilisation and culture. At least one major economic historian, David Fischer, has developed what he calls his 'long wave' theory of European cultural development on the basis of it.[7] According to Fischer's analysis, the gradual accumulation of agricultural surpluses leads to relative wage and price stability. The prosperity which this generates creates a trend to a lower marriage age and larger families. But this causes a population explosion (as occurred in Europe in the eighteenth century), which puts pressure on the food supply in a subsistence economy and creates inflation. If this then coincides with significant crop failures, there are liable to be instabilities and periods of social confusion, sometimes leading to wars and to revolutions. These last are often accompanied by famine and pestilence, the latter generated by lowered resistance within the population to the vector-borne plagues which are endemic in human communities and always waiting for their chance to explode.[8] This experience, in its turn, invariably seems to stimulate social and technological innovation to escape from its consequences.

Fischer identifies the key points of this pattern in European history as falling in the sixth century, when the Roman Empire finally collapsed in Western Europe; the fourteenth century, the period of the Black Death and the Hundred Years War between Britain and France;[9] the seventeenth century, characterised by civil war in Britain and the horrendous Thirty Years War in Germany; and the long famine of the eighteenth and early nineteenth centuries. He notes that these crises have tended to come more rapidly over the centuries as the waves have shortened. It is an interesting and beguiling point of view, not least because it supplies a framework within which to consider the cultural and technological responses to the particular crises which afflicted Europe from the mid-eighteenth to the mid-nineteenth century. The knock-on effects of these are particularly relevant to an understanding of the development of our cuisine.

The first of these responses was the introduction of new food crops. It was during this period of European history that rice and maize were introduced into southern Europe and potatoes into northern Europe as the food staples of the poor. This often happened in the face of widespread opposition from the prospective consumers. The deployment of Frederick the Great's army at Kolberg in 1774 to force the Prussian peasantry to plant potatoes at gunpoint is only the most dramatic and best-known instance of this resistance.[10] Many landholding contracts of the period stipulated the planting of these new crops as a condition of renewal of tenure.[11]

Although the proponents of such agricultural 'improvements' as the introduction of new crops and new systems of land tenure liked to characterise their opponents as either ignorant or ill-informed reactionaries, or superstitious peasants, the opposition of the poor to these changes was perfectly rational. Such changes degraded their diet; they had been used to living on much better and more varied foodstuffs. The change in staples was also bad for their health. An exclusively maize-based diet, for instance, leads almost immediately to the deficiency condition pellagra, which by the middle of the nineteenth century was endemic in rural southern Europe in particular. Poor people knew that there was a relationship between what they ate and this condition. They also knew that a food culture dependent on a single crop exposed them to a high level of risk. If the crop failed for any reason — as was the case in Ireland in the 1840s — the outcome would be disastrous and even fatal.[12]

The second thing that happened as people looked for ways out of the food crisis was the industrialisation of food production. Innovators began to explore how, through the application of what they called

Boxty

The poor quickly adapted themselves to the new foodstuffs and invented ways of cooking cheap but filling dishes from them. This Irish dish takes its name from the Gaelic *bochty* or *boch*, meaning poor. But it could also be something of a luxury meal as well, as the traditional Irish rhyme illustrates: 'Butter on the one side/ Gravy on the other/ Sure, them that gave me boxty/ Were better than me mother.'

  250 g raw grated potatoes
  250 g cooked mashed potatoes
  100 g self-raising flour
  salt and pepper
  milk
  lard or oil for frying

Squeeze the starch out of the grated potato and mix with the mash, flour, salt and pepper, and enough milk to make a stiff batter. Heat the lard or oil in a pan and fry large spoonfuls for about 5 minutes on each side or until browned and cooked. You can add a little grated onion to the mixture if you like. And then, as the verse says, butter on the one side, gravy on the other . . . There are many variations on this theme: Dublin coddle, pan haggerty (with cheese), stovies, or the Jewish latkes. You'll find all of these and more in Lindsay Bareham's *In Praise of the Potato*.

Kidneys in Potatoes

Some of the expedients the poor used to get some nutrition and a hot and filling dish inside them were very imaginative. This is one of the cheapest of all dishes, though it requires an oven for cooking. It also happens to be nutritious and tasty. It was particularly popular as a 'bought' item in the taverns of Portsmouth during the Napoleonic War, eaten with the sailor's tot of rum.

4 large potatoes
4 lamb kidneys
butter, salt, pepper and mustard

Trim the kidneys of their fat and core, but leave them whole. Cut the potatoes in half lengthways, scoop out a cavity, season it, and fit the kidney inside before re-assembling the potato. Bake in the oven on a tray at 220°C for about 1 hour and serve immediately with butter and mustard.

'scientific' techniques, they might best bring marginal land into intensive cultivation, and how they might improve crop yields to get much more food out of the existing available land. These innovations were largely successful in achieving these objectives. The French social historian Fernand Braudel points out, for example, that the productivity of grain planting went up from 1:4 to 1:10 between 1760 and 1820.[13]

Those exploring new ways of raising food quickly also made the unsurprising discovery that much higher capital investment in larger units was the best way to obtain greater productivity. This meant, of course, that considerably fewer people were required to work on the land, and that the patterns of landholding had to be simplified. This was also a period of widespread land enclosure in which large landowners used their political power to drive many small landholders off the land and into cities. The Highland clearances are the most dramatic and best known instance of this phenomenon, but it was much more widespread than in Scotland alone, and led to an even more fundamental change in agricultural society in both Britain and in Ireland.[14] A customary culture which had flourished and been central to much social life in both countries for centuries was torn apart within the space of two generations.

THE HUNGRY POOR

That created its own problems.[15] Many of those displaced were absorbed by the developing industrial towns which were themselves an outcome of the same eighteenth-century crisis. These grew at an astonishing rate. Manchester, already by 1800 a town of 75,000 was, by 1850, home to 400,000.[16] Not the least of these problems was feeding people once they had been physically separated from the source of their food. The diet of industrial workers during this period is a notorious by-word for inadequacy and malnutrition. We know quite a lot about this, not only because there were regular official enquiries into working-class diet (some of which were conducted by the workhouse authorities and designed to see how *little* people could live on) but there were also a large number of published private investigations, and subsequent collections of first-hand reminiscences, some of which make harrowing reading.[17]

A fascinating source of information for the earlier part of century is a budget prepared in 1810 by a group of London printers' compositors, reckoned to be the best paid of all the urban workers.[18] They received £1 19s 2d a week on average, and on the basis of their budget they argued that they needed at least £2 7s 6d for a man, his wife and two children to live any sort of life at all. This budget contains what we would regard as the absolute minimum by way of diet. It comprised bread, a very small quantity of meat, a little bit of butter and cheese, tea and a few vegetables. What they actually ate on the wage they received beggars the imagination.

One of the most interesting accounts covering the period was published in 1904 and entitled *The Hungry Forties, or Life Under the Bread Tax*. As its name suggests, it was a compilation of the memories of those, now old, who had been young adults during the worst of the famine times of the previous century. No doubt memory was blurred by time, but the consistency of the experiences described is notable. A typical contributor to this book, a skilled labourer named Charles Robinson, described how, in the earlier part of the century, when his wages were 9s a week and a loaf of bread cost 1s 2d, he and his family lived on what was known as 'crammings'. These he described as 'what was left of the grain after the flour and bran was taken away. We made a sort of pudding with it. You ask how the people did get on? Well, they got into debt and then again they lived on taters, but butchers meat we never heard of and never saw it except in the shops.' And Charles Astridge who also spoke of crammings said: 'They made your inside feel as if 'twas on fire, and sort of choked 'ee. In those days we'd see children come out into the streets and pick up a piece of bread and even potato peelings.'

Often people stole swedes or turnips from fields, or food left out for pigs, merely to survive. The Poor Law Commissioners, reporting in 1843, commented: 'The food of a labourer and his family is wheaten bread, potatoes, a small quantity of beer but only as a luxury, and a little butter and tea.' A doctor who also gave evidence to this enquiry said that four out of five working people who consulted him were really suffering from malnutrition, and their medical problems would be resolved if they ate decently and regularly.

The numerous anecdotal accounts which survive from this period and on into the century are confirmed by a similar plethora of statistical studies. These are also remarkable for their consistency. Tannahill cites the weekly diet of an average semi-skilled worker in 1841 earning 15s a week as comprising, in good times, five loaves, about two kilograms of

Cullen Skink

The poorest of the poor ate soup which was little better than scummy salt water with a few potatoes in it. But in some areas it might also incorporate a cheaply available local product. One of the best resultant soups was Cullen Skink from the Firth of Moray, home to the Finnan haddock. This is a slightly upmarket version.

1 onion, chopped
50 g butter
500 g smoked fish, cut into morsels
600 ml water
250 g mashed potato
600 ml fish stock
250 ml cream
chopped parsley, salt and pepper

Soften the onion in the butter, then add the fish and the water, and simmer for 20 minutes. Take out the fish and flake it. Return it to the water with the potato, stock, cream, parsley and seasonings. Cook for a further 10 minutes.

meat, seven pints of beer, 20 kilos of potatoes, and a little butter, sugar and tea. In bad years the meat, the beer and the butter were dispensed with.[19] The statistical explorations of diet are voluminous and by no means confined to those with a political point to make such as the works of William Cobbett and Friedrich Engels.[20] Many of them are the published outcomes of official investigations, particularly by local authorities.[21] Others are ancillary to enquiries into working conditions in mines and factories — the meal breaks allowed to workers at a time when 14-hour days were commonplace, and what workers ate when they were allowed them. Often they had to make do with a crust of bread, taken standing at their workplace or even on the job. As a result, this inadequate food was frequently supplemented by an unwelcome quantity of dust or other additives, some of it dangerous to health.

Other studies are simply the work of philanthropists, horrified at the conditions their fellow human beings were forced to endure, and driven to statistical investigations by the disbelief of other more prosperous citizens who refused to countenance the anecdotal evidence of inadequate diet among town workers, usually insisting that these were extreme cases attributable to the improvidence of the workers themselves.[22] Typical of these was James Kay, who published *The Moral and Physical Condition of the Working Classes Employed in the Cotton Manufacture in Manchester* in 1832, and S. R. Bosanquet, who published *The Rights of the Poor and Christian Almsgiving Vindicated* in 1841. Both found that the poor lived mainly on bread, potatoes and a little bacon, supplemented by tea, sugar and butter when times improved. Although some social commentators like to think of the nineteenth century as a period of continuous improvement in the condition of British working-class life, this situation persisted well into the century's third quarter.[23]

THE GORGING RICH

The contrast between the diet of the poor, even when they were continuously in work, and of those who were more comfortably off is almost obscene. In one study conducted in 1824, a well-to-do family of three adults with two maids and a manservant as well, and who regularly gave dinner parties, spent £65 a year on meat, £25 on fish and poultry, and £20 on fruit and vegetables. For comparison, a regularly employed

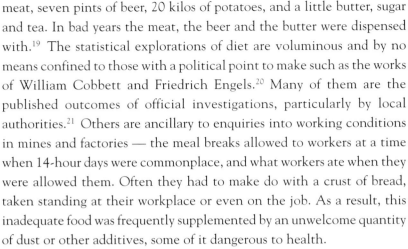

Lobscouse

Some of these poorer dishes became regionally or locally celebrated, and eating them a mark of identity with your community, as with this famous dish from Liverpool which lies behind the appellation 'scouse'. The irony is, of course, that you now have to order these cheaper cuts of meat especially, because they're too 'poor' for the butcher to stock regularly.

50 g lard
450 g brisket of beef, the fattier the better, cut up into chunks
1 kg potatoes, peeled and cut in chunks
600 ml water
1 bay-leaf, salt and pepper

Melt the lard in an iron pot and brown the meat. Add the potatoes and turn to coat with lard. Cook for 5 minutes, then add the water, bay-leaf and seasonings. Cover tightly and simmer for an hour, then uncover and let the water simmer away, browning the bottom of the dish. Serve this with pickled red cabbage.

There is a German version of the same with fish (*Fischlabskaus*), and a Dutch version with carrots, salt meat and fried onion.

artisan with a wife and two children spent about £7 pounds on meat, never ate fish, and had about £3 pounds worth of fruit and vegetables per annum.[24] According to the same source, when the rich ate their dinner it was a bad day 'when there are not at least five varieties: a substantial dish of fish, one of meat, one of game, one of poultry, and, above all, a ragout with truffles. They form the absolute minimum and *sine qua non* of a dinner for one person.' There was usually a sweet course of pies, tarts and puddings to follow, the last so rich in its composition as to be described by the French gastronomic survey, the *Almanach de Gourmands*, as a 'mélange indigeste et bizarre plutôt qu'une préparation savante et salubre'.

The well-off not only ate sumptuously but copiously. Breakfast, an informal meal, was served from 8 am. This was followed by a luncheon between 1 and 2 pm, a tea at 4 or 5 pm, and dinner at 7 or 8 pm. For those who were still hungry there might be a supper at 10. The contents of each of these would today be regarded as making a substantial meal in its own right, and the dinner a veritable feast. Bills of fare which survive for the formal dinners of the nineteenth century can only be described as astonishing. One such from 1830 features five servings in two courses and a mammoth 32 dishes for 18 people. These include not only the usual roast of beef, a calf's head in sauce, chickens and game birds, but beef palates, a lark pâté, and a matelote of carp [i.e. stewed in wine with aromatic herbs and vegetables].[25] And the Speaker of the Commons, John Denison, was to reminisce in 1899 of the appetite of the 82-year-old prime minister Lord Palmerston who, at a pre-session dinner earlier in the century,

> ate two plates of turtle soup; he was then served very amply to cod and oyster sauce; he then took a pâté; afterwards he was helped to two very

Galantine of Chicken

A galantine is essentially a stuffed chicken. This recipe is from *The Gastronomic Regenerator*, written by one of the most famous of all Victorian cooks, Alexis Soyer, the chef at London's Reform Club. You can probably buy a boned chicken, but boning is easy enough to do once you get the hang of it. There is a very good description of how to do it in the first volume of *Mastering the Art of French Cooking* by Beck, Bertholle and Child. It's quite a good, cheap way to earn a reputation as a cook, but the Victorians took it rather seriously. This is one of their dinner classics.

1 large boned chicken
4 slices fatty bacon
4 slices cooked ham, cut in strips
a few large black mushrooms, chopped
some shelled pistachio nuts
about 1 litre chicken stock
2 carrots
2 onions
a bouquet garni
salt and pepper

Season the chicken and stuff it with about 500 g of good-quality forcemeat made in the proportion of 1 cup minced veal, to 2/3 cup suet, 1 tbsp butter, a couple of eggs, salt and pepper, and a grating of nutmeg, interspersed with the pistachios and mushrooms, and layered with the bacon and ham. Don't overstuff the chicken. Sew it up and poach it for a good hour in the stock with the vegetables and the bouquet. It should be served cold on a bed of chopped aspic. This can be made from the cooking stock, strained, boiled down, and with a little gelatine mixed in. Alternatively, it can be roasted, well buttered and wrapped in foil, at 160°C. Allow about 20 minutes for each 100 g of bird, and then a further 20 minutes without the foil to brown.

greasy-looking entrées; he then despatched a plate of roast mutton (two slices) . . . there then appeared before him the largest, and to my mind the hardest, slice of ham that ever figured on the table of a nobleman, yet it disappeared just in time to answer the enquiry of the butler, 'Snipe or pheasant, my Lord?' He instantly replied 'Pheasant', thus completing his ninth dish of meat at that meal.[26]

Potted Hare

Potting meats to keep a surplus fresh was very common prior to the invention of the refrigerator. This very simple but delicious recipe comes from Elisabeth Ayrton's *The Cookery of England*. She, in her turn, got it from an Edinburgh manuscript of 1780. The Victorians liked to eat a savoury dish such as this at the end of a meal.

1 kg hare meat
½ kg fatty pork
½ tsp each marjoram and thyme
a sprig of parsley
grated nutmeg
salt and pepper
clarified butter

Mince all the ingredients finely, except the butter, and put in ovenproof pots, leaving room at the top. Bake in the oven for 2 hours at 140°C, and then cover with melted clarified butter. Keep it in the refrigerator until you need it, or even in a cool larder. The butter will keep it fresh for quite a long time. You can make the same with veal or venison.

This was extreme, but even the less well-off among the middle class did well enough for themselves. The chef Alexis Soyer, in one of his several books, cites the case of a shopkeeper's wife who in the course of a single week kept a table which carried roast and hashed beef, pork, lamb chops, fish and steak, with copious green vegetables and potatoes, and sweet dishes besides.[27] As the prosperity of this family increased, Soyer was able to quote the wife as saying of their daily fare that it comprised 'a soup or a fish, one remove, either joint or poultry, one entree, two vegetables, a pudding or tart, and a little dessert'. And a curious little book *What Shall We Have for Dinner*, published under the name of 'Lady Maria Clutterbuck' but actually penned by Mrs Charles Dickens, provides unwitting evidence of the plentitude of what the comfortable middle classes ate at home. This collection of dinner menus for parties of up to 24 guests recommends, for a group of eight, three soups, four fish dishes, eleven dishes of meat and game, three different cream puddings and a savoury.[28] Even contemporaries such as Jane Carlyle, who dined with the Dickenses from time to time, was moved to private protest at what she considered the insufferable vulgarity of such an overloaded table.[29]

LEAVING HUNGER BEHIND

To say that this was a food culture of contrasts, with some enjoying a varied, abundant and well-developed diet, and others continually malnourished and hungry, seems, in consideration of the facts, something of an understatement. Neither can there be any argument that in the nineteenth century the great majority of people in Britain and throughout Europe fell into the second category. The outcome of this was sometimes simple starvation, occasionally on a widespread scale. More usually, however, the outcomes were less obvious and more pernicious: endemic illness, a miserable scraping life and a premature death. Working people in Britain in the nineteenth century found that their standard of living was so degraded by their circumstances, whatever they did to ameliorate their condition, that they were confronted with two stark choices. Either they stayed and put up with it or they emigrated.

Whenever the opportunity to do the latter presented itself, that is exactly what they did. Between 1853 and 1876 more than 4 million outwards emigrants are recorded in the official statistics as leaving Britain. These figures are notoriously inaccurate; probably the numbers were about double that. This phenomenon was paralleled by developments in Ireland in the wake of the potato famines, particularly those of the 1840s. Between 1841 and 1925, 5.8 million people left Ireland because there was no prospect whatsoever of their earning a living there.[30]

Many English, Scottish and Irish people fetched up in the antipodes as a result. During the third quarter of the nineteenth century, 804,366 people are recorded as leaving Britain as emigrants for Australia and New Zealand. This too is probably a gross underestimate. In New Zealand alone between 1861 and 1876 net immigration — that is, those arriving minus those leaving — amounted to 207,000 in a non-Maori population in 1876 of just under 400,000.[31] The great preponderance of these immigrants were from England.[32] The gold rushes of the mid-century also contributed their share.

Hunger, in one form or another, drove our European ancestors out of Britain. That hunger has had a significant effect on the development of our national eating habits cannot be doubted. But to understand what that has meant in day-to-day practice we need to go more deeply into the process of migration which resulted. The people who came here were mostly people of a particular kind, and that determined what they chose to do to assuage their hunger when they got here — in other words, it meant not only that they would want to eat a good deal more than they'd been used to at home, but also that they would choose particular food items. What underlay this development was the globalisation of international trade.

People speak of the globalisation of international trade as if it is a new phenomenon. In fact a very good case can be made — and has been made by Paul Hirst and Grahame Thompson in their 1996 study, *Globalisation in Question* — that during the period from about 1870 to the First World War the international economy was much more highly globalised than it is now or is likely to be even under the auspices of the

World Trade Organisation.[33] There is quite a lively debate among economic historians as to whether one of the underlying causes of the First World War was a serious international trade imbalance in agricultural commodities. Proponents of this view argue that because one of the principal consequences of the industrialisation of food production which arose from the experience of famine and hunger was the internationalisation of food delivery, any significant change in this system was bound to have profound consequences.[34]

What is important from our point of view is that unlike the experience of famine, the globalisation of food production *was* an entirely new phenomenon. Until the middle of the nineteenth century, most food consumed locally was produced locally. It wasn't uncommon for people to be starving literally a few score miles from a food surplus. All of that changed, first with the building of a canals network and then a railways network in Britain, and then through the creation of an international shipping network. This last was also new. Although there had always been some international trade by sea, the nineteenth century saw an explosion in the volume of traffic, the number of routes available and the quantity of staple foodstuffs carried. Food could now be brought considerable distances to feed large populations concentrated in centres of industrial activity. This not only allowed cities to grow exponentially, but also allowed particular countries to concentrate on and specialise in aspects of feeding them.

This had a notable impact on British farming. Until the mid 1840s, British farmers were protected by the Corn Laws — a very high tariff barrier imposed on imported grains. This made farming quite lucrative for large landowners, although it also meant that the price of bread, as a staple of the British worker's diet, was very high. The Corn Laws were repealed in 1846. The effects of this were not immediately felt, but between 1850 and 1880 three important things happened.

First, during that period the vast arable lands of the American Midwest, of Australia, of western Russia and the Argentine came steadily and increasingly into wheat cultivation. Secondly, these countries built extensive railway networks to transport their immense quantities of grain to the ports. Thirdly, the international shipping network which developed was based mainly on the returning immigrant ships which had brought in the labour for these new farms and for railway construction. The process therefore fed on itself and created its own dynamic expansion.

As the new wheat sources began to deliver their harvests, these were absorbed at first by the needs of the Crimean War, then by the American Civil War, and then by the huge market for beef- and pork-fattening which developed around Chicago. But from 1870 the new wheat harvests became increasingly available for international consumption. What made these grains particularly attractive was their relatively cheap price, even taking into account the costs of shipping. Between 1860 and 1900, for instance, the cost of transporting grain from Chicago to Britain fell by 72 percent. British farmers could no longer compete, and between 1870 and the First World War were forced to go through fundamental structural changes in order to survive in their new situation.

POOR FARMING MEN

British agriculture did survive, largely through a shift from arable to pastoral and horticultural production. As had happened a century earlier, farming became even more capital intensive. This in its turn meant a significant fall in the demand for farm labour and the development of considerable unemployment in the British farming industry. Between 1870 and 1904, areas in grain production in Britain fell from 3.8 million acres to 1.7 million. Over more or less the same period the numbers of agricultural labourers required in British agriculture fell from 3 million to 2 million.[35] The result for the displaced farm labourers was poverty, falling wages, desperation, industrial unrest and mass emigration. By a quirk of history a significant proportion of the agricultural labourers who emigrated ended up in New Zealand.[36]

The period from 1870 to 1880 was an intensive period of government-underwritten capital development in New Zealand's communications and development infrastructure — the so-called Vogel period. Parallel with this development, the government was also encouraging mass assisted immigration. Between 1870 and 1875, the most intensive period of nineteenth-century immigration to New Zealand, the country took in well over 100,000 people. And because of an arrangement worked out with the agricultural unions in the wake of a series of widespread but failed strikes in protest at the reduction of agricultural wages in southern and central England, almost all these people and their families were members of agricultural unions. These two factors are significant in the development of our national diet.

All of the accounts seem to agree that farm labourers ate even more badly in the nineteenth century than their town counterparts. They may have been responsible for the production of the meat and dairy produce which the burgeoning middle classes enjoyed, but these items rarely appeared on their own tables. Nor could they easily supplement their inadequate diet by their own efforts. They were mostly forbidden to use the land surrounding their cottage (often a rural slum) to grow their own food, or they were obliged to pay the farmer for whom they worked, and who usually owned their home and its surroundings, for the privilege.

There are many first-hand accounts of rural labouring life throughout the nineteenth century. For the earlier decades we have the writings of William Cobbett to give us some insight into how the rural poor lived in the period following the wars with the French. Cobbett, whose life (1763–1835) more or less spanned the 'century of hunger', had himself been a rural labourer and gardener, and could personally recollect the introduction of potatoes to the village of Farnham where he was born and grew up. He 'very well remembered', he wrote, 'that even the poorest of the people would not eat them. They called them hog-potatoes; but now they are become a considerable portion of the diet of those who raise the bread for others to eat.'[37] Thus he had the first-hand experience to understand the rural workers' predicament when, as a radical journalist, he took up his pen to excoriate those he saw as being responsible for it. So miserable indeed were the circumstances he described in his periodical the *Political Register*, and his subsequent *Rural Rides* and *Cottage Economy*, that his middle-class readers could scarcely countenance what he had to say of the lives of rural workers. Of the village of Cricklade in 1821 he wrote:

> The labourers seem miserably poor. Their dwellings are little better than pig-beds, and their looks indicate that their food is not nearly equal to that of a pig. Their wretched hovels are stuck upon little bits of ground on the road side where the space is wider than the road demanded. In many places they have not two rods to a hovel.[38]

And he went on to say that in his whole life 'I never saw human wretchedness equal to this'. But Cobbett was always careful to point out that where common land had not been enclosed for private purposes by large landowners, and where villagers had retained customary rights to use land around their cottages for cultivation as a supplement to their diet, they lived much better. If there was a return to this way of life, he suggested, then much rural poverty and deprivation would disappear.

Some of his readers were even more sceptical when in November 1829, in the wake of disturbances in Surrey, Cobbett warned the landowners of England:

> You and the taxgatherers have taken from the labourers, by degrees, every article of decent clothing and of household stuff; you have taken from them their cows and pigs and hens and bees; you have cut them off from every inch of common; you have enclosed all, you have grasped all to yourselves; and after this you complain that they will not stir to extinguish the flames that are consuming your barns and your stacks.[39]

The following winter there was widespread rioting and rick-burning following a poor harvest and the laying-off of rural workers because of it. The response of the authorities was to accuse Cobbett of fomenting this uprising, when his only crime had been to draw attention to the general distress which had preceded it. Central to his message was the relationship between the meagre diet of the rural workers and their families, and their low and wholly inadequate wages, when many farmers could have afforded better but would not pay.

That matters had not materially changed by the other end of the century is clear from Flora Thompson's *Lark Rise to Candleford*,[40] which covers the period up to the First World War. Far from being hostile to the rural life, this is an affectionate account of an almost idyllic rural childhood. What it does make clear, however, is how very close to subsistence rural labouring families lived even into the twentieth century, and how little of the food they were instrumental in producing fell to their lot. For instance, most labouring families kept pigs, but they ate them only rarely. Instead, the animals were sold to meet cash needs such as the rent. The family might get a ham or two out of this annual process, but this was all the meat they might see in a year. Thompson recounts how the children of rural labourers had a single main meal each day which habitually began with a Yorkshire pudding to take the edge off hunger before the meat was served.

Potato and Bacon Hotpot

The ingenuity of the nineteenth-century poor in making their meals stretch to feed their families is impressive. Many of these expedients have survived because they are not only cheap and nourishing but also delicious. One of these traditional recipes, for a potato and bacon hotpot, is given by Jocasta Innes in her *Paupers' Cookbook*. She remarks, 'I got it from my mother who can't remember where she got it from.' When I first encountered it, I was surprised to note that it is very similar to one made regularly by my own grandmother, born in Central Otago in 1876. This is my granny's variation.

10 large potatoes, peeled and thinly
   sliced
3 onions, peeled and sliced
3 tart apples, peeled, cored and sliced
6 rashers of bacon with the rind
   removed, chopped
salt and pepper
nutmeg
a *roux* sauce made of 1 tbsp each of
   butter and flour with 600 ml of milk

Layer half the potatoes in a large casserole, then put in a layer of the onions, bacon and apples well mingled, then the balance of the potatoes. Add salt and pepper and a good grating of nutmeg. Make the sauce by melting the butter and blending in the flour. Let this cook for a few minutes and then add the milk and a little more salt and pepper. Cook gently until it thickens, and then pour it over the ingredients in the casserole, shaking it well down. It should just cover. Bake covered in an oven preheated to 200°C for 1 hour; uncover it and give it another hour at 180°C.

Many poor people would not have had an oven but they would take this dish, obviously for festive occasions, to the village baker and it would be cooked in his cooling bread oven along with many others.

Yorkshire Pudding

A good Yorkshire pudding is a delight rarely encountered these days. It goes best with a roast, although that was not its function in the nineteenth century, when it was eaten to take the edge off the appetite so that less was eaten of the dishes which followed. It will not only take the edge off your appetite but will also add inches to your waistline. Do it anyway.

    300 ml milk
    125 g plain flour
    salt
    2 eggs

Make a batter by gradually beating the milk into the seasoned flour and then beating the eggs into this mixture. Let it rest in a cool place for about half an hour. Pour some of the fat from the roasting dish into another small tin; return it to the oven until it is really hot, and then pour in the batter. Return this to the oven (which should have its heat raised to brown the meat), and cook for about 30 minutes until it is puffy and golden. If you have a double oven this will make life easier, in which case cook the pudding at 200°C.

Dorothy Hartley, who claims that this pudding can only be made successfully in Yorkshire or Lancashire and that this has to do with the 'brisk bright coal of the Black Country and the way they hang their roasting meat over the pudding below', has a most interesting but complex recipe in her *Food in England*. This involves separating the whites and yolks of the eggs, beating the former stiff before making the batter, and cooking the pudding underneath the beef so that it incorporates the juices in the pan. This recipe is not for the amateur.

Alongside such anecdotal accounts there is the usual plethora of statistical material available on the income and thereby the diet of rural labourers throughout the nineteenth century. The revision of the Poor Law in 1834 which put an end to a system of 'outdoor relief' in which local taxes were used to top up the wages of agricultural workers to subsistence levels was touted by its proponents as freeing up the labour market in ways which would permit wages to rise, thus ensuring that rural workers got the benefits of agricultural improvement. This did not happen, and agricultural workers continued to exist in grinding poverty.

Select committees of the House of Lords in 1836 and 1838 found that wages still fell far short of providing comforts. Labourers were now engaged by the day, instead of by the year as had been the case for centuries, and were turned off when there was no work or times were bad. Their diet was meagre in the extreme, comprising little more than bread, potatoes and beer, with a few green vegetables when they could get them. These reports continue to paint the same melancholy picture in 1843 (Report of the Special Poor Law Commissioners on the Employment of Women and Children), 1863 (Report of the Medical Office of the Privy Council), 1870 (*The Agricultural Labourer: A Short Summary of his Position*) and in 1893 (Report of the Royal Commission on Agricultural Labour).[41]

When these people came to New Zealand in the latter part of the nineteenth century, they brought with them both this experience of agricultural poverty and hunger, and a determination that they would not, in their new country, starve as they had done in the old. Notwithstanding the hunger which drove them out, it is important to remember that they also left behind a burgeoning Victorian tradition of good eating in both town and country which was not solely confined to the rich, or even to the comfortably off. This was new and distinct for its era, and also had its influence on the diet the immigrants adopted in the new land.

Lamb chops and oysters

It is perhaps now a matter of astonishment that we can read Sam Weller saying in 1837:

> Poverty and oysters always seem to go together . . . the poorer a place is, the greater call there seems to be for oysters . . . here's [in Whitechapel] a oyster stall to every half dozen houses. The street's lined with 'em. Blessed if I don't think that ven a man's werry poor, he rushes out of his lodgings and eats oysters in reg'lar desperation.[42]

What is notable about this is not that oysters were regarded as food for the poor (they were very common and cheap in London until the mid 1800s, when the pollution of the Thames became so bad that it poisoned the beds) but what it tells us about the eating habits of the ordinary urban working population. Mostly they lived in lodging houses and took their meals in the street or in eating houses.

The social reformer and observer Henry Mayhew, writing in 1851, particularly remarked upon the wide variety of produce and comestibles regularly available from small street stalls or itinerant vendors.[43] These included not only shellfish of every variety, but also bread and butter, baked potatoes (sometimes stuffed with a kidney), pies, boiled eggs and soup. Eels and whelks were regularly available, the former both jellied and, rather less usually to our taste, as a very popular soup flavoured with mint and celery.[44] A wide range of dairy produce was common, even in the largest cities, where cows were kept in enclosed sheds, often in circumstances which would today have the health inspector calling at once.[45] These supplied not only milk and cream, either for use directly or in fresh syllabub (cows had been kept in St James' Park since the seventeenth century for this purpose) but also yoghurt and curds and whey (a treat sufficiently popular to feature in *Tom Brown's Schooldays* as the ordinary thing to eat on an excursion).

Those with a little more cash in their pockets could dine at an eating house. These were so common that, according to a writer in *Household Words*, the magazine owned and edited by Charles Dickens, there was scarcely a street in London without one. In the earlier part of the century the standard of hygiene in these left a great deal to be desired. They were characterised, according to contemporary descriptions, by wooden stalls which afforded a modicum of privacy, and a sand- or sawdust-covered

Beef with Oyster Sauce

One of the most interesting but least-known English contributions to the international cuisine is the teaming of certain meats and shellfish. The last survivor of this tradition is the so-called 'carpet bag steak' which combines beef and oysters. Originally the associations were much more widespread and common: lamb with crab, for example, or chicken with mussels, or pork with anchovies.

This dish was commonly eaten in the chop houses of Dickensian London, but was obviously out of the reach of the poor, who would have had to content themselves with just the oysters.

6 rump steaks
1 dozen oysters in their liquor
120 g softened butter
1 tbsp plain flour
salt, pepper and a little grated nutmeg
200 ml milk

Grill the steaks to your taste (about 5 minutes each side). Warm the oysters in their juice and blend the butter, flour and seasonings. Strain the oyster liquor onto this in a small pan and add the milk. Cook this until it thickens, return the oysters to it, and pour a little over each steak to serve.

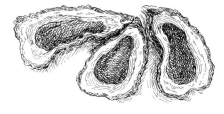

Mutton Pies

Hot pies were a staple of the street vendors in the nineteenth century. Sometimes they were made of mutton chops with apple, but this version from Elizabeth Ayrton's *The Cookery of England* was more common.

1 kg short pastry
800 g lean chopped mutton or lamb
2 onions, very finely chopped
chopped parsley
800 ml good leftover beef or mutton gravy
an egg yolk

Line small soufflé dishes with the pastry. Fill with the mixed meat, onion and parsley, and season if you have to. Pour over the warmed gravy, cover with a round of pastry, make a hole in the top, and gild with the yolk. Bake at about 160°C for about an hour. Best served hot.

A Joint of Mutton

Oddly, in a sheep-producing country, mutton, which the Victorians ate as a meat quite distinct from lamb, is sometimes quite difficult to get. Nathaniel Hawthorne should have stayed out of the railway hotels and found his way to an establishment where they knew how to cook it.

In her *Food in England*, Dorothy Hartley gives an intriguing recipe for boiled mutton joint.

Put mint and thyme with onions and a good dash of pepper and salt into water, and let them boil till the liquid is well flavoured before putting in the meat . . . See that the meat is completely covered and then withdraw the pan and let it only simmer thereafter. A few minutes after putting in the meat, skim, and again at intervals, as you want to lift the meat out clean and very white-looking.

She doesn't say how long to cook it (use your judgement and a skewer) but suggests serving with a hot caper sauce. Mr Pickwick would have approved. 'A select company of the Bath footmen,' it will be recalled, invited Sam Weller to 'a friendly soiree consisting of a boiled leg of mutton, with caper sauce, turnips and potatoes'.

Stewed Eel

It's always seemed to me astonishing that when our waterways teem with eels we don't do more with them. Our English forebears would not have made this mistake. This recipe has been adapted by Jane Grigson for her *Food With the Famous* from the diary of the Rev. James Woodforde, a gourmet (some would say guzzling) parson who lived in the late eighteenth century (1740–1803), and who always recorded the meals he had and often who supplied them. His Norfolk landlord, who was a miller, sometimes sent him a string of eels from the mill race.

A *beurre manié* is a variant of the more familiar *roux*: the flour and butter are moulded together 'dry' and by hand, and then stirred into the sauce so it thickens afterwards.

1 kg eels for 4 people
milk to cover
2 onions, sliced
a bay-leaf
butter and flour to make a *beurre manié*
300 ml or more of cream
juice of a lemon
some slices of fried bread
salt, pepper and a little chopped parsley

Wash the eels and skin them. Chop them into pieces and simmer them in the milk with the onions, bay-leaf, salt and pepper until they are cooked. This should take about half an hour. Remove and keep warm, and add the *beurre manié* to the liquor with the cream and lemon juice. Simmer until it thickens. Serve the eel pieces on the fried bread with a few of the onions, with the sauce over and with a sprinkling of parsley.

Mock Turtle Soup

Turtle soup was one of the curiosities of nineteenth-century cuisine, and certainly led to one of its oddest trades. Ships at sea, if they encountered a turtle, or if they were able to call at an island where they were known to be, would capture as many as possible and bring them back alive in seawater tanks to London where they would be sold to restaurants. They made a thick green unctuous soup, much favoured for mayoral banquets, but demand soon outstripped supply and a substitute had to be found. Thus 'mock' turtle soup.

This nineteenth-century recipe is from Elisabeth Ayrton, *The Cookery of England*. Forcemeat balls are usually made from breadcrumbs, minced meat, onion and seasoning, and rolled into floured balls. They should be popped into the soup to cook towards the end.

half a calf's head
1 litre beef stock
8 shallots
90 g butter
60 g flour
300 ml dry sherry
1 tbsp each of chives and parsley, well chopped
salt, pepper and a pinch of cayenne
2 tsp soy sauce
1 tbsp mushroom ketchup
juice of a lemon
20 or so small forcemeat balls

Boil the rinsed head for about an hour and a half, and strain, keeping the broth. Remove the meat from the bones and cut into small pieces. Discard the bones. Meanwhile, fry the shallots lightly in the butter and add the flour to make a *roux*. Add this to the kept broth and bring to the boil. Reduce the heat and add the other ingredients, including the chopped meat. Simmer for 20 minutes and serve.

This will explain why John Tenniel, in illustrating Lewis Carroll's *Alice*, chose to depict the Mock Turtle as a calf. 'Beautiful soup, so rich and green,' the creature sang mournfully. It sounds even better in the German translation of 1867: 'Schone Zuppe, so schwer und so grün.'

floor, rarely refreshed and designed to catch all manner of dirt. For about a shilling one could get a meal of boiled beef, a dried pea mash, new potatoes and bread, with coffee or beer. One of Dickens's writers in *All the Year Round* visited an eating house in Lambeth which he described as a 'low roofed, dingy, dirty hole, littered with sawdust and grease. The table cloth was inconceivably dirty; the knives, forks, plates etc., were of the rudest description, and clogged with black dirt.' Understandably he did not wait to try the food. Even in the better establishments eating out was not a very elegant experience. In a mid-century description of a Leadenhall Street eating house specialising in turtle soup, a popular but expensive dish, the writer remarked that 'the steam of thousands [of meals] hung, in savoury grease upon its walls. I could have inscribed my name with a penknife if I had been so disposed, in the essence of innumerable turtles.'[46]

As the class of diner moved upwards, so the standard of the eating house tended to improve. Those at the upper end of the social spectrum had always eaten well when out of their own homes, but their habit was to dine at one another's houses. Their main contribution to Victorian cuisine was the country-house breakfast, the influence of which on subsequent New Zealand cuisine was significant but attenuated, and is dealt with in subsequent chapters. But as the middle class grew, and the century progressed, so too did the demand for an improvement in the standard of public eating establishments.

One of the main influences on this development was the growth of the railways. Fresh food ingredients could now be brought quickly from their various sources to developing town and city markets; even fresh fish could be regularly obtained in inland places. There was too, a significant increase in regular travel by train, both for business purposes and as whole middle-class families adopted the fashionable habit of taking family holidays. We forget in this age of travel that until the invention of the railways, leaving one's place of birth even temporarily involved an arduous, sometimes dangerous journey. Until the middle of the nineteenth century, most people never left their home town or village. Even as late as the 1960s alcohol could only be served to *bona fide* travellers in Scotland on a Sunday if they were also taking a meal. What is interesting about this quaint survival is not the requirement in itself but the definition of a traveller: someone who was more than five miles

Syllabub

The syllabub, a thickened and enhanced cream confection, was a characteristic part of the English cuisine for three centuries and then unaccountably disappeared. Nor did it translate, as might have been expected, to New Zealand, at least in this form. This recipe is from Hannah Glasse's *Art of Cookery Made Plain and Easy* (1760).

600 ml cream
200 ml sherry
juice of 2 oranges
zest of an orange and a lemon
350 g caster sugar
some good claret, i.e. cabernet
    sauvignon

Mix all of the ingredients except the claret and 100 g of the sugar, and beat until this is stiff. Serve in tall glasses on top of some of the claret sweetened with the remaining sugar. (This is perhaps not to modern taste.) Glasse also suggests thickening the liquid with gelatine rather than beating it. Does this survive in disguise and fugitive form as the Spanish Cream of my childhood, I wonder?

Barley Soup

The Victorian philanthropists were great ones for offering soup to the poor, but didn't scruple to eat it themselves. This recipe for a cheap but nourishing soup has an interesting history detailed by Jane Grigson. It comes from a manuscript book of recipes kept by Emily, Lady Shaftsbury, wife of the reforming 7th Earl, Anthony Cooper, between 1855 and 1872. Despite his title, Cooper was perennially short of money and Emily bent her best efforts to supporting him domestically by feeding him frugally but well. This recipe, says her manuscript, she got from her mother Lady Cowper, whose bohemian lifestyle was one of the features of Regency London. Lady Cowper's second husband, Lord Palmerston, was reputed by gossip to be Emily's father during the currency of the first husband. Daughter or stepdaughter, the Palmerston household often came to the rescue of the straitened Shaftsburys by having them to stay for extended periods.

60 g pearl barley
2 litres veal or chicken stock
60 g butter
4 leeks, sliced finely
2 or 3 sticks of young celery, chopped
150 ml cream
1 egg yolk
salt, pepper and nutmeg

Cook the barley gently in half the stock for about an hour. Stew the leek and celery gently in the butter until it softens, and then add the remaining stock, simmer until cooked and combine with the barley. Flavour and season. Beat the egg and cream together and then stir it very carefully into the hot soup. Serve it at once and don't let it boil or it will probably curdle.

from home.[47] This new-found freedom of movement, in its turn, created a demand for hotels of a superior standard, usually with their own dining facilities on the premises. The nineteenth century heralded the great age of the railway hotel, with all its conveniences.

This also met a need for places in which women might respectably dine in public. Eating out began to move up the social scale. In Dickens's time, certain London taverns, particularly those on the river towards Greenwich, were becoming known as places where the respectable could eat either as an entertainment for friends at lunch, or after the theatre. The food, however, still fell far short of what later generations were to expect at the Cafe Royal. Nathaniel Hawthorne, American consul in Liverpool from 1853 to 1857, remarked 'the living at the best of English hotels, so far as my travels have brought me acquaintance with them, deserves but moderate praise, and is especially lacking in variety. Nothing but joints, joints, joints.'[48] He was one of a long line, including Dickens, who commented on or complained about the ubiquitous mutton.

Even the miserably poor enjoyed a few of these improving developments. In the 1860s a Dr Edward Smith, who had an interest in nutrition, conducted a survey of over 60 workhouses. He found that in most workhouses meat and vegetables were offered at least three times a week, and that soup or broth were common. This was something of an improvement on the earlier years of these establishments when porridge, skilly (watered skimmed milk, sometimes served warm), and bread and cheese had been the only available commons. Interestingly, Smith disapproved of these improvements because he thought that such luxury encouraged a dependent attitude in the poor.[49]

Outside the workhouse, the arrival of the railways may not have been as great a boon to the working classes as it was to their putative betters. The ability to transport fish rapidly from place to place before it spoiled made it the staple of working-class diet. Mayhew in particular commented on this in 1851, remarking that both its relative cheapness and the ease with which it could be cooked made it attractive. But this is not to say that it was liked. Pickled or smoked herring or mackerel, if produced en masse for cheap consumption, is not an appealing proposition:

The rooms of the very neediest of the needy of our population always smell of fish; most frequently herrings. So much so that, to people like myself, who have been in the habit of visiting their dwellings, the smell of herrings even in comfortable homes, savours from association so strongly of squalor and wretchedness, as to be often most oppressive.[50]

A lack of cooking facilities also militated against the eating of fruit and vegetables. Prejudice against raw food continued (and was even rational in an era when clean conditions of transport and storage were not at a premium), and the sugar required to make fruit palatable to Victorian taste was too expensive.

Mostly the poor ate potatoes. One consequence of combining these with that other staple, fish, was the development of the archetypal working-class dish, fish and chips. There is heated controversy over its origins. Claudia Roden, in her magisterial survey of Jewish cooking, traces the habit to a legacy of the Portuguese *marranos* who came as refugees to Britain in the sixteenth century.[51] But it remained a habit confined to the upper classes until Joseph Malin, an Eastern European refugee, opened a cooked fish business in Bow in 1860 and took the obvious step of cutting up potatoes and adding them to the oil in which the battered or crumbed fish was done. Others dispute this. John Walton, in the standard work on the subject,[52] gives credit to Malin, whose business survived well into the 1960s, but locates the origins of the dish at least 20 years earlier, although more obscurely and in the northern industrial towns as well as in London. The potatoes may originally have been baked, although the fried chip appears in, for instance, Soyer's *Shilling Cookery* of 1854. Whatever may be the truth of the matter, the association of fish with poverty was to have a significant influence on its place in the nineteenth-century New Zealand cuisine.

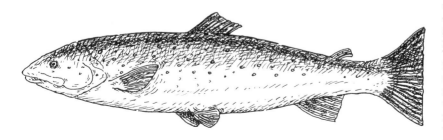

Fried Fish

In her *Book of Jewish Food*, Claudia Roden remarks upon the specifically London Jewish practice of frying fish in batter and eating it cold. This she tracks to Portuguese Marranos who came to England in the sixteenth century, and cites a reference to this as early as 1544. The first traceable Jewish cookbook published in England, Judith Montefiore's *Jewish Manual* of 1846, also refers to the practice, as does Thomas Jefferson from a visit to England in the early nineteenth century. Probably we'll never really know the full story of the connection between this and fried battered or crumbed fish. But interestingly, in her *Modern Cookery* of 1845, Eliza Acton includes a section on Jewish cookery and gives a recipe for fried salmon, to be served cold. This is her recipe.

**sufficient olive oil to deep-fry the fish
about 800 gm salmon fillet**

Clean and dry the salmon and fry it gently until it is cooked right through. This should take about 5 minutes. This should be lightly browned at most. She also recommends sole, plaice or turbot as a substitute, and suggests that it should be eaten either hot or cold with 'a Mauritian chatney (sic)', and 'garnished with a light foliage' arranged symmetrically round a portion of larger fish.

Grilled Herrings with Mustard

Herrings are getting harder to obtain, not because there aren't any in this part of the world but because the retailing of food is becoming increasingly homogenised. Unless it is a mass product with a fixed profit margin the main outlets are not prepared to stock items such as whole herrings, for which there is only a small market. Assuming that you have got them, and they are cleaned and gutted, dip each in seasoned oatmeal, brush them with melted butter and grill them. These should be served with plain boiled potatoes and a mustard sauce. This can be made by first making a flour and butter *roux* using 1 tsp of dry mustard with the flour, and then adding about 300 ml of milk and seasonings, and simmering it to thicken. Alternatively, the fish can be painted with a paste of mustard and white wine. If you can't get herrings, smoked fish can be substituted but it isn't as good.

In the countryside fish as a source of protein was much less available. Only poaching could guarantee any regular intake, and poaching was a risky business. A man might easily lose his living, his home, his freedom or even his life to a spring gun or in an affray with keepers if he persisted.[53] Bread and porridge alternating with porridge and bread, or in Scotland kale brose (a miserable green vegetable soup), was the more usual fare. And then, the labourer, if lucky enough to accompany the farmer to the nearest town on market day, might get an additional treat — the scraps left over at the inn back door after his employer had dined. It was not a diet calculated to make a man fat, nor a life much to be hankered after. Small wonder, then, that so many of the urban and rural poor took the chance when it offered itself, and emigrated in search of a better fed existence.

3

SALT BEEF AND THE FARMERS' ORDINARY

ETWEEN 1861 AND 1881, 556,156 immigrants entered New Zealand.[1] Because of a bizarre administrative decision taken in the 1970s to destroy the original nineteenth-century census records, the detail of where they came from is largely anybody's guess and seems for earlier historians to have been informed by the reified belief, dating from the period of the First World War, that since being British is best that is where a racially superior people such as ourselves must have come from.[2] We know only that most seem to have come from the British Isles, provided one includes Ireland within that rubric (which the original formulators of our mythologies probably would have preferred not to do). What is more important for the purposes of this exploration is to note that three of the most significant years for immigrant numbers during the nineteenth century were 1874, 1875 and 1876. During that period 94,116 immigrants are recorded as entering the country. Only the period from 1862 to 1865 (when 119,867 people entered New Zealand) surpasses it.[3] These latter were probably mostly, although by no means exclusively, miners attracted by the newly opened goldfields. This probably explains why the net immigration figure for that period is 76,947; that is, the influx was matched by an outflow of 42,920. Many probably left in subsequent years as the gold petered out.

But the influx of the mid seventies was of a different order. Not only was the outflow much lower, at 18,785, but a very high proportion of those who came during that period were distressed rural labourers.[4] Their arrival happened to coincide with a change of policy in New Zealand

Ochra Soup

A century and a half after Evelyn, the American statesman Thomas Jefferson performed a similar service for the nascent United States. You can read about this in Jane Grigson's *Food With the Famous*. Ochra is an African vegetable which probably came to the Americas with the slave trade. It was soon in regular use, as this recipe, adapted from Mary Randolph's *The Virginia Housewife* (1825), illustrates.

Take 2 double handfuls of young ochra, wash and slice them thin, and add 2 finely chopped onions. Put these in a pot with salt, pepper and 3 litres of water, and simmer for 2 or 3 hours. Add a handful of lima beans and simmer for a further hour and a half, then add 3 small custard marrows cleaned and cut into pieces, some chicken pieces, 2 or 3 pieces of veal shank with the bone, a piece of boiled pork, chopped, and half a dozen skinned tomatoes. Let it cook until the meat is done, then thicken with *beurre manié*, and serve with boiled rice.

Ochra used to be hard to get fresh but is now seen quite regularly in city greengrocers. It can always be bought in tins, although for reasons unfathomable these are usually too large for a single use. Fortunately tinned ochra freezes quite successfully. Custard marrows are smaller, and much firmer than their traditional counterparts, and are generally available in New Zealand.

associated with Julius Vogel's government, which borrowed heavily for public works and immigration, and was willing to offer assisted passages.[5] The farm labourers and their families brought with them an approach to food production and consumption which had a key influence on the development of our national cuisine. This approach focused on small-scale production for domestic consumption. It was a market-garden culture.

A MARKET GARDENING CULTURE

The European notion of the garden as a self-conscious location of culture came to Britain in the seventeenth century, mainly through the work of the diarist John Evelyn, a foundation member of the Royal Society, who has already been noted for introducing or popularising in England many of the salad vegetables now in common use. During the parliamentary interregnum he had travelled in Holland and Italy to pursue his interest in gardening, and following a visit to France in the 1650s translated a number of the classic French gardening books of his day into English. All over England landowners, from the grandest to the most humble, took up his ideas on gardening and forestry.[6]

By the end of the eighteenth century there had grown up in European polite society a whole philosophy of gardening, which ranked the garden with dancing, architecture and sculpture as a component in the elegant arts. Some familiarity with gardening became an element in the makeup of any cultivated person.[7] It was in this period and into the nineteenth century that the English developed their characteristic but ambiguous relationship with their countryside. As one cultural historian has recently remarked:

> Though ways of seeing and understanding landscape and nature are visual and literary, closely tied to the culture of the age, we can understand the particular forms they assumed in the eighteenth century only by moving beyond the landscapes, verses, and gardens themselves, to trace the changing mental and material contexts in which they were made. For the transformation in eighteenth century economic, social and cultural life, enormously affected how people saw nature. The urbanisation of Britain, the declining number of people working on the land, a new, more distanced, and scientific view of the natural world, the development of agricultural

'improvements', the development of domestic tourism among the polite classes . . . irrevocably transformed the relationship between the British, nature, and their landscape.[8]

The high seriousness with which all of this was treated found its satirist in Jane Austen whose General Tilney in *Northanger Abbey* does duty in caricature for a generation of enthusiastic aristocratic gardeners.

But this enthusiasm was not just a hobby for a few over-refined eccentrics; it also had practical implications of some significance. James Cook placed immense store by his efforts to introduce European domestic vegetables to New Zealand at the very moment that his colleague Joseph Banks was collecting exotic flora to carry in the other direction. And in Britain the art of gardening found its more humble and domestic philosophers in Gilbert White at Selbourne and Philip Miller at Chelsea, then a garden village on the outskirts of the metropolis and long home to the Physicke Garden, sheltering herbs brought back from around the globe for the benefit of the London apothecaries. (It still does, and may be visited by tourists from New Zealand who will find the descendants of plants brought from here to there by Banks.)

Miller described his ideal kitchen garden in 1731 as requiring at least an acre of ground:

> This ground must be walled round, and if it can be conveniently contrived, so as to plant both sides of the walls which have good aspects, it will be a great addition to the quantity of wall fruit; and those slips of ground which are withoutside of the walls, will be very useful for planting of gooseberries, currants, strawberries, and some sorts of kitchen plants.[9]

Cobbett, in his rural rides, regularly deplored the disappearance of the cottage garden tradition (or praised it when it still existed); and even in the burgeoning industrial towns it was not unusual to find among the dwellings strips and tiny plots devoted to kitchen gardening, a customary use which eventually developed into the vigorous urban allotment movement.

This is because the workers who had suffered the consequences of the land enclosures of the late eighteenth and early nineteenth centuries were determined to restore what they saw as their lost rights to use of their garden land.[10] The restoration of these lost rights was central to the political programmes first of Chartism and then of radical Liberalism.

Raspberry Pie

General Tilney would certainly have recognised this dish.

puff pastry
500 g raspberries
120 g white sugar, plus a little more
300 ml cream
3 egg yolks

Line a deep pie plate with pastry and put in the raspberries and the sugar. Cover with a pastry lid and make a hole in the top. Trim with a few shapes and brush the lid with a little egg white. Sprinkle with sugar. Bake at 180°C for about 45 minutes. Meanwhile, heat the cream to almost boiling, remove from the heat and quickly whisk in the yolks. Take out the pie as it nears the end of cooking and pour as much of this custard as you can into the pie through the hole. This is a tricky operation and you might like to raise the lid very carefully instead. Give the pie another 10 minutes. Serve it with what remains of the custard (or caudle as it was called in the nineteenth century).

Apples in Batter

In the period prior to the enclosures of the commons the villagers would usually have access to common fruit trees, most typically apples. There was a very wide variety of these available, and most villages made a distinctive cider. The surplus would be used in a variety of dishes, of which this is fairly typical.

6 large cooking apples, peeled and cored
raw sugar
2 cups wholemeal flour
4 eggs
salt
2 cups milk

Pack the fruit in an ovenproof dish. Fill the centre of each apple with sugar. Make a smoothly blended batter with the other ingredients and 1 tbsp of sugar, and pour this over the apples. Bake at 180°C for about an hour, and serve hot with cream.

That rural dwellers in particular retained a vivid recollection of what they thought life had been like before workers had been deprived of these rights is clear from a passage in *Lark Rise to Candleford*. Flora Thompson, a beneficiary of the compulsory education reforms of the previous decade, was called upon to assist the elderly owners of a cottage in her village (an unusual situation) with certain business affairs they could not cope with for themselves. She won the confidence of Old Sally and Dick, then in their eighties, and was admitted to the secrets of their family history. Her later recollection of this is worth quoting at length, because it encapsulates a rarely expressed popular memory of the way life had been and ought to be for ordinary rural people:

> Sally could just remember the Rise when it had stood in a wide expanse of open heath, with juniper bushes and furze thickets, and close, springy, rabbit-bitten turf. There were only six houses then and they stood in a ring round an open green, all with large gardens and fruit trees and faggot piles . . . Country people had not been so poor when Sally was a girl, or their prospects so hopeless. Sally's father had kept a cow, geese, poultry, pigs, and a donkey cart to carry his produce to the market town. He could do this because he had commoners' rights, and could turn his animals out to graze, and cut furze for firing, and even turf to make a lawn for one of his customers. Her mother made butter for themselves and to sell, baked their own bread, and made candles for lighting . . . Sometimes her father would do a day's work for wages, thatching a rick, cutting and laying a hedge, or helping with the shearing or the harvest. This provided them with ready money for boots and clothes; for food they relied almost entirely on home produce. Tea was a luxury seldom indulged in, for it cost five shillings a pound. But country people had then not acquired the taste for tea; they preferred home brewed. [11]

In the course of the century this way of life virtually disappeared, and as the labourers lost their common rights, their access to gardens and their ownership of their cottages, one of the most significant effects was the impoverishment of their diet. They also lost their independence and were forced to rely on the goodwill of the local farmers, the squire, and his professional and religious supporters, the local lawyer and clergyman. These worthies, and especially the vicar and his wife, often arrogated the right to interfere in the detail of the private lives of the labourers, determining what they could and could not eat and using this power as a much-resented opportunity for a patronising and humiliating form of personal charity.

The agricultural workers who came to New Zealand with their families in the seventies were determined not to recreate the social relationships they had suffered in Britain, and they also brought with them significant recollections of what they felt their ordinary lives would have contained had they not been unjustly deprived. Some of these elements of the lost culture they sought to recreate had continued to exist in attenuated form well into the nineteenth century. The most significant of these were the harvest home feast and the weekly tradition of the ordinary.

Harvest home and the ordinary

In the eighteenth century, as noted, it was customary for single farm labourers, but often their families too, to eat as family members with their employer. All enjoyed the same food.[12] By the period of the great migrations from Britain in the nineteenth century, this custom had largely died out as land was enclosed, and workers moved to the new industrial towns or into separate, and often poor and unsanitary, accommodation on the land. Provision for the supply of food in contracts of employment, particularly in rural areas, was often not honoured, or honoured so miserably that the labourers quit, often to the accompaniment of considerable acrimony or even legal action for breach.

In a reported case as late as 1891, we find William Burchell, a carter,

Currant Bread

For obvious reasons harvest home was characterised by special breads. Many recipes for these came to New Zealand, and survive in nineteenth-century and later cookbooks until well after the Second World War.

    25 g yeast
    150 g sugar
    650 g white flour
    2 tbsp gluten
    salt
    100 g softened butter
    milk
    200 g mixed dried fruit
    30 g chopped candied peel

Cream the yeast with a little warm water and sugar. Mix the sugar and the dried ingredients and then work in the butter and enough milk to make a firm dough. Let rise, break down, knead in the dried fruit, and let rise in a tin again before baking at 180°C for about 20 minutes, or until it is cooked. Bread with sugar in it has to be carefully watched so it does not burn. The dough can also be shaped as buns.

Harvest Tart

Apples and other fruit, for similarly obvious reasons, were also closely associated with harvest home. In particular this applied to apple tarts, although over the centuries they were cooked with varying accompaniments. These might have included rosewater and dates (in the sixteenth century), or lemon slices and quince (in the eighteenth).

50 g raisins
jigger of rum
short pastry for the base
1 kg cooking apples and 1 quince, peeled, cored and sliced
200 g sugar
lemon zest
½ tsp cinnamon
1 vanilla pod
60 g butter
beaten egg and caster sugar

Soak the raisins in the rum overnight. Line a pie dish with the pastry. Cook all of the other ingredients (including the rum and raisins, but excluding the egg and caster sugar) in the butter until the whole is slightly caramelised, and then pile this in the case. Decorate with pastry strips and glaze with the egg. Sprinkle the sugar over. Bake for 40 minutes at 200°C, watching to make sure it does not overcook. Serve hot or cold with cream.

Gloucester Lardy Cake

Special bread cakes were also made for harvest-home feasts. They come from most English regions; this one from the south-west is fairly typical.

1 tsp salt
450 g plain flour
25 g creamed yeast
100 g lard
100 g brown sugar
120 g mixed currants and sultanas

Make a dough from the flour, salt, creamed yeast and water. Let this rise once. Break it down, and on the surface spread a third of the softened lard, and a third of the sugar and mixed sultanas and currants. Fold this well in, and repeat twice more. Let it rest and rise, then roll it out and shape it into 2 cakes. Put these in 2 cake tins and let them rise again. Bake at 200°C for 45 minutes and turn out onto a cloth while still hot.

summoned to appear before the magistrates for leaving the employ of Joseph Reffel, complaining that of the potatoes he had been promised at the time of engagement he had received not more than six during his whole hiring, and that the boiler he had been promised for cooking his food was old and rusty 'and not fit to cook the food of pigs'. In addition he had had to find his own firing.[13] All that remained of the sense of communal responsibility borne by the local rural land-owning and tenant-farming classes which had previously impelled eating habits was the once-yearly 'harvest home'.

This curious remnant, which might traditionally be held any time between the end of August and mid October, marked the completion of the harvest, and was probably in its origins a survival of the medieval feast of Lammas, a celebration of the first communion using the bread of the new corn. Obviously this predates Christianity and had much more to do with the agricultural cycle and the worship of the spirit of fertility. During the English church reformation it had gone the way of many other traditional festivals, but by the middle of the nineteenth century the church had reclaimed it. It entailed not only religious observance but also feasting.

Thus in 1863 in Berkshire, the Rev. Charles Kingsley preached a sermon and at midday shared dinner in the fields with 340 labourers and their wives. This was followed by games and other organised pastimes. There are many such events recorded even quite late in the century. In 1883, for example, more than 150 harvesters sat down to a feast a Fawley Court.[14] These feasts were lavish, and usually entailed the consumption of quantities of meat which the labourers did not see at any other time of the year. According to one reminiscence from Haddenham in Buckinghamshire:

> No institution was more popular or more deeply rooted in our village sentiment than our annual feast, which fell on the first Sunday after the 19th of September . . . It should be remembered that as lack of plenty to eat was the normal experience of the poor a century ago, so a day given to fill the belly with good food was a delight. The ancient celebration was really of that character, a literal feast of good food and drink, with the mirth that goes with these things.[15]

Some of this mirth, which was fuelled by copious quantities of beer and cider, was frowned on by the church, but the drinking which accompanied the harvest home remained a principal feature of it.

Interestingly, by the later decades of the century some farmers were commuting this feasting into a cash payment known as the 'horkey', but the custom itself continued, now organised by the labourers themselves and centred as often as not on their injury benefit insurance mutual society (by now quite a common feature of rural life) and its annual dinner. This normally took place in the local public house, and quite deliberately excluded the local farmer or landowner and the parson, whose patronage was sometimes deeply resented by the labourers.[16]

Thus, throughout the nineteenth century, alongside the poverty and deprivation experienced by most farm labourers and industrial workers, there existed in rural areas or among those with memories of rural life an alternative tradition of plenty upon which those who subsequently emigrated could draw by way of a cultural comparison.

Nor was this the only opportunity the rural poor had to observe how the 'other half' lived. There was also the tradition of the farmers' ordinary. This was the midday dinner traditionally served to farmers at the local inn at the end of the weekly market day. It was essentially a fixed-price meal served to anyone who had the wherewithal. It is best described as 'hearty', usually comprising a thick soup, a pie or savoury pudding, roast meat or poultry, and a sweet pie or pudding, with cheese to follow. The main course would be accompanied by quantities of vegetables, often creamed in winter, and savoury puddings served with the meat, along with large helpings of potatoes.[17] Unless they had a particularly generous employer, the labourers did not take part, although they might be vouchsafed the scraps or remains at the inn back door. But they were certainly well aware of what they were deprived of; it was before their eyes if not in their bellies.

Once the rural poor had taken the long step to emigration, those who left the British Isles had these contrasts fixed in their mind's eye. And the voyage to the new land itself created a further opportunity for comparisons. If they came to New Zealand in steerage, as most did, then they would have lived in daily close proximity to their cabin-class fellow passengers. In those circumstances they quickly became aware of how much better the middle and upper classes fared at table than they did.

Savoury Pudding

The savoury puddings of rural England were rather grand affairs. This recipe, given in Elisabeth Ayrton's *The Cookery of England,* is from Cumberland, and would have been eaten in Carlisle on market day, probably served with pork or goose.

700 ml milk
120 g fine oatmeal
120 g breadcrumbs
2 eggs
100 g flour
120 g suet
chopped sage, thyme and parsley to taste
240 g chopped onions
a handful or two of raisins and chopped prunes
salt and pepper

Pour the heated milk over the oatmeal and breadcrumbs and let it stand for about 10 minutes, then beat in the eggs, and mix in the other ingredients to a smooth batter. Bake for about an hour in a preheated oven at 180°C.

The other traditional pudding eaten as a part of the ordinary, particularly in the north, was Peas Pudding. This is easily made by soaking 250 g of dried peas overnight, draining them and boiling them until soft with mint, thyme, parsley and marjoram. Drain them again, blend to a smooth paste, add some melted butter and seasoning, and boil in a pudding basin for about an hour.

Dried Pea Soup

Pulses need not be a horror either. This soup
would have been eminently suited to
catering at sea. The English traditionally
make it with a knuckle bone, but this would
not have been available to the steerage at
sea; nor would the eggs probably, these being
reserved for the cabin.

  200 g dried green peas
  1500 ml water
  100 g tapioca
  50 g butter
  salt and pepper
  some chopped hard-boiled eggs
  chopped parsley

Simmer the peas in half the water until soft,
then purée. Add the remaining water,
seasoning and tapioca, and bring to the boil.
Put in the butter and simmer for about 20
minutes. Scatter the eggs and parsley on each
serving.

LIFE ON THE OCEAN WAVE

The contrast between the diets of steerage and cabin passengers on nineteenth-century immigrant ships is one of the most immediately notable
features of the emigration experience. Strictly speaking, the diet of the
steerage was regulated and a certain minimum had to be supplied as a
condition of the sale of a ticket. But this was often observed in the breach,
and provided many opportunities for unscrupulous captains, owners and
crews to profit at the expense of the passengers who were largely powerless
once at sea.

The American immigrant traffic was particularly notorious in that
regard, and this is dramatised by the scandal of the *Washington* in 1851.
It should be noted that this was no unsafe hulk converted to the emigrant
business, but a purpose-built and well-constructed vessel which had made
many such voyages. It came to public attention only because the
philanthropist Vere Foster, a relative of Lord Hobart, who had made it
his business to improve conditions on these ships, took passage aboard
for the sake of first-hand experience. No food was served to the steerage
for the first five days of the journey, and only then when Foster
complained. His initial complaints were met with threats, and when he
persisted he was knocked down by the mate, told by the captain he was
'a damned pirate and scoundrel', and threatened with strangulation and
a journey on bread and water in irons. Foster had also taken the precaution
of bringing with him scales in which he measured the food doled out,
and he found it seriously deficient in weight. Only those prepared to tip
the cook in money or whisky could get their food cooked in the galley,
although this was supposed to be freely available to all. Despite a House
of Commons enquiry and the revelation that several of the deaths of
children on board were from starvation, that the doctor had sided with
the captain in his treatment of the passengers, and that this sort of
treatment was commonplace, it took several decades for any significant
improvement in conditions to occur.[18]

The situation of emigrants to New Zealand and Australia never
reached these depths, partly because the journey was much longer and
had to be more carefully planned, but mainly because it was largely
controlled by provincial and national governments, or semi-official
ventures such as the New Zealand Company and its various offshoots,
and was therefore better conducted than the private business ventures

which characterised the American emigrant trade (which was really little more than an adjunct to the timber industry). The adequate but unexciting dietary for steerage passengers on New Zealand Company vessels was set out in a schedule to the Company publications, and its putative generosity was emphasised by them. It was up to the passengers to prepare this food as best they might.

Usually the 300 or so steerage passengers who crammed the converted cargo space on a typical emigrant ship were divided into messes of 10 or a dozen, who deputed one of their number as 'mess captain' to collect the rations, and another to undertake the cooking or to oversee the ship's cook to ensure that there was no theft or other monkey business. This responsibility could be onerous: 'a task of no honour and very great difficulties from the various tempers you have to please,' recalled F. W. Leighton on board the *Bloomer* in 1853.[19]

The duties involved were described by E. Cuzens, who travelled on the *Travancore* as a boy of 10:

> The rations were served out once a week, and meat twice a week by the Chief Officer. At this function the family was not a name but a number. In the mate's book was entered the quantity of each article to be supplied and when the number was called out some representative of the family was expected to step forward and take what was coming to them. [The meat was then tagged for subsequent cooking.] The next step was to carry the meat to the galley which was presided over by a big negro who threw them together into the boiler and left them to stew until dinner time. At about half past twelve forty or fifty people assembled at the galley, each with a tin dish for their dinner meat, when the cook also arrived with a big three pronged fork thrust into the boiling mass, brought out a joint, called out the number on the disc, which was quickly claimed, and so on until the boiler was empty.[20]

The chaotic scenes which followed this rush to the galley do not need to be imagined. They have been described by John MacKenzie, a cabin passenger who observed from the poop what he characterised as a rush to the galley 'like so many dogs in a kennel let out to get food'.[21] John Fenwick on the *Lightning* in 1854 drew attention to the problems this created for male messes who had had no previous experience of cooking for themselves.[22] Another mess captain in 1875 failed to draw his ration of pork and so his mess had to make do with pea soup and preserved

Boiled Salt Beef

The salt beef served out to steerage passengers was of variable quality. Sometimes by the end of a voyage it was becoming rotten. The early settlements in New South Wales virtually subsisted on it for the first couple of years of their existence, and one of the officers, Watkin Tench, has left a mindboggling description of how it was eaten; apparently it was so hard it had to be held over a naked flame for some time before it became sufficiently soft to consume. Understandably boiled salt beef developed an unsavoury reputation as a food for the poor, to be eaten only from necessity. But this need not be so, as this recipe illustrates.

2 kg piece of corned beef
2 onions, peeled and stuck with cloves
(3 or 4 each)
1 tsp mace and 1 tsp crushed allspice
grated nutmeg
a dozen or so peppercorns
800 g small carrots, peeled but left
whole (spring carrots are best)

Put the beef in a large pot and cover with water. Bring to the boil and skim. Pour away the water and refill the pot adding the spices and onions this time. Simmer closely covered for about 2 hours, then add the carrots for a further hour. This can be served hot or cold sprinkled with chopped parsley, and accompanied by pickled cucumbers and boiled potatoes.

The nineteenth century invented many ways of making salt beef palatable. A method outlined in Dr Kitchener's *Cook's Oracle* involves putting it in a pan with a quart (1200 ml) of water, covering the meat with about 3 lb (about 1.3 kg) of thickly shredded mutton suet, and a couple of minced onions, then putting a flour and water paste crust over the top, and baking in a moderate oven for 6 hours. The *Colonists' Guide* suggests stuffing it 'by making deep cuts in it filled with a stuffing of soaked bread, squeezed dry and flavoured with a little fat and various seasonings. Tie the meat up in a cloth and boil — for 10 pounds the time required will be about 3 hours.'

Pork at Sea

In her *Food in England* (1954), Dorothy
Hartley gives recipes for two dishes which
may very well have been the sort eaten by
steerage passengers. In the first, a joint of
pork is boiled with vegetables — carrots,
turnips, parsnips, swedes, onions, celery
tops, a cabbage, 'in fact any vegetables you
have except potatoes' — and this is then
seasoned with a few peppercorns, a spoonful
of treacle, and a cup of cider. The failure to
add salt suggests that we are dealing with
salt pork here. A muslin bag containing a
couple of handfuls of dried peas and half a
sprig of mint is suspended in the pot also.
This is then simmered gently for several
hours. The meat is carved and served with
the vegetables, (which must have been like
nothing on earth after several hours of
boiling), and the pease pudding is divided in
half and flavoured with a knob of bacon fat,
black pepper and some of the hot broth.

The second recipe is for pork dumplings
which, Hartley herself remarks, 'has a very
galley aroma'. In this a suet pastry crust is
stuffed with chopped pork, sliced onion and
apple, some sage leaves and a spoon of
honey. Again no mention of salt. Instead, a
thick slice of salt bacon is recommended as a
substitute for the pork. The whole is then
sealed up with a crust lid, and boiled well.

potatoes that day.[23] This was not always the fault of the mess captain.
Sometimes the food distribution arrangements were so chaotic that
drawing bread at one place meant missing meat at another.

The cooking facilities themselves could also leave a great deal to be
desired. The galley was often small with little room to manoeuvre, and
cooks, some of whom knew little of their trade, were not above refusing
to oversee the cooking or to allow it at all without generous tipping. In
1857, on the *Ann Wilson*, which actually had a pig sty on the galley roof,
the waiting time for food to be cooked could be up to five or six hours.[24]
By the end of a ship's voyage the galley could be virtually unusable. Martha
Adams noted a deputation to her ship's captain to complain that the
iron work on the fireplace was all burned through and was incapable of
further use. The captain could only say that he had already replaced the
grate once and had no more iron on board. Until he found some other
expedient the steerage was obliged to go hungry to bed.[25]

The monotony of the food also seems to have been depressing,
although at least one passenger, Antoine Fauchery, who subsequently
wrote up his voyage on the *Emily*, was able to wring a laugh from the
dreary state of provisions: 'In the morning salt beef with dried potatoes;
at noon salt pork with rice; at two o'clock dried potatoes with salted
beef; at four rice with salt pork. Lord bless you, if we wanted we could at
six o'clock have both salted beef with potatoes and salt pork with rice.'[26]
Some could barely tolerate the food at all. Emma Hodder on the *Hydaspes*
bound for Lyttelton in 1869 complained pathetically, 'I feel weak for
want of something nourishing. I am going to remain on deck while they
all go down to dinner which consists of cold rice and sour bread. I cannot
take it today.'[27]

Those who fell ill seem to have been in particular difficulty. Even
Martha Adams, usually most unsympathetic to the steerage, was moved
to protest about the situation in which these unfortunates found
themselves:

If this vessel was properly regulated there ought to be a nurse or two to
attend to the sick below, who also should have preference before all others
at the galley fire: as it is now 'might is right' and those who can see to their
food being cooked get it, those who cannot must go without, unless some
compassionate neighbour help them. When the doctor has ordered Mr
Jones a canister of preserved meat to make into broth for him he has to

wait until nearly tea time before the saucepan which has no owner can be accommodated at the fire, while the strong and healthy were having their dinner and tea and their little nick nacks got ready for supper.[28]

One passenger seems to have died of starvation as a result of the failure of food supplies for the sick on board the *Anne Wilson* in 1857.[29]

The set scales of rations were not lavish. The intending passenger would receive a pound (450 grams) of biscuit and three quarts (about 3.5 litres) of fresh water a day. On alternate days they would receive half a pound of either salt beef or pork, and minimum quantities of flour, raisins, suet and peas. This might be supplemented by rice, potatoes, sugar, butter and, as a scorbutic, pickled cabbage. Small quantities of tea and coffee would be available.[30] This dietary improved somewhat as the century progressed, with some greater emphasis on fresh fruit and vegetables, but not much. Passengers were advised in the many books published for the guidance of would-be emigrants to take their own supplementary rations with them, and most did. However, because access to their trunks was restricted for long intervals during the voyage, it was not unusual for these additional rations to spoil before they could be consumed.

But it was the contrast between the messing arrangements of the steerage and the cabin passengers which is the most notable feature of nineteenth-century emigrant life at sea. To say that the cabin ate lavishly is a considerable understatement. In 1839 the gentleman Alexander Marjoribanks made the long journey to New Zealand with about 150 other emigrants on the *Bengal Merchant*:

> We, who were in the cabin, or cuddy, as it is generally called at sea, consisting of nineteen individuals, fared sumptuously every day; a circumstance highly creditable not only to the New Zealand Company, but to the liberal captain of the ship. In fact it may be said that we did little else but eat, drink, and sleep, during the whole voyage. We had four meals per day, and at dinner always had five or six dishes of fresh meat, with a *carte blanche* of claret and other wines, besides a dessert of fruit.[31]

This fresh meat was supplied by an astonishing 60 sheep, 21 pigs, and 900 head of poultry carried on board. The noise of the hungry pigs demanding food was, he added, 'almost equal to that of a clap of thunder'. Presumably it lessened as the journey proceeded.

The social historian Helen Simpson quotes an unsourced cabin diarist

Boiled Fowl and Sauce

Anne Cobbett gives this suggestion for a dinner dish in her *English Housekeeper* (1851), illustrating neatly the variety of sauces the nineteenth-century middle class ate with their boiled chicken. Oddly, she fails to mention the most famous of all, a sauce of mussels:

> A fowl put in cold water should simmer by the side of a fire for twenty five minutes to half an hour. Some cooks boil a little fresh suet sliced, and also slices of lemon peel with fowl. Some boil them with milk and water. The water must be well scummed. Boiled fowls go with white sauce or mushroom, oyster, celery, lemon or liver sauce, or parsley and butter. A pretty remove of fish or soup is a small tongue in the centre, a boiled chicken on each side, and small heads of broccoli, asparagus and French beans to fill the spaces. Serve any of the above sauces. Garnish with lemon.

For a duck she advises: 'Choose fine fat ones. Some persons salt them slightly, for two days, others boil them without. Smother them with onions, or serve onion sauce.'

Plum Pudding

Where would the nineteenth-century English have been without plum pudding? There are numerous recipes for this standard. This one is from Mrs Beeton, who claims that a plum pudding is really a Christmas pudding but became known as a plum pudding from the Tudor habit of adding prunes.

100 g apple, cooked
200 g dried figs, chopped
100 g currants
200 g seedless raisins
100 g blanched almonds, chopped
100 g pine kernels
200 g of dried white breadcrumbs
1 tsp mixed spice
100 g soft brown sugar
100 g mixed peel
zest and juice of a lemon
1 tsp of salt
100 g butter
100 g honey
3 beaten eggs

Grease a couple of pudding basins. Mix the fruit, nuts, breadcrumbs, spice, sugar, peel, salt, and the lemon zest and juice. Warm the honey and butter until liquid, and beat in the eggs. Stir this well into the dry mixture and then turn into the basins. Cover tightly and steam for about 3 hours. This quantity should serve 6, says Mrs Beeton, and may be served with flaming brandy.

in 1842 as saying that first-class passengers at sea:

> load their stomachs with the most incongruous mixtures. At dinner for instance, after rich pork, they will take roast duck with boiled ham, currant jelly and perhaps pickles, with boiled fowl, currant jelly and caper sauce; or roast mutton with tongue and pickles, plum jam; to say nothing of several sorts of stale vegetables. Rich tart or plum pudding, often a plateful of both, follow. They just leave a corner in the stomach for a piece of new bread and strong cheese, thus preparing a foundation for a plate full of almonds and raisins and other dessert, larger than economical ladies would put upon table for a party of 4 or 5 people.[32]

Further detail of this ongoing feast is added by Martha Adams who sat down at the cuddy dining table with 16 others in 1850 and had:

> roast beef, as good as if just fresh from the hands of a country butcher, and your own cook: mashed potatoes and carrots, stewed beef-steak, boiled salmon, green gooseberries and damsons all from the cases; then we have every day four if not five dishes of meat at dinner including the above, with fresh pork and mutton in joints, meat pies, poultry and curry: and the plum pudding we had today weighed I should think six pounds. At tea we have fresh bread, for which the passengers find marmalade and preserves in preference to the salt butter; and our breakfasts are quite as abundant in proportion as our dinners. In the way of drinkables water only is provided: but ale, and porter, wine and spirits are sold, and I find the lime juice and a little sugar in my water the most agreeable beverage possible.

'So,' she concluded smugly, 'altogether, we lead a very comfortable life.'[33]

Many similar accounts could be added to these, among them Alfred Fell's from 1841:

> We had an excellent dinner: a salmon preserved and as fine as ever I tasted, soup (and sailors make capital soups), a roast goose, a saddle of mutton, a Westphalia ham, plum pudding and apple tarts, cheese and bottled porter, champagne and sherry, with dessert consisting of apples, nuts, almonds, raisins &c. We had some capital port. The officers of the ship dined with us (altogether twenty two of us) and a really elegant affair it was.

A storm at sea during dinner even gave him an opportunity to fall into verse: 'The mad potatoes soon the deck o'erstrew/ And knives and forks the general chase renew;/ Beef, ham and mutton from their stations prance/ And frantic biscuits round the table dance.' Streams of gravy flowed across the floor with the soup and the wine, the pork ribs and the hams followed suit, and 'The restless beef no mortal arm can stay/ Roast goose and mutton pies pursue their slippery way.'[34]

By way of contrast, passenger Warren Adams described the indignation which reigned in the cabin on an occasion when the fresh provisions supplied to the first class on the *Canterbury* in 1851 failed and they were reduced to the same dietary for the final three weeks of their journey as the steerage. Adams described the salt meat they were obliged to dine upon as 'almost uneatable', but made no observation of the fact that most of those on the ship had been living on it for three months or more.[35]

Because they were far fewer and had their own cooking space, a few cabin passengers whiled away their time learning new skills, some of which stood them in good stead when they arrived in their new land. Muriel Aitchison on the *Olympus* bound for Wellington in 1841 learned how to make bread: 'The steward gave me a small piece of dough and showed me how to mix it, and from time to time I save a piece and by that means have a constant supply of fresh bread.' She thought that if far less biscuit and much more flour was issued by way of rations, this would make for a better diet on board, but she had obviously not thought through the logistics of so much daily baking. She bemoaned her failure to bring spices and bicarbonate of soda with her on the voyage.[36] She also felt the need of cheese, her small supply having long run out.

This contrast between the messing arrangements of the steerage and of the cabin is one of the lasting central impressions of the experience of nineteenth-century emigration to New Zealand and elsewhere recorded in surviving letters and diaries. Combined with the central place of land and to whom it should be available for use in nineteenth-century British political discourse, it constituted a powerful and key element in the creation of the food culture of new lands everywhere. This is as true of New Zealand as of Australia, the United States, Canada or anywhere else the British poor fetched up.

LAND, SETTLEMENT AND WORKING PEOPLE

We forget or neglect these influences, not only because we are accustomed to having more than enough to eat, but also because in our century

Boiled Ham and Salmon

Alfred Fell's Westphalia ham would most probably have been boiled. Eliza Acton gives comprehensive instructions for boiling a ham in her *Modern Cookery* (1845).

It should be soaked first through several changes of water over a day to extract some of the salt. It should then be scraped and brushed, and any black or rusty parts carefully pared away. It is then to be put into a large pot of cold water and brought very slowly to a simmer, skimming away any froth. Once the water has cleared, it should be simmered 'softly but steadily' until tender and on no account permitted to boil. A bunch of herbs and three or four carrots cooked with it improve the flavour. It is ready when a larding pin will go in easily, and should be taken out, the skin stripped off, and placed in a hot oven for a few minutes to dry the surface. It can then be glazed, if people prefer. She also recommends simmering the ham in cider and vinegar with a bay-leaf and a bunch of herbs.

Martha Adams would have had her boiled salmon cooked in a fish kettle in a court bouillon — a combination of wine, vinegar, vegetables and aromatics boiled together and strained, a method much favoured by the Victorians. A fish about 5 cm in thickness should cook in about 20 minutes if the liquid is simmering when the fish is lowered into it. It can be eaten hot or cold.

Pakeha, in particular, do not associate politics and land in the same way as in previous periods. When we think about land, we see it largely as an economic resource; its significance lies with the overall place of agriculture in the economy and, to a degree, with how it is owned and what these patterns imply for the environment, rather than with any effects on our immediate daily lives. In the nineteenth century land occupied a very different place. Not only was it the key to the long-running political battle between Liberals and Conservatives in Britain, but the question was as much a moral one as an economic one. That it had resonances in nineteenth-century New Zealand should not surprise in the least.

Even those who came from urban backgrounds often had direct recollections of living rurally, or had parents or other relatives who had enjoyed the unenclosed common rights noted earlier.

Furthermore, this moral nostalgia was underpinned by a widely disseminated philosophical and political tradition. From Thomas Paine and William Cobbett at one end of the century to Henry George at the other, radical political thinkers erected a coherent intellectual framework within which this adherence to a rural or semi-rural moral economy of self-sufficiency could sustain itself.[37] Some of this was specifically built into political programmes which were implemented with greater or lesser degrees of success. Perhaps the most comprehensive of these was the attempt by the Chartists to set up a land company which operated between 1845 and 1850, the intention of which was to settle labourers as small proprietors on self-sufficient agricultural smallholdings.[38] This attempt came to grief on the rock of business inexperience, but it was widely admired and imitated during the nineteenth century, especially but not exclusively in the United States.[39]

That the same attitudes came to New Zealand has been amply explored and demonstrated by our own historians.[40] Most recently, Miles Fairburn has explored the mythologies this created in New Zealand both contemporaneously and subsequently, and has made this matter central to historical debate. Fairburn cites a range of sources on the importance of getting hold of land in the new colony both for the gentlemen investors who got a good deal of it by one means or another, and for small proprietors. Among those he notes are I. R. Cooper in 1857:

Those who arrive in the colony without capital will, if they enjoy good health, are sober and economical in their personal expenses, and are able and willing to work at any one trade as farm servants, boatmen, shepherds, or house servants, soon realise a sufficient capital to invest in land, cattle or sheep, and thus render themselves and their children independent.[41]

Or Alexander Bathgate in 1874: 'In Dunedin very many working men live in their own freehold cottages, and some of the suburbs are almost exclusively filled with neat little houses owned by working men.' Or the *New Zealand Handbook 1888*, which sagely remarks that although an immigrant might not be assured of a fortune, 'yet a comfortable living, a home in healthy surroundings, a fair start for their children, and a reasonable provision for their own future are within the reach of emigrants if they are careful and industrious'. Quite literally dozens of other writers could be cited on the same theme of the ease of small land ownership and a comfortable subsistence for those in modest circumstances. By 1885, fully 60 percent of adult males in New Zealand owned a land freehold or a Crown leasehold.[42] This astonishing statistic in anecdotal form is one of the most generally encountered commonplaces of contemporary writing about nineteenth-century New Zealand and those who have written about it since.

What makes Fairburn stand out is that he has interrogated the meanings of this pattern, and in particular the use to which the smallholders put this land once they had got it. First and foremost, he remarks, it was a way of ensuring that in the event of unemployment or other calamity, the home was not lost. During the 'long depression' of

Blackcurrant Jam

Once they were settled in a house of their own, one of the first acts of the smaller settlers was to plant soft fruit bushes. These invariably included currants (black, red and white), and these in their turn inevitably ended up in the preserving pan in one form or another. Blackcurrant jam was a standard. This recipe is from *Brett's Colonists' Guide*.

Strip from the stalks, and place in preserving kettle adding small quantity of water. Steam for about ten minutes; then add sugar in the proportion of three quarters to one pound for every pound of fruit. Stir constantly as the jam is very liable to burn, and boil until the preserve jellies when a little is poured onto a plate. This will probably be in about an hour from the time it begins to boil.

Stirring jam for an hour would be quite tiring work; no doubt the children were recruited. Brett gives 26 recipes for various fruit preserves including quince, carrot, peach and melon.

Fried Marrow and Other Vegetables

The nineteenth century used its vegetables rather differently from us, probably because of the cooking technologies available. Marrows, which were usually called 'gourds', were sometimes fried, as in this recipe from Kitchener's *Cook's Oracle*.

'Take six or eight small gourds,' he says, 'as near of a size as possible. Slice them with a cucumber slice, dry them in a cloth, and then fry them in very hot lard; throw over a little pepper and salt, and serve up on a napkin.' The lard must be very hot and the slices done in a minute, he advises, otherwise they will be greasy and tough.

He also gives a recipe for a celery purée for eating with a boiled turkey. Brett, for his part, suggests a dish of fresh young turnip tops, boiled for 20 minutes.

the 1880s the Stout–Vogel government bent strenuous efforts to settling the unemployed on smallholdings where they could raise their own food and generally look after themselves — a policy cancelled by the incoming and highly conservative Atkinson government in 1888.

The keystone of this security and its release from the anxieties which must have induced many to emigrate in the first place was the production of food.[43] In late nineteenth-century New Zealand in particular, everyone who could kept livestock of some sort: usually chickens and pigs, and for the better-off, a cow. This had been forbidden to the rural poor in Britain, and was the aspiration of many urban dwellers. Now free to do as they pleased, they seized the opportunity with such enthusiasm that the town ordinances of this period seem obsessed with the problems of wandering livestock, of the smells and effects on the state of the water of keeping pigs in the midst of other people's suburbs, and of the crowing of cockerels. It sometimes seems that the men who owned these smallholdings spent every leisure moment growing fruit and vegetables, while the women of the household took care of the animals. The nineteenth-century agitation for a half holiday for working people on Saturdays, for instance, seems largely to have been informed by a desire for time to cultivate gardens; Sunday, of course, was reserved for religious observances.

There is a fascinating survey conducted by the Department of Labour in 1892 which explores the household expenditure of working people.[44] Many failed to include entries for vegetables, bacon, jam or pickles. It is hard to believe they did not consume these items and much more likely they did not note them because they never had to buy them: they produced their own. Thus the cultural significance of the quarter-acre section stands revealed. It was the parcel of land required to keep a garden sufficient in size and scope to live virtually a subsistence life with little recourse to other than casual or seasonal employment, both of which were key features of the nineteenth-century labour market in New Zealand.[45] During periods of economic downturn, the possession of a productive garden and laying hens must have been a significant lifeline for many who would otherwise have gone hungry to bed or worse. It is interesting to note that this tradition had sufficiently deep roots to survive the century and to surface once again in the depression of the 1930s.[46] What can be observed at work here is the transplanting from one end of the earth to the other of a culture of market gardening which had existing among working people, and rural working people in particular, for centuries.

This tradition came early to New Zealand and flourished among the mission settlements, but it was after 1840 that it really came into its own. The early Wellington settler William Mein Smith was reporting to the New Zealand Company as early as January 1841:

> We are now enjoying vegetables, such as greens, peas, cabbage, and turnips in as high perfection as I have ever seen them in England. Many seeds of more tender nature perished on the voyage, or, from late sowing, did not gather strength to resist the grasshopper, with which we are troubled at this season of the year. The peas thrive wonderfully, as do beans of all kinds. The former are growing in my garden upwards of six feet high, and producing abundantly.[47]

Of course, as an official of the company he was bound to write in glowing terms, but in a personal letter a few days later to his father, to whom he had no need to dissemble, he also mentioned the abundance of lettuces (badly ravaged by insects), endive, radishes, mustard and cress, potatoes and pumpkins. Research undertaken into the early settlement of Wellington has revealed the existence of a nursery garden, Portobello Gardens, in Nairn Street just below Brooklyn Hill, very early in the history of the settlement.[48]

Edward Jerningham Wakefield at a similarly early period praised the exhibits at the newly formed Horticultural and Botanical Society exhibition held in 1842, referring to cabbages weighing 21 pounds, and the enormous turnips, radishes and kidney potatoes which would grow in the Hutt Valley. To Wakefield we owe an evocative description of early working-class Wellington:

> They [the workers] used to work at their little patches of ground after their labour for the day was over; and Wade's Town, which had before looked a very bleak hill, of poor soil and denuded of timber by the clearing of former years, soon boasted a population of 200 working people, whose neat cottages and smiling cultivations peeped from every nook among the picturesque hills.[49]

These descriptions find their counterparts in all of the early settlements well into the early years of the twentieth century. Their tone is generally one of astonishment at such bounty and such plenty.

Cabbage and Milk

'It is scarce 100 years since we had cabbages out of Holland,' says a gardeners' handbook of 1699. Cabbages afforded, it went on to say, 'a gross and melancholy juice, yet loosening if moderately boiled. It is seldom eaten raw except by the Dutch.' Those of us familiar with institutional cooking will be cheering for the Dutch at this point. However, in the nineteenth century cabbage was sometimes finely chopped and lightly cooked with milk and a knob or two of butter. It was then drained and tossed with more butter, and the milk remaining in the pan thickened with a beaten egg and poured over, to be eaten with hot buttered toast as a light meal on its own. Cabbages were also made into salad, one variety of which, Yorkshire Ploughboy, used red cabbage, treacle, vinegar and black pepper. This was traditionally eaten with cold corned beef. It isn't actually as bad as it sounds.

Cooking Vegetables

The instructions given for cooking vegetables in nineteenth-century cookbooks are largely at variance with today's practice, and read oddly to us. They would not have improved Judge Chapman's cabbages at all, and reflect a centuries-old belief that unless vegetables were thoroughly boiled they might be a danger to digestive health. The Whitcombe & Tombs publication, *Colonial Everyday Cookery* recommends cooking vegetables with the lid off the pan (although it does not say why) and adding salt only after the vegetables have begun to soften. Cabbage and cauliflower should be cooked for at least 20 to 30 minutes, and any loss of colour might be corrected by adding 'a piece of washing soda the size of a pea'. A crust of bread tied in muslin or a piece of charcoal might also be added 'to stop the objectionable smell'. *Mrs Kirk's Cookbook*, a manuscript and clipping collection held by the Alexander Turnbull Library (undated but certainly prior to 1905), suggests cooking green vegetables in two steps. They should be first blanched in boiling salted water. This should then be poured away, and the vegetables brought to a simmer in another potful and kept there until cooked — for how long it does not say. For reasons also unclear it recommends pouring the cooking water on the garden afterwards.

The problem of abundance

From the very outset of European settlement, the wealthier settlers in particular thought New Zealand a veritable paradise for gardeners, and were often to be found agreeing with one another that the common people had no business complaining about their lot as a result. This is clear from many of their letters and diaries. Thus Charlotte Godley writing from Dunedin in March 1850:

> There are already a great number of people settled outside the town up every little valley and along the beach too, and *all* well off. Everything is dear, wages 4s a day, bread 9d. the 4lb loaf, meat the same as in London and *very good*, milk ditto, fresh butter 2s a pound, and such washing bills! — about 3s a dozen for everything, we pay, for a few things we have brought up to have washed. The poorest people have fresh meat at least once a day, but still there are plenty of grumblers.[50]

Her friend Conway Rose was similarly astonished at the good food so readily available. Describing his new house in Canterbury in 1851, he alluded to 'a fine crop of potatoes waving gaily on every side' and the good fertility of the soil for vegetables. 'I have a lot of hens and chickens,' he went on, 'three pigs, two dogs, one horse and two drays', and he continued with a lively account of a gentleman selling potatoes from the back of a dray and the children of clergy selling their surplus of butter door-to-door.[51] Despite this, or perhaps because of it, Rose did not much care for New Zealand, and after some years of living here returned to England with his family. But others of the middle classes stayed and made the country their home, no doubt attracted by the healthy diet they could enjoy. Judge H. S. Chapman, who came to Wellington in 1844, was one of these. 'Our cabbages from the garden are so sweet,' he wrote to his father from Karori that year, 'so unlike their namesakes from Covent Garden that I who never ate cabbage in London am now a decided cabbage eater.'[52] He bought potatoes, which he pronounced 'excellent', from the local Maori for 9d a basket, and paid 1s 6d a pound 'for as good fresh butter as the world can produce'. Lady Barker concurred, in her often quoted description of the typical daily intake:

> Porridge for breakfast with new milk and cream *a discretion*; to follow — mutton chops, mutton ham or mutton curry, or broiled mutton and mushrooms, not shabby little fragments of meat broiled, but beautiful tender

Haricot Mutton

This recipe is a curiosity, a haricot of mutton being usually what we would call a casserole. This, from the handbook *Colonial Everyday Cookery*, seems to be a descendant of this dish, but one which has removed itself rather far from its origins.

3 neck or loin chops
2 onions
1 carrot
some diced turnip
2 cups stock
60 g dripping
2 tbsp flour
salt, pepper and 'herbs'

Trim and beat the cutlets out flat. Season with salt, pepper and herbs (some rosemary perhaps, or a little marjoram), and brown these and the vegetables in the dripping. Remove the cutlets and keep warm. Stir the flour into the dripping and vegetables, and cook for a short while, then add the heated stock and a little boiling water, and simmer until the vegetables are cooked and the sauce thickens. Finish off the cutlets under the grill, and then serve on a platter with the sauce poured over.

steaks off the leg; tea or coffee and bread and butter, with as many new laid eggs as we choose to consume. Then, for dinner at half past one, we have soup, a joint, vegetables and a pudding; in summer we have fresh fruit stewed instead of a pudding, with whipped cream . . . We have supper about seven; but this is a moveable feast consisting of tea again, mutton cooked in some form of entree, eggs, bread and butter, and a cake of my manufacture. I must, however, acknowledge, that at almost every other station you would get more dainties such as jam and preserves of all sorts than we can boast of yet . . . [53]

Most of the poorer settlers, including labourers, would have recognised this menu as not dissimilar to their own. They were astonished at the abundance which confronted them. Grace Hurst, farming at Bell Block in 1858, wrote home to her sister: 'We have almost everything within ourselves — milk, butter, eggs, flour, potatoes, ducks, fowls, vegetables, fruit.'[54] Louisa Johnson, who landed in Dunedin in October 1874, wrote home to her friends in Grandborough: 'I wish a lot from Grandborough would come. Joe says he would get you all a meal such as you never had at home.'[55] Two years later Michael Cook, a farm labourer who had settled near Geraldine in Canterbury, wrote to friends in his old village of Pyewipe of his establishment of a garden and his new pig sty, and concluded: 'You said I was to send you word if we kept Christmas up. Of course we do, and we had green peas, new potatoes and roast beef for dinner, and that will puzzle you at Pyewipe.'[56] His wife, who had resented dressing poultry for others at home in England, now found it not nearly so tiresome, for 'what she dresses now she helps to eat'. George Catley, a shoemaker, wrote to a friend at Nettleton: 'This is the place for beef steaks and mutton . . . What with one good thing and another I am getting quite stout, and have every reason to like this country.'[57] The letters go on and on. Some could barely believe that they could stay in bed until six, rise and eat a hearty breakfast, and then begin work at eight, and finish at five in the afternoon. Others gloried in the gardens they could now cultivate without any interference from squire or farmer. Twelve-year-old Helena Barker addressed herself to her old Sunday school companions:

Our section is all under cultivation now, that is the one acre. We have apples, plums, black currants (sic) bushes, and strawberries planted and the remaining part will be potatoes and corn, and mother is cultivating a

Beefsteaks and Oysters: Roast Rolled Beef

Eating beef regularly was the subject of much astonished comment among the settlers of the 1870s in particular. Most of them had never seen beef on their own plate in England from one year's end to the next, and probably had to pinch themselves to believe that they could have it every day. But they were not slow to adapt to this new situation. 'Brown a pound and a half of steak in two ounces of butter,' says Mrs Murdoch in her *Dainties or How to Please Our Lords and Masters* (1887). 'Add half a pint of stock, pepper and salt, and the liquor from about a dozen and a half of oysters. Stew until tender, add a glass of port, and beurre manie to thicken. Add the oysters and stew until they are done. Then serve it very hot.'

The Whitcombe & Tombs cookbook carries this recipe for a grand dinner dish.

> 2–3 kg sirloin of beef
> 2 glasses each port and vinegar
> 'a rich forcemeat'
> 1 tsp ground allspice
> salt and pepper

Marinate the beef in half the liquid for two days, then trim, season, stuff and roll it. Roast in a medium oven, allowing 20 minutes to each 500 g, basting regularly with the other half of the liquid. The book recommends making a gravy from the juices, and serving the meat with this and a redcurrant jelly. The serving of spiced beef in this form can be traced back to at least Elizabethan times. Most usually it was eaten at Christmas. A similar but much more elaborate recipe is given in S. Paston-Williams, *Christmas and Festival Recipes* (1981).

The Whitcombe & Tombs book is also of interest because it sets out the general methodology for roasting beef, including before an open fire with a meat screen. In that case the roast was hung from a 'bottle jack', i.e. a revolving vertical spit. This method, says the book, requires 'a very bright, clean, fire'. The meat was set very close to this in the first instance for browning, and then moved back to cook.

small flower garden in front. Father has a nice black horse and we have killed one little pig about 10 stone.[58]

Eating their meals as one of the family with the farmer and his wife for whom they worked is mentioned by a number of those writing home to friends, but it is the quantity and quality of the food which is mentioned again and again. 'This is the country for living — beef, mutton, butter and eggs and everything else that is good,' wrote one labouring man. 'We are as happy as the day is long. I would not come back on any account, for we can get something to lean over, no water broth, but a good belly full of beef.'[59] 'We can go to the shop and get a bag of sugar and half-chest of tea, and pay for it with ready money, and anything else without any trouble,' wrote another.[60] And perhaps most telling of all, George Tapp from Taranaki and previously an official of the Kent Labourers' Union: 'Working people don't eat sheep's and bullock's heads or liver here. They have the best joints as well as the rich.'[61]

It is fair to record that there were some sour notes. The pseudonymous 'Hopeful', writing from Christchurch, probably in 1885, on the quality of the food in the colony, allowed that the bread was excellent and that the eggs, milk and cream were good and cheap, but was sniffy about the butter ('would not touch the Britanny') and the lack of choice between dairies, and thought the cheese 'indifferent'. She was particularly scathing on the subject of meat: 'Pork and bacon cannot compare with home productions; the pigs are mostly large and coarse and, from the extreme cheapness of meat and food generally, are coarsely fed; that is they get the refuse from the slaughter yards; and the same rule applies to fowls, they are dry and tough as a rule.' This, she thought, was because they were not fattened properly with grain but fed on scraps. Bacon, too, was pale and second rate. 'Beef looks very good as it hangs but it cannot compare with *good* beef at home; it is deficient in gravy and eats dry. If a joint is baking, you never smell that rich smell that a good joint at home will send forth; and when sent to table you notice the absence of a good gravy.' 'Hopeful' thought the mutton good enough for the price if you were a lower class of immigrant, and the lamb beautiful, but she commented rather disapprovingly on the very large consumption of meat (which she described as 'a craving', attributable to the climate and to its cheapness). Vegetables, she went on, quickly withered up when cut and displayed because of the hot winds. There had also been game available of late — hares, pheasants and wild ducks — and particularly rabbits which were sold cheaply because they were vermin. She thought the meat and vegetables served in restaurants 'uneatable'.[62]

'Hopeful' and others were minority detractors. But while the abundance and freshness of the produce was typically welcome, it created some problems for poorer settlers in particular, who had no experience of such bounty and no ready response to the question of how it should be served. It has already been remarked that the culinary tradition from which they came placed considerable emphasis on eggs and butter, and these were readily to hand. But the sheer quantities now available provided a new challenge.

Before them, however, was the experience of the way their immediate 'betters' had dined, both in England and on the voyage to New Zealand. There is little doubt that the immigrants from rural areas in particular recollected the rare feasts and the diet of their farmer employers in their old homes, and responded by emulating these on a daily basis. One difficulty they confronted was that the seasons were the wrong way around if they wanted to mark a particular event, such as the end of harvest, and to fit it to the traditional European agricultural calendar. But they soon adapted these as necessary. Celebrating Michaelmas without a goose (because in the antipodes it was spring, and geese were an autumn phenomenon), for instance, led to the invention of 'colonial' goose, i.e. a boned and stuffed roasted roll of lamb. No doubt the separation of season and observance contributed to the decline of these festivals as the culture itself secularised. Besides, as it was possible to eat heartily every day in any event, the basis of festival eating gradually disappeared, leaving only Christmas as a season for traditional good eating. (Attempts are made from time to time to revive other associations — at Easter, for example, or to celebrate at the winter solstice — but none have much caught on.)

Similarly, the poor who came steerage had not far to look for examples of how they should eat when they encountered the plenty which their new home in New Zealand supplied. The result was an extraordinary cuisine which persisted, particularly in our rural districts, for over a century, and which found its apotheosis in the daily culinary round of

Colonial Goose

Geese in rural England were divided into 'green' and 'stubble'. The former were fed only on greenstuffs; the latter were turned into the wheat field after the harvest and the gleaners had finished with it, to fatten on the grains left behind by both processes. In *County Recipes of Old England*, Helen Edden remarks that the custom of eating a stubble goose at Michaelmas arose partly because the tenant sometimes brought a goose as a 'sweetener' to the landlord when paying the post-harvest autumn rent. In his *English Huswife* of 1615, Gervase Markham says that a green goose needs a sauce based on sorrel and billberries (or some other tart fruit such as gooseberries), but a stubble goose needs something a little sweeter made of apples. Unfortunately, there was no goose at Michaelmas in the southern hemisphere, and so the spring lamb had to do service. Every New Zealand cookbook worth its salt has a recipe for Colonial Goose. This one is adapted from David Burton's *Two Hundred Years of Food and Cookery*.

    a leg of lamb
    120 g new breadcrumbs
    75 g suet
    1 large onion
    1 tbsp of parsley, finely chopped
    a little sage and thyme
    salt and pepper
    1 beaten egg
    milk

Bone the leg. Make a stuffing with the crumbs, suet, onion and herbs, seasoned to taste and moistened and bound with the egg and milk. Stuff the cavity in the leg, sew up, and roast at 180°C for about an hour, depending on how well done you like your meat.

Burton gives a number of variations both as to meat cut and stuffing, including one made with apricots and honey. He comments that he doesn't know the origin of the name and therefore suggests using mutton (as does the magisterial *Edmonds Cookery Book*), but that would have been hard to combine with Michaelmas in nineteenth-century New Zealand. It ought properly to be a lamb cut that is used.

Fried Liver

Despite George Tapp's strictures, liver *was* eaten and appears in most cookbooks in nineteenth-century New Zealand. Norma McCallum's *Great Grandmama's Kitchen* (1977), a collection of nineteenth-century New Zealand recipes which she does not, regrettably, individually source, gives the following, which was originally labelled 'a cheap dinner'.

> 2 large onions
> 500 g liver
> 120 g fat beef
> 80 g oatmeal
> a half dozen or so potatoes, peeled and sliced
> salt and pepper

Chop the onions and cut up the liver and beef into small pieces. Layer the beef and potatoes in a heavy pot, season well, and sprinkle the oatmeal on top. Fill up with water, put on a lid and stew on a fire for an hour and a half. 'This will make a very substantial dinner for five people.'

The consumption of offal meats was not confined to liver as a curious letter in the *Lake Wakatipu Mail* of 17 September 1864 makes clear:

> Sir — I must beg sufficient space in your newspaper to allude to an occurrence which I witnessed a few days ago. Whilst taking a walk in the immediate vicinity of the Arrow township I observed a female washing tripe in the race which conveys water to the reservoirs from which the townspeople obtain their supply for domestic purposes. Had it been a man thus engaged I would have remonstrated with him. but having a wholesome dread of a woman's tongue, I forebore. However, I earnestly hope that this hint will prevent a repetition of so flagrant a disregard for the commonest precepts of decent housewifery.

Washing tripes in the public water supply is an ancient European tradition upon which Elizabeth David also comments. I am indebted to Philip Temple for the reference to this letter.

Lamb in Nineteenth-century New Zealand

One of the curiosities of the available cookery books from nineteenth-century New Zealand is that they don't give many recipes for lamb, although they abound in instructions for cooking mutton. The Whitcombe & Tombs book, for example, gives none out of 900 recipes of every description. Perhaps lamb was cooked so often and regularly that it was felt not to need a recipe — or only for exceptional dishes such as this for Minced Lamb with Poached Eggs, courtesy of the Napier Rowing Club.

> Take the remnants of some cold roast lamb, a good cup of stock, some chopped mint, salt and pepper, and 2 eggs for each person. Mince the lamb, season and add the mint, heat the stock and stir in the mince. Thicken with flour, and serve with the eggs on hot buttered toast.

Rabbit Soup

This recipe is given here verbatim from *Mrs Kirk's Cookbook*:

> The inferior parts of the rabbit will answer for this, while a pie or stew can be made of the loin and legs. Wash the joints well in warm water, especially the head which is liable to be bloody. Put them in a saucepan with a bunch of parsley and just cover with water. Add an onion stuck with two cloves and simmer gently until the rabbit is quite tender. Now take out the joints and remove the flesh from the bones, pound it in a mortar with the yolk of an egg, and the crumbs of a roll soaked in milk. Return to the saucepan [presumably containing the strained stock] and add sufficient water to make it to the required thickness. If a little cream can be procured it will wonderfully improve the taste and colour of the soup as it should be quite white. Season to taste with pepper and salt. Boiled rice is sometimes in the tureen with it, or may be served separately.

It is unlikely that this dish would have reconciled 'Hopeful' to life in Christchurch. More interesting is the similarity of this to the white soup eaten in *Pride and Prejudice* and noted earlier, and of which it is clearly a variation.

Eggs and Asparagaus

6 eggs
60 g butter
2 tbsp milk or cream
nutmeg, salt and pepper
some cooked asparagus tops
2 slices toast

Beat the eggs with the milk or cream and the seasonings, and pour onto melting butter in a pan. As the dish thickens, add the asparagus and serve on the toast, well buttered and kept hot.

Savoury Eggs

Most of the recipe books of the period contain many recipes for eggs, some of them also incorporating milk or cream. These often entail ways of serving eggs which are not longer in use.

6 eggs
herbs
30 g butter
2 tbsp minced ham or anchovies
salt and pepper

Boil the eggs, cool, shell and halve. Pound the yolks with the other ingredients, refill the cavities with this mixture, brush with some raw egg and roll in breadcrumbs. Fry in boiling fat and serve on a napkin with a chopped parsley garnish.

Plain Custard and Orange Jelly

Mrs Murdoch's book of dainties furnishes many recipes for milk and gelatine desserts. These two are fairly typical. Take a pint of milk, she says, and boil it with 2 oz (60 g) sugar. Take from the heat, and let it cool. Beat in 2 egg yolks mixed with a little milk and then cook in a double boiler until it thickens, 'adding any flavouring you like'. She goes on to suggest that a tablespoon of cornflour can be added to the eggs and milk 'if the custard is required very thick'. For the jelly, gelatine was soaked in a little cold water for an hour. This was then dissolved in a pint (600 ml) of boiling water, to which the juice of 9 oranges and a lemon was then added, together with sugar to taste. This was then strained into a mould to set.

Simnel Cake

One tradition which did not transplant, but which ought to have, is the eating of Simnel Cake at Easter, notwithstanding that an autumn Easter makes little sense. Perhaps it was the custom of servant girls taking this cake home to their mothers on the fourth Sunday in Lent which failed the transplant. Many of the mothers were a world away — and who wanted to be a servant in the new country anyway?

500 g marzipan
150 g butter
150 g raw sugar
3 eggs
250 g self-raising flour
1 tsp each nutmeg, cinnamon and mixed spice
salt to taste
120 g each currants, sultanas and mixed peel
milk and jam

You can make your own marzipan from crushed almonds, icing sugar, egg yolk and almond essence, but for this recipe the manufactured variety does as well. Cream the butter and sugar, and beat in the eggs. Mix this cream thoroughly with the sieved dry ingredients and the fruit, with enough milk to make a stiff mixture. Put half of this into a greased cake tin, roll out half the marzipan, and cover the mixture. Put in the rest of the mixture and bake at 150°C for about 2½ hours. Let cool, brush the top with jam, and cover with the rolled-out balance of the marzipan.

established farmers as typically described by Judith Miller, who encountered it when living for extended periods with her grandparents in the Taranaki of the 1940s:

Whoever got up first, which I think was grandfather, set the fire and of course the porridge was soaked the night before, so that was put on to cook, and then the bacon and eggs. At 7.30 you were called and you were faced with a plate, a huge plate, of porridge. Breakfast was all over by about eight o'clock, and then nana would go and do the dishes and get all that tidied up, and then she would rush and do the housework and then she was back in the kitchen preparing scones for morning tea. And straight after, or even before morning tea, the roast was put into the oven, and the vegetables like potatoes and carrots were prepared, and all sort of left there to cook. The greens were put on later. Jellies made the night before, and custard which you could carve, and which was lovely . . . So we would fight our way through this enormous meal. Now it was invariably summertime when I stayed with them and you ate your way through all sorts of vegetables, greasy fatty meat, which I loved, and greasy gravy which again I loved. The plate was handed around, you helped yourself to vegetables. Occasionally grandfather would bring out a bottle of cider, he was a great cider person, and while you were still wiping your face on your napkin the pudding was brought on, which would again take about three or four dishes. Then they used to have a siesta; they'd go and lie down until something like a quarter to two and nana would then get up and start preparing for afternoon tea which was at three o'clock. In the morning, depending on the day of the week, she would make fruit cakes and so

Gooseberry Chutney

Making sauces and pickles from surplus seasonal produce was a major domestic industry in nineteenth-century New Zealand. All of the cookbooks of the period contain recipes, 23 in the Whitcombe & Tombs book alone, including chutneys and catsups of mushroom and walnuts. This is for a surplus of gooseberries, a common fruit when most households grew a bush or two.

2 kg green gooseberries
100 g salt
300 g stoned raisins
120 g each mustard and garlic, peeled and chopped
200 g green ginger, peeled and chopped
500 g brown sugar
1 tsp each cayenne and turmeric
1500 ml vinegar

Chop the gooseberries and mix thoroughly with the other dry ingredients. Boil in the vinegar until soft, press through a sieve, and bottle for use. The original of this recipe gives a much higher quantity of salt, which would be inedible to us.

forth. Come three o'clock my uncle and grandfather would appear, didn't have to be called, and there'd be this enormous afternoon tea which actually went on for about half an hour, and then grandfather would be back in the house just before five, scrubbed up and sitting down to tea at six o'clock, and that was how the day went.[63]

This could easily stand beside the description of a typical day's food from Lady Barker, quoted above. Miller was astonished to recollect the level of organisation required and the amount of time her grandmother spent in the kitchen: if she was not there cooking for that day, she was making jams, chutneys, pickles and preserves of every description. Truly this was a culture based centrally on food and its consumption. But it was not only the experiences of poverty and of emigration which created this culture. There was a range of other influences at work to which we need now to turn if our picture of the basis of our cuisine is to be complete.

4

TAME BEASTS, GAME BEASTS AND GOOD KING EDWARDS

THE LAND OF NEW ZEALAND, as subsequent experience has amply illustrated, is ideally suited to certain types of industrial agriculture. It has a temperate climate, good soils, and a range of topographies over a considerable longitude. Most things to eat that grow in Europe will grow here, along with much else besides. But it did not appear quite in that light to those who arrived in the first part of the nineteenth century, as is graphically illustrated by the memoir of the early Wellington settler, Alfred Saunders:

> With very long faces we saw what a fearfully rough country we had come to . . . We strained our eyes in the hope of seeing some level land, but could see nothing but the roughest mountains. 'What a country,' said Mr Cullen, a Somerset farmer. 'But see what a fine harbour we have got,' said the Deal boatman (who had come out to act as pilot). 'Dang the vine harbour.' said Farmer Cullen; 'What's the good of a vine harbour whar you can't graw nothing?'[1]

His words were echoed by Frederick Hunt, another early settler: 'If this is the country we are to sow and reap from, it will tire many a poor ploughman . . . This land may do well for cattle and sheep . . . but it will require the transition of ages to render it available to plough and harrow.'[2]

Matters were not quite as parlous as Hunt depicted them, but large areas of New Zealand were in a virgin state and required much work to bring them to regular cultivable standard. Perhaps even more to the point, for a wholesale agriculture to develop and sustain itself, the immigration of large numbers of people, and of their flora and fauna, was required. The European settlers of the nineteenth century who encountered these problems were not, as it happens, the first to do so.

KITCHEN GARDENERS OF THE SUNRISE

The Polynesian people who had arrived in New Zealand perhaps 1000 years before farmer Cullen would have understood his apprehensions very well. They too were faced by a land which had limited sustainable food resources. A significant number of these they had been obliged to bring with them. At least one recent major study of the human history of New Zealand has located the origins of its Maori culture in that overriding factor.[3] Certainly those who first arrived here from somewhere in the Eastern Polynesian triangle some time in the eleventh century of the Christian era or thereabouts brought with them both their own horticultural foodstuffs and a vigorous cultural tradition of kitchen gardening.[4]

Wherever the original Polynesian inhabitants of New Zealand may have come from in the immediate sense, the agricultural and food tradition they brought with them was a very sophisticated one, with its own lengthy history stretching back through the Lapita culture of what is now Melanesia to south-eastern Asia. This was a gardening and fish-eating culture which had travelled across the Pacific from west to east and brought its staple crops with it. These almost certainly included taro and yams (but not initially the sweet potato which was introduced later from South America by means which are not clear). In the islands closer to the equator there were breadfruit, coconuts and bananas, as well as a number of tree fruits not unlike apples. Root crops were carefully and intensively raised in enclosed and well-irrigated gardens. These crops were stored in pits. Gourds were grown for storage and transportation of foodstuffs and liquids, although the Lapita culture also had pottery. The gardens were probably enclosed to protect them from the inroads of the marauding pigs and chickens which were also kept for food.[5]

All of these characteristics of the Polynesian islands were noted by Cook and other explorers who penetrated the Pacific in the eighteenth century, and have been largely confirmed by subsequent archaeological investigations. But the same explorers noted differences once they had

Muttonbird

Some of the birds traditionally eaten by the pre-European Maori, such as the moa, are extinct; others are now protected, except in rare circumstances. The only one still generally available is the muttonbird or titi, the young of the sooty shearwater. Harvested from burrows before it grows to flight age, and thus very fat, it is too strong a flavour for some tastes. It can be cooked in a number of ways: roasted, as one would a duck; grilled after a brief boiling; or boiled for about an hour in several changes of water. It is best served with puha, cabbage, kumara and potato, which should be cooked in the same water as that used to boil the bird.

In his *Two Hundred Years of New Zealand Food and Cookery*, David Burton gives a number of recipes for muttonbird. These include the following for Muttonbird Pie:

1 muttonbird
450 g cooked mashed potatoes
2 x 30 g butter
50 ml and 100 ml milk
parsley, chopped
1 tbsp flour
salt and pepper

The muttonbird should be boiled for about 30 minutes in several changes of water and then boned and the meat chopped. Mix 30 g of melted butter with 50 ml of milk and the mashed potato, and line a greased dish with this, reserving some for the top. Make a *roux* sauce with butter, flour and 100 ml of milk. Pour over the chopped muttonbird in the potato case, sprinkle with chopped parsley and season to taste. Cover, pat down and bake at 200°C for about an hour or until the top is browned.

Raupo Bread

The preparation of bread using raupo pollen was described shortly after the signing of the Treaty by the Rev. Richard Taylor and involved the collection of the pollen, or pua, first at dawn and then at dusk by large parties. This description is repeated in *The Maori Cookbook*, a collection of traditional recipes introduced by Joanna Paul and published in 1996. The dish made from this can be recreated by making a stiff paste from about 500 g of raupo pollen, shaken from the raupo heads, with about ½ cup of water. Wrap this in raupo leaves and steam it (in a hangi if possible) or in a steamer on the stove, until it is cooked — about an hour.

Bread was also made from hinau berries, Taylor noted, although it was rather too oily for European taste.

Seaweeds

The aquatic weed known as sea lettuce to Pakeha is called parengo by Maori, and is a close relative of the European delicacy laver or the Japanese nori. It should be eaten either steamed with butter, or boiled for about 30 minutes with dripping.

Shellfish

Maori ate all manner of shellfish. Mussels are now commonly eaten throughout New Zealand, but their commercial availability has developed only recently, in the wake of their farming for export. Perhaps for this reason most Pakeha are unaware of the existence of a freshwater mussel, kakahi. These make a delicious soup. If you can't get kakahi, pipis will do as well.

2 dozen kakahi
2 large onions, chopped
oil for frying
2 carrots, grated
2 tbsp each brown sugar, Worcester
  sauce and vinegar
a dash of cayenne pepper
salt and pepper
cornflour

Boil the mussels until they open, then shell them, retaining the juice. Fry the onions in oil until soft, then add this with the other ingredients, including the boiled mussels, but not the cornflour, to the mussel liquid. Thicken with the cornflour and season as desired. A little chopped parsley sprinkled on top adds to the flavour.

arrived in New Zealand. Many of the food items they had noted in warmer areas were not apparent. There were no bananas, coconuts or breadfruit, for example, nor the domestic animals which abounded in Tonga or Tahiti. Nevertheless, Cook in particular was impressed and gave many descriptions. Of one typical site in Queen Charlotte Sound he wrote in 1769:

> The ground is completely cleared of all weeds — the mold broke with as much care as that of our best gardens. The Sweet potatoes are set in distinct little molehills which ranged in some in straight lines, in others in quincunx [a five-sided pattern]. In one Plott I observed these hillocks, at their base surrounded by dried grass. The Arum is planted in little circular concaves, exactly in the manner our Gard'ners plant melons as Mr . . . informs me. The yams are planted in like manner with the sweet potatoes: these Cultivated spots are enclosed with a perfectly close paling of reeds about twenty inches high.[6]

It is clear that the staple crops of Polynesia had been transplanted to New Zealand by careful transfer by the original settlers, probably in mulch; and that those which would take in the new environment were being raised by the same techniques as were used elsewhere.

If animals were also brought they had largely not survived. The only ones to have done so appear to have been the dog and the ubiquitous rat. This must have posed something of a problem for the original Polynesian settlers. New Zealand is not rich in varieties of native fauna. Some of what was there would have provided abundant sustenance, at least for the first couple of hundred years, as archaeology also confirms. Available for food were birds (including the flightless moa, although this was hunted to extinction within a relatively short time), and, around the coasts, seals and shellfish, perhaps an occasional beached whale, and a plentiful inshore fishery. Freshwater eels also abounded. At a pinch the original arrivals could also eat fern root, and they discovered a range of other edible berries and vegetable plants — although this must have been a rather hit-and-miss affair, involving experimentation with items similar to those familiar from their home islands. By the time Europeans arrived, the Maori were utilising, among this range, raupo pollen, hinau paste, the berries of the tawa, the juice of the tutu, karaka pulp, sow thistles (puha), watercress, a wide range of seaweeds, and a form of spinach unique to New Zealand (*Tetragonia expansa*).[7]

James Belich conjectures that the eating habits of these first settlements developed in response to a threefold need to exploit the natural fauna, to establish gardens and to ensure access to the stone quarries crucial to Polynesian technology. He dismisses the notion that New Zealand was naturally abundant in food, and tartly suggests that dropping contemporary exponents of this view into the bush, foodless and in the midst of winter, would quickly disabuse the survivors of any such romanticism. But his conclusion is that in the era of early Polynesian settlement 'an all-year-round living could be wrested from New Zealand nature, even in the absence of game or gardens, but it took an immense effort and organisation, aimed at a wide range of targets'.[8] However, he goes on to point out that by perhaps the sixteenth century the growth of population was putting considerable strains on the food supply, which was reaching its potential limits.

Archaeologists and historians have drawn attention to what one of them calls 'the bleak contrast between the richness and diversity of the early hunting middens and the monotonous uniformity of later rubbish dumps, composed almost entirely of fish and shellfish'.[9] This may be an exaggeration but by 300 years ago the earlier major sources of hunted foods had probably largely been exhausted. This may explain the development of the distinctive warrior culture of the Maori encountered by Tasman and Cook, with its emphasis on command of land and its food resources. It may also explain the alacrity with which Maori adopted the potato following its introduction by Cook, initially at Motoara in the Queen Charlotte Sound.

PORK AND POTATOES

The scientist Georg Forster recorded in his journal that:

> Cook, who was determined to omit nothing which might tend to the preservation of European garden-plants in this country, prepared the soil, sowed seeds and transplanted the young plants in four or five different parts of this Sound . . . he chiefly endeavoured to raise such vegetables as have useful and nutritive roots, and among them particularly potatoes of which we had been able to preserve but few in a state of vegetation. He had like-wise sown corn of several sorts, beans, kidney-beans and pease, and devoted the latter part of his stay to these occupations.[10]

Paua, Kotoretore and Kina

Kina roes are generally eaten raw, either scooped directly from the case, as a relish to meat and potatoes, or on brown bread with butter. Kotoretore is sea anemone jelly. The anemones should be soaked for about 3 hours in cold water to remove sand, and then scored and simmered in fresh water for about an hour. The resulting jellyfish liquid can be used as a stock for fish soups or as a sauce base. But it is the paua which continues to delight above all other shellfish. Because they are common (as abalone) to the Pacific area there are many recipes including, among others, a Chinese soup in which the abalone are made into fish balls with white fish and shrimp and cooked in a strong chicken stock (for this recipe see Kenneth Lo's *Chinese Food*), and as a filling for empanades or little pastries in Argentina (Elisabeth Ortiz, *The Book of Latin American Cooking*). They are usually eaten in New Zealand as fritters. When I was a boy these could be had at the Greymouth piecart for sixpence each. Usually we alternated them with whitebait fritters which covered the whole plate at the same price.

450 g minced paua
1 egg
1 tbsp flour
1 tsp baking powder
1 small onion, grated
milk
salt and pepper

Make a creamy batter with the egg, flour and other ingredients, and stir in the minced fish. Fry dropped spoonfuls in oil, about 4 minutes each side. Traditionally these should be eaten with boiled puha or sow thistle. The smooth-leafed variety is sweeter, and should be washed well in running water, and then steamed for about 30 minutes, seasoned with salt, butter and a dash of vinegar.

Kumara Soup

Maori quickly adapted their own root
vegetable, the kumara, so that it could be
eaten in combination with the newly
introduced flora and fauna. Kumara is an
excellent basis for soup.

> 500 g kumara
> 3 onions, sliced
> 30 g butter
> 600 ml milk
> 500 g corn (creamed or not)
> salt, pepper and parsley, chopped

Peel, dice, cook and drain the kumara. Mash,
gradually adding about half the milk. Fry the
onion in the butter until it clarifies, then add
the kumara mixture, the corn and the
remainder of the milk. Bring slowly to the
boil, season to taste, and serve with parsley
sprinkled on top.

This same simple soup can be made with
potatoes, with the addition of a little
chopped silverbeet.

Pumpkin Cake

The use of vegetables to bulk out a cake was
another European technique to which
Maori quickly adapted.

> Cream ½ cup of butter with
> 1½ cups of sugar, and beat in 2 eggs.
> Sift together 2 cups of flour, 1 tsp of
> baking powder, and ½ tsp of baking
> soda, with 1 tsp of cinnamon and ½ tsp
> of ground cloves. Mix this thoroughly
> with a cup or two of cooked and mashed
> pumpkin and a cup of raisins and ½ cup
> of mixed nuts. Turn this into a greased
> tin and bake at about 180°C for 50
> minutes.

In addition, Cook planted turnips, cabbage, carrots, parsnips, parsley,
onions and leeks, and went to some trouble to demonstrate their method
of cultivation to local chiefs. When he returned in 1773 he found that
some had been foraged by rats, but otherwise the gardens were flourishing.
This was not from deliberate cultivation by the locals, but rather the
result of natural profusion. His lessons seem to have fallen mostly on
deaf ears at Queen Charlotte Sound.

But someone must have taken note, because as he went further afield
he found these initial plantings had been emulated throughout the
country, and many of the vegetable plants Cook introduced had spread
far and wide long before the beginning of organised settlement. In 1813,
a Captain Williams, for example, reported well over 40 hectares of
potatoes in cultivation as far south as Bluff. And the botanist Dieffenbach,
who visited the Queen Charlotte Sound in 1839, reported that the hills
around were yellow with cabbage in blossom and were to be found all
over the Cook Strait area.

Together with the cabbages and other vegetables planted by Cook
and other early Pakeha navigators and whalers (garlic was, appropriately,
introduced by the French navigator du Fresne in 1772), the potato
revolutionised Maori society, a fact particularly noted by Charles Darwin
when he visited in 1835. Potatoes could be cultivated in areas of the
country previously not suited to large-scale root crop production, and
did not require the intensive gardening activities of taro and kumara.
They were more easily stored, and they produced a far more abundant
crop than anything else available. They could be used for purposes of
trade with Europeans, and may also have increased the tendency to

territorial aggression inherent in the culture because enough potatoes could be grown and stored in a season to sustain a war party through several seasons of warfare — something not previously possible.

By the time missionaries and others began to settle in numbers, most of the European vegetable staples were already introduced. Samuel Marsden spoke of a large area of potatoes in cultivation on the 100 acres or so of flat land surrounding one of his early encampments. And the painter George Angas, after remarking that the potato was the staff of life to the Maori by the time he came to New Zealand in the 1840s, described rather charmingly, how

> before putting the potatoes in the oven they are washed by the slave women in the stream which runs past every village. The woman, having the potatoes in a flax basket or kit with two handles, goes into the stream, and putting one foot into the basket with the roots, takes hold of the handles and commences shaking them furiously, her foot acting as a scrubbing brush; in this way the potatoes are effectually cleansed in a few minutes.[11]

By this time, Angas thought, the kumara had been virtually reduced to a minor crop cultivated for ceremonial purposes.

Cook also went to some trouble to introduce the smaller European domestic animals. His first attempts, with pigs and goats, were unsuccessful. The stock from which he hoped the Maori would breed were simply slaughtered and eaten before they had a chance to multiply. Never daunted, Cook tried again. 'I took four hogs, three sows and one boar, two hens, and three cocks, and carried them a little way into the woods at the very bottom of West Bay where I left them as much food as would serve them a week or ten days. This I did in order to keep them in the woods, Lest they should come down to the shore in search of food and be discovered by the natives.'[12] This and subsequent liberations in uninhabited areas in both islands were highly successful, and within a few years of Cook's third voyage the released animals had begun to breed and spread rapidly. Pigs in particular were enthusiastically taken up by Maori, becoming a principal source of protein and a valuable item of trade.

By the 1830s this trade was extensive. Edward Markham, the rakish grandson of an Archbishop of York who lived in New Zealand for eight and a half months in 1834, recorded that the going rate on

Sugared Kumara

Rather less usually, Maori also learned how to make comfits using sweet potato, a trick common in the English cuisine until the early nineteenth century, but which now survives only as candied citrus peel and angelica. You'll need 2 large peeled and boiled kumara. Split these lengthways and put them in a roasting dish. Boil together about 100 g of brown sugar, 1 tbsp of lard or bacon fat and a little grated nutmeg, and pour this over the kumara. Bake this in a medium oven (180°C) for 5 minutes each side.

Pork and Kumara Casserole

The complementary combination of the pork and kumara was an early discovery. This is a later recipe but would certainly have been recognisable in the early nineteenth century.

1 small tin pineapple pieces
2 tbsp wine vinegar
2 tbsp cornflour
500 g pork, diced
2 large kumara, cubed
2 onions, sliced
salt and pepper

Mix the syrup drained from the pineapple with the vinegar and cornflour and pour over the meat, vegetables and pineapple in a casserole. Season. Bake covered at 180°C for a little over an hour, adding a little water if necessary. This dish can be made equally successfully with apricots, and is an analogue to the medieval sweet and sour dishes noted earlier.

the ground was two large pigs for a blanket.

> The sows at stated times go into the woods, and find their lords, and having done rural for some time return to more civilised life and better food and bring up a squeaking family fully proving that they had loved. Vessels come up the Hokianga and buy and salt all the pork they can, say 20 tons at a time and take it up to Hobart Town and Sydney, and get sixty pounds a ton for what stood them in three or four and in the same way they have bought potatoes at 12 shillings a ton and sold them at 12 pounds . . . [13]

For that most crucial of all trade goods, the musket, Maori were prepared to offer eight pigs and 150 baskets of potatoes apiece in 1827.[14]

Markham included in his picturesque account much incidental detail about the food eaten by Maori in the pre-Treaty period. Kumara were still relatively common during his sojourn (he saw about 4000 flax kits of them in one store) and he also described the use of sand pits for storing carrots. Although he initially wearied of the universal diet of pork and potatoes he developed a taste for it and missed it after he left the country. He described it as 'amorous food', and rather impishly drew attention to the fact that the missionary Henry Williams lived on it and had nine children — an implication which might well have scandalised Williams and his colleagues had they been aware of it. Bread-eating, however, had not caught on in Markham's time despite the efforts of the missionaries. He did not eat it in New Zealand until he was five months into his stay, at dinner with James Busby (where he also had a bottle of port which he considered a great treat).

Maori also quickly adapted some food items to their own purposes. Markham particularly mentioned rotted corn, which he said 'stinks terribly' and thought was responsible for the spread of tuberculosis. Angas also included a description of this culinary curiosity:

> Railed enclosures of some twenty feet square are erected in the water near river side settlements, expressly for the purpose of preparing the favourite stinking corn. The cobs of maize are placed, when in a green state, in flax baskets, and put under the water for some weeks, until quite putrid; they are then taken out as occasion may require and made up into disgusting cakes . . . at other times the putrid mass is put into a *kohue* or large pan, and, when mixed with water and boiled over the fire, is converted into a

Kaanga Wai

That sounds much better than rotted corn, but that's essentially what it is. Maori still make and enjoy this dish, using a similar technique to that described by Angas. Curing corn in this way entails putting corn cobs in a sack of some sort and leaving them in clear running water for a couple of months. The kernels are then stripped from the husk, cleaned, mashed, brought to the boil and simmered for about 2 hours or more. This can be eaten with a little salt, sugar and cream as a porridge, or it can be dried in the oven after squeezing out the moisture and used as a base for other dishes. One of these is a custard made by beating together an egg, 200 ml of milk, 100 g of the dried corn, 30 g of melted butter, and sugar and salt to taste. This is then baked in an ovenproof dish at 140°C until the top is browned (about 40 minutes).

species of gruel that sends forth an effluvia over the whole settlement. No-one who has been fortunate enough never to experience the vile odour arising from the corn thus prepared, can form any idea of its extreme offensiveness.[15]

Notoriously, one culture abhors some of the food habits of another, and the Europeans of pre-Treaty New Zealand were no exception. We do not know what Maori thought of the notion of eating rotted milk, i.e. cheese, but their view might well have been the same as that of the Europeans when it came to rotted corn.

THE MISSIONARY INFLUENCE

The earlier settlers were, as it happened, quite confident of the superiority of their particular brand of civilisation and worked to introduce it to their Maori neighbours as a saving grace. The missionaries especially tried very hard to convert their new communicants to the virtues of European farming, supplying them with ploughs and milking cows. Even before the establishment of his mission in the Bay of Islands in 1814, Samuel Marsden was showing Maori visitors to Sydney over his model farm, introducing them to grain cultivation and supplying wheat seed for the return home. Some of those he patronised took up his suggestion, though the new crop initially caused much derision. Many Maori who had not had the advantage of Marsden's stern lessons in the origins of civilisation apparently remarked that it seemed a great deal of effort to produce something with no edible root.

It took some time to overcome this conservatism, but by the 1830s many Maori had become enthusiastic farmers in the European mode. In 1826, the mission supporter Taiwhanga, at Paihia, is recorded as having a thriving garden in which he grew cucumbers, pumpkins, melons, onions, peas and parsnips; he also had vines and a peach tree, and an acre of wheat. By 1837 he was operating New Zealand's first dairy farm, with 20 head of cattle, seven of them in milk, and was regularly selling butter for between 1s and 2s 6d a pound. By 1841 he had added a small flock of sheep.[16] John Gorst's and Lady Martin's subsequent descriptions of the flourishing European-style farming economy of the Waikato people in the 1850s are well known.[17]

But there is similarly ample evidence that the missionaries not only knew little about the significance of food hospitality as a key element in Maori culture, but also frowned upon the practices it entailed as wasteful and leading to idleness and profligacy. That this hospitality could be offered on a grand scale is clear from many accounts. Markham's is particularly evocative:

> The feast was about to commence. Moyterra [Moetara] mounted on Oakes old mare came on the ground. Rubbed noses with the chiefs and Europeans and then proceeded to distribute his potatoes, baked pigs, sharks, muttonfish [paua], and pippies dried, and a cow had been bought and killed and cut up. Moyterra had some 4,000 bags of potatoes stowed in long line, three bags high like a wall; supposing them to contain 60lb each kit worth £18 a ton, they were computed to be worth £2,000 in Sydney market, independent of the baked pigs spread eagle fashion tout les agremens. He served out the potatoes to the chiefs, according to their followers, and when that was done, the potatoes were carried to the different encampments, and speedily each party was hutted, and then cooking began for that evening; next morning pork and potatoes was the order of the day, and I had brought salt and grog so I was all right . . . [18]

His words were echoed by the trader Joel Polack, who described similar quantities of potatoes set out in two long rows, with kumara, watermelons, taro, karaka kernels, dried fish, preserved turnips and baked ti-tree roots.[19] In another account he added onions, peaches and grapes to his catalogue of foodstuffs.

No account of the Maori cuisine was complete without a description of what Edward Markham called the 'coppre Mourie' or oven. Readers of his journal might have been more confused than enlightened by his description, however. That of Joel Polack is more coherent:

> Some of the lads had collected stones, and deposited them in a hole, previously dug in the ground, near the beach, over some firewood which had been ignited. The stones having been made red hot, the provisions, which consisted of fish procured at Moperi, after being cleansed and bound up in the leaves of the *kaha* or wild turnip, which covers almost every spare surface of vegetable soil in the country, together with the potatoes and kumeras, were all placed in a basket on the hot stones, which were arranged so as to surround the food. Some leaves and old baskets were

placed over the first that had been deposited in the hole, and pouring some water from a calabash, the steam that arose as a consequence was speedily enclosed, by earth being thrown over the whole so that the steam could not escape — every gap being carefully closed up. Within twenty minutes the provisions were excellently cooked, and fit for eating.[20]

Perhaps what most fascinated the early explorers and travellers about the use of the hangi was the existence in what they would almost certainly have thought of as a primitive and even savage society of cooking techniques at least as sophisticated as those of contemporary Europe (where much cooking continued to be conducted over an open fire), and in some ways significantly more efficient. They certainly thought it worth commenting on if they did not emulate it.

Given the obvious key significance of activities relating to food, it is not surprising that the Maori feast was described by the anthropologist Raymond Firth in his classic work on Maori life and economy as

an institution of great cultural importance. It was always an affair of excitement and pleasure, it represented the pinnacle of satisfaction in community life. The focus of interest for months ahead, it gave scope for generous display both of provisions and of the personal accomplishments of those who attended. It offered too, a peculiarly favourable opportunity for selective friendship and sexual choice. The feast also played a valuable social role in providing the occasion for the meeting of different groups and promoting harmonious relationships between them. Food had a very mellowing influence when it was a question of patching up tribal differences.[21]

Firth went on to describe, in a lengthy passage devoted to this central Maori institution, its role in dividing and distributing the economic surplus, in creating complex patterns of reciprocal obligation which helped to hold Maori society together, and in marking events of both personal and communal significance. These might include the naming of a child, a tattooing, a tangi, the conclusion of planting, the harvesting of the crop, first fruits in hunting seasons, the annual appearance of the Pleiades in June, peace, war, the arrival of visitors of note, or some significant capital undertaking such as the construction of a communal building or a canoe.

Cabbage Tree

The inner blanched leaves or hearts of the cabbage tree were sometimes served as a vegetable for those without any other food. *The Maori Cookbook* gives three methods of preparing this. The first involves breaking out the heart and stripping it of its leaves or grass, to reveal the firm white centre. This, when boiled until tender, gives a slightly astringent vegetable which goes well with roast meat. Similarly, the centre can be boiled with puha, in which case it goes well with pork or corned beef. Finally, the same white core when sliced finely can be eaten as a salad with a French dressing, in much the same way as finnochio.

EUROPEANS AND THE MAORI LARDER

Food continues to serve all of these functions, and more, in Maori life, but the Europeans who came to colonise and settle New Zealand in great numbers after 1840 were largely wilfully ignorant of such things. There were some attempts, it is true, to draw on the food resources the land supplied. George Earp's 1849 handbook for intending settlers[22] carried information on the use of tawa berries, and suggested the boiling of the unripe fruit of the kiekie to produce a food rather like egg albumen. It also warned against the extremely poisonous tutu, although a form of wine was made by Maori from the extracted juice. Canon W. J. Stack, who once tried some, did not repeat the experience when after just a few sips he felt numb in his extremities, the room revolved, and he fell over. His wife Eliza also recorded the eating of ripe kiekie flowers, of which she 'found the flavour very agreeable'.[23]

Stewed fuchsia berries were also widely eaten during the early colonising years. The Auckland missionary Vicesimus Lush recorded in his diary that on 18 November 1850 he went with Maori and other friends on a fuchsia berry-gathering expedition. 'The lads quickly dispersed themselves over the wood and climbed up the fuchsia trees, many of which were exceedingly lofty and laden with a small, black berry, the fruit of their small scarlet blossom. We gathered upwards of a gallon . . .' These were made into a pudding for his dinner four days later, and he 'thought it good'.[24]

Sweet kumara was crystallised or baked in a tart as Marianne Williams, wife of the missionary Henry, recorded in her journal, but this had long been a common practice in Europe, so owed nothing to Maori lore.[25] What was more interesting was the use of the nikau tree to produce not only a boiled vegetable (which Eliza Jones described as having 'rather a nutty flavour, the best parts being drawn as with artichokes from the bottom of the central frond'), but also a form of sugar which could be extracted from it when cane sugar ran low. There is an interesting description of this process in *Earliest Canterbury* by James Hay, one of the first European settlers on Banks Peninsula.[26] But mostly these native foodstuffs were regarded as curiosities and fell out of use as the more familiar European items became readily available.

The Bohemian settlers at Puhoe might have eaten boiled nikau hearts to save themselves from starvation, but this was the action of those with no alternative, and the Pakeha settlers of New Zealand drew little from the accumulated food lore of their predecessor and now companion culture. It has taken well over a century for the Pakeha to overcome this cultural arrogance, and to relearn and understand the value and pleasure of the traditional Maori foodstuffs which the land provides.

Rather than adopt the food of the indigenous inhabitants they preferred to import their own. They also tended to eschew fish, and ate it regularly as a staple only when they could not avoid it. Where they had come from, fish was, with notable exceptions, the food of the poor, and they had come to better themselves. This meant an ambition to be regular meat-eaters, as has been seen. The pig they already had, but the early European settlers aspired to a great deal more edible protein on the hoof, both for farming and as game.

BEAUTIFUL MOUNTAINS FOR SHEEP

When Samuel Butler came to the Canterbury settlement in 1860 to take up the land which was to make his fortune and settle him back in England as a literary gentleman for the rest of his days, one of his very first conclusions was that whatever else New Zealand might possess, it had beautiful mountains for sheep.[27] He was by no means, of course, the first settler to appreciate this, although most of his predecessors lacked his capacity for irony. It *was* good country for sheep, and before long the land was to support a great many of them.

Cook had released two merinos in 1773 but they failed to survive. Marsden also brought in a small flock but this too failed to prosper. It was not until the 1840s that sheep were imported in numbers. The first significant shipment is usually attributed to Charles Bidwill, who imported 1600 sheep from Australia (where they could be had for 2s 6d a head) in 1843, and, with his partners Frederick Weld and Henry Vavasour, ran these first in the South Wairarapa and then in Marlborough. His example was quickly followed by many others, like the Deans brothers in Canterbury and George Duppa in Nelson.[28] It was a hazardous business. Overcrowding and stormy conditions in the Tasman meant that many sheep were lost on the passage; death of livestock in sea transit is no new phenomenon in this part of the world. But Canterbury, Marlborough, and later Hawkes Bay and Otago (where the ex-whaler Johnny Jones took up sheep raising in 1844) proved ideal for sheep, so that the flocks had grown to over 2.7 million by 1861, 11.6 million by 1874, and 19 million by 1895.[29] It was wool that the sheep herders were initially interested in, but sheepmeat was an obvious source of protein. New Zealand became overwhelmingly a mutton-eating nation early in its colonial history and remained so well into the twentieth century.

Beef cattle were a less favoured introduction. Horned cattle numbers amounted to 193,285 in 1861 and to 494,113 in 1874, but a lot of these beasts were bullocks which provided the main motive power for heavy transport and for stumping. Cattle raised for meat consumption never took on in the same way as sheep, and New Zealanders are not even now primarily beef consumers.

The principal use of cows in the nineteenth century was for milk and its by-products. These were entirely for domestic, and mainly local, consumption. A very high proportion of early settlers kept a cow or two, along with a hen coop. This is wholly understandable from a culture in which the food traditions emphasised butter, cheese and eggs, and which many immigrants had been denied the opportunity to eat regularly, either because they had lived in towns (where the milk was liable to be adulterated or unsafe for human consumption), or because they had been rural labourers whose grasping employers had refused them the right to do so. Chickens had been carried on board sailing ships since at least the fifteenth century, usually under the watchful eye of the ships' officers to prevent crew from making off with the eggs. This practice became so standard in the nineteenth century that the passage of fowls of various kinds was taken absolutely for granted, and there is no record of by whom or when they were again introduced following the experimental introduction by Cook in 1773 (which seems to have been a failure: the wild hen is unknown in New Zealand).[30] They seem to have been here from the outset, and to have flourished. The crowing of roosters heralded the New Zealand dawn in every part of the country, rural or urban, well into the twentieth century.

The importation of game animals proved rather more problematic. Henry Petre, a director of the New Zealand Company who, rather unusually, decided to settle in the colony he was sponsoring, brought a collection of pheasants and peacocks with him, but it remained for the twentieth century to raise the former in commercial numbers. He also

Egg and Cheese Dishes

The availability of cheap eggs, cheese, butter and cream in quantity was commented on by many of the settlers. The nineteenth century tended to be more adventurous in its use of eggs than we are. Anne Cobbett's *The English Housekeeper* of 1851 lists 14 different ways of presenting them, including (among the usual poached, fried, scrambled, and omelette), eggs prepared 'a la tripe' (which contains no tripe but is an onion dish), and 'Swiss eggs', made with cheese, nutmeg and white wine. There is also an egg fricassee (hard-boiled eggs in a hot white sauce with sippets), and a dish in which boiled eggs, and onions and mushrooms fried in butter, are simmered in thickened stock flavoured with mustard.

The nineteenth century also enjoyed Welsh Rarebit (or Rabbit) as a cheese savoury, a dish that can be traced back to Andrew Board writing in the fourteenth century. 'Put a lump of butter in a saucepan,' runs an old recipe, 'add twice as much ale, and a pinch of salt and pepper. When heated grate in enough cheese to make a stiff cream. On no account allow the mixture to boil. Have ready a slice of toast fried in bacon fat and buttered. Pour the rabbit quickly over, and give it one second under the grill or hold the red hot fire shovel over it.'

imported red deer in 1854 and in 1860. In 1861, Prince Albert sent more. Gentlemen who had made their homes in New Zealand were attracted by the thought of hunting deer here. In 1847 Colonel William Wakefield had remarked that 'the sport of hunting them would be highly attractive and would conduce to the breed of horses, and afford a manly amusement to the young colonists, fitting them for the more serious life of stock-keeping and wool-growing'. John Godley, one of the more prominent of the Canterbury settlers, harboured similar pretensions, having, as the principal historian of acclimatisation has remarked, 'an irresistible urge to be on a horse and chasing things'.[31] During the century the very active provincial acclimatisation societies which sprang up everywhere seem to have competed with one another in the introduction of deer varieties and their release into the wild. There, they quickly became a nuisance and highly destructive of vegetation, so that by the early twentieth century hunters were being paid a bounty to shoot them. It was not, however, until the practice of farming them began in the later twentieth century that they figured as other than an occasional item of diet. Some of the more exotic animals brought to New Zealand have never been taken up or flourished, and, with the exception of goats, and those rarely, are never eaten.

The acclimatisation movement in fact brought in a wide range of edible animals and poultry, although the birds, with the exception of ducks, did not much figure in the nineteenth-century New Zealand kitchen. Lady Barker refers to raising and eating pheasants at Broomielaw, but similar references are rare:

> This is one of the very few stations where pheasants have been introduced, but then, every arrangement had been made for their comfort, and a beautiful house and yard built for their reception on a flat, just beneath the high terrace on which the house stands. More than a hundred young birds were turned out last spring, and there will probably be three times that number at the end of this year. We actually had pheasant twice at dinner; the first, and probably the last time we shall taste game in New Zealand.

This is a curious remark from one whose husband was a regular pig hunter for their larder, but she feared that the pheasants would be hard put to escape the depredations of the hawks which abounded.[32]

Stuffed Venison Flank

Nicola Fletcher's *Game for All* (published in London in 1987) gives what she describes as a traditional New Zealand recipe for venison flap ('flap (pron. flep)' as she expresses it, in a vain attempt to capture the local vernacular), and which is the flank of the deer — about 2 kg of meat. This may or may not be traditional. I have never encountered venison prepared in this way, although the style of preparation is typical of the nineteenth century.

    a boned venison flank
    6 deer tongues
    2 onions
    beef stock
    sage, salt and pepper

The tongues should be boiled in some of the stock and skinned when cool. The inside of the flank is then seasoned with the sage, salt and pepper, the tongues laid on it, and the whole rolled up and tied securely and enclosed in a cloth. It is then to be simmered in stock for 3 hours, and served cold.

Pig's Head Brawn

Nineteenth-century cooks were far more frugal than we are and used all edible parts of an animal, rather than turning them into fertiliser meal or recycled animal cake. Your butcher may look at you curiously if you order a pig's head, but they're readily available and quite cheap. Ask for it to be split into two or it's too cumbersome to handle in the first part of the operation.

> a pig's head
> 2 trotters
> 450 g shin of beef on the bone
> a clove of garlic, chopped
> bouquet garni
> a handful of black peppercorns
> 2 tbsp wine vinegar
> salt
> juice of a lemon
> 2 onions, stuck with a few cloves
> 2 carrots and 2 leeks, cut in pieces

The head and the trotters should be brined for a couple of days if you can manage it. Make your brine by boiling together 3 litres of water, 400 g each of salt and brown sugar, 50 g of saltpetre, some juniper berries, nutmeg, a bay-leaf, some mixed herbs and 6 cloves. Rinse the meat after the second day, and put it in a large pot with the beef and the vegetables, spices and herbs. Cover with the water and bring to boil, then skim. Simmer until the meat is cooked and can be easily removed from the bone. Strip the meat from the bones and cut it into bite-sized pieces. Strain the stock and boil it down. Add the lemon juice and a little gelatine if you have insufficient faith in the setting powers of the stock. Simmer this for 20 minutes. Pack the meat into a mould and pour over the stock jelly. Leave to set in a cool place overnight and turn out to serve.

Stuffed Wild Rabbit

You don't have to be poor and desperate to eat rabbits. One of the lesser-known gourmets and cooks of the nineteenth century, and one of the most creative, was the French painter Henri de Toulouse-Lautrec, whose collected recipes were published after his death by his friend and fellow chef, Maurice Joyant (translated and republished in 1966 as *The Art of Cuisine* by the Metropolitan Museum in New York). The most difficult part about this recipe will be getting the rabbit.

> 1 whole dressed rabbit
> liver and kidneys of the rabbit
> 100 g each beef mince, pork mince and
>   sausage meat
> 100 g stoned black olives
> salt, pepper and thyme
> mustard

After salting it well inside and out, stuff the rabbit with the other ingredients mixed to a firm consistency, and sew up the belly of the rabbit. Brush the outside with mustard and, if you have it, cover with pork rind (I keep and freeze the rind from the Christmas ham for this sort of use). Roast in a hot oven for 20 minutes and then reduce the heat to medium and give it another 40 minutes or so, depending on how you like your meat.

Wild Pork

This dish was understandably popular with the settlers, especially as it was free for the shooting. *Brett's Guide* gives quite a number of recipes for cooking it; they include several pies, along with a recipe for sucking pig which is worth citing. The pig should be about three weeks old, says the author, scalded to remove the hair, and cleaned thoroughly, then it should stuffed with a mixture of breadcrumbs, sage and butter, seasoned with salt and pepper. It should then be rested by the fire so that it dries out, rubbed all over with melted butter, and then roasted in a medium to hot oven for 2 hours or so with regular bastings with oil or butter. The *Guide* also gives a recipe for a pig's head brawn.

Game Custards

The Victorians ate much more game than we are used to doing, and in many more forms. Some of these are now being rediscovered. This unusual recipe comes from the cookery notebooks of Emily Cooper, Lady Shaftsbury, who had it from the novelist Emily Eden in 1857. To make, it requires a strong game stock made of bird carcasses, a glass of white wine, a base of beef stock, and some aromatic herbs and vegetables to your taste. For each 100 ml of strained stock, allow 1 egg yolk. These should be beaten into the stock and the whole seasoned to taste, then poured into ceramic custard ramekins and stood in a pan of simmering water on top of the stove for about half an hour or until the custard thickens. This should then be served with toast.

Potted Pheasant

Lady Barker probably had her pheasants roasted. Our forebears also commonly potted them. In her *Modern Cookery* of 1845 Eliza Acton has the following recipe:

Roast the birds as for table, but let them be thoroughly done, for if the gravy be left in, the meat will not keep half so well. Raise the flesh of the breast, wings, and merrythought, quite clear from the bones, take off the skin, mince, and then pound it very smoothly with about one third its weight in fresh butter, or something less if the meat should appear of a proper consistence without the full quantity: season it with salt, mace and cayenne only, and add these in small portions until the meat is rather highly flavoured with the two last; proceed with it as with other potted meats.

By which she meant that a seal of clarified melted butter should be poured on top so that it can be kept in a cool place until called for.

Eel Pie

In the nineteenth century a favourite recreation was an excursion up the Thames to Twickenham Eyot, better known as Eel Pie Island, where the inn was famous for its eel pies. This recipe comes from William Kitchener's *The Cook's Oracle*, published in 1843.

2 eels
2 shallots
50 g butter
2 glasses dry sherry
a handful of parsley, chopped
60 g more of butter and the same of
   flour
juice of a lemon
2 hard-boiled eggs
nutmeg, salt and pepper
puff pastry

Skin, clean and bone the eels and cut them into pieces. Fry the chopped shallots in the butter until they are transparent, and then add the parsley, a few gratings of nutmeg, and salt and pepper to taste, together with the sherry. Put in the eels, add water to cover, and bring to the boil. Take out the eels and lay them in a buttered pie dish. Add the butter and flour to the sauce and let it thicken, then stir in the lemon juice. Chop the hard-boiled eggs and put them with the eels. Pour the sauce over, and make a pastry lid to cover. Bake for 20 minutes at 230°C, then lower the heat to 180°C and give the pie another 30 minutes or so. It can be eaten hot or cold.

Trout

When I asked a piscatorially inclined friend the best way to cook trout he replied, 'immediately'. That's quite right, of course, but not all of us can take it straight from hook to pan. Trout is best grilled, lightly coated with seasoned flour or oatmeal, and wrapped in bacon, vine leaves or the green leaves of a leek. The nineteenth century had many other ways of preparing it, however, including stuffing it and then baking it in pastry.

  puff pastry
  a salmon or brown trout (probably about
    2 kg)
  100 g breadcrumbs soaked in a little
    boiling milk
  90 g butter
  some chives, tarragon, parsley and
    thyme, chopped
  1 tsp mace
  salt and white pepper
  150 ml cream
  120 g shrimps, cooked and shelled
  lemon for garnish

Roll out the pastry and position the fish on it so it can be enclosed by it. It is best to do this on the dish you will be using to bake the fish. Make the stuffing from the crumbs, butter, herbs, mace, salt and pepper, and pack this into the fish. Brush the fish all over with the cream, sprinkle with salt and pepper, and spread the shrimps around the belly. Fold the pastry to cover, sealing well. Bake at 200°C for about 20 minutes to brown the pastry, then reduce the heat to 160°C and cook for a further half hour. If the pastry is looking too dark, cover lightly with foil. Let it rest a few minutes before serving it garnished with lemon wedges.

The least successful of the imports was almost certainly the rabbit. This was not because they failed to adapt, but rather the contrary. 'In New Zealand,' said Mark Twain, 'the rabbit plague began at Bluff. The man who introduced the rabbit there was banqueted and lauded; but they would hang him now if they could get him.'[33] Even before introduced diseases made both rabbits and hares distasteful, they were seldom eaten because of their status as vermin. Several nineteenth-century writers on New Zealand noted them as food for the hard pressed — apparently they sold for about sixpence apiece. This parallels the experience in Australia, where rabbits are commonly sold in butchers shops, and have always found a ready market during economic downturns.

Of all the other introductions of edible fauna by the acclimatisation societies, the only ones to catch on widely in the nineteenth century were the freshwater brown trout, which was successfully released in New Zealand in either 1867 or 1868; the rainbow trout, introduced in 1883; and the Atlantic salmon, which was released in quantities between 1868 and 1889.[34] Some brook trout and quinnat salmon were also introduced. Brought in as game fish, these species could not be farmed, could be caught only by those with a licence and could not be sold commercially. It was not until the twentieth century that they were much eaten outside the fishing fraternity and their friends, of which there were doubtless many during the season. Perhaps because of these restrictions the general prejudice against the consumption of fish in New Zealand as a poor second to meat has never applied to freshwater game fish.

Some immigrants thought the range of available fish a poor one in any event. Writing in 1887 of the fish on sale in Christchurch, 'Hopeful' imagined the disappointment of an English fishmonger cast up in New Zealand:

> He will see oysters, certainly, but beyond that I don't know what to say; no soles, no shining mackerel, no whiting, no plaice, no brill, no turbot, herring, sprat, salmon, crab or lobster to be seen. There is a crayfish which answers to the lobster in appearance but it is hard and very indigestible; and a small fish called flounders, about the size of a small plaice that they seem to think a great deal of out here . . . and sometimes some black evil looking things of the eel tribe, most uninviting to the eye.[35]

Crayfish Salad

In 1864 the food enthusiast Edward Abbott published, under the pen name 'The Aristologist', what has become the most famous nineteenth-century Australian book about food, the *English and Australian Cookery Book*. This had a section on New Zealand and included a recipe for a crayfish salad.

Cooked crayfish meat, cut into small pieces, was to be mixed with the yolk of a hard-boiled egg, a mashed, well-cooked mealy potato, a tablespoon of vinegar and two of oil, a dessertspoon of mustard, and a little salt. This was to be mixed with a shredded lettuce and a tablespoon of cream.

The days when as much crayfish as one liked was virtually there for the taking are gone, but not as far away as one might think. When I was a boy crayfish bodies could be had for the asking at Akaroa, where the fishermen were interested only in the tails, kept a few to bait their pots, and threw the rest off the wharf and into the water. One alternative still available for the taking is crabs, but New Zealanders do not much catch them for themselves. Crabs have an illustrious history. They were a favourite of the American president Thomas Jefferson, also a noted cook and gourmet.

Freshwater Crayfish Sauce

Most people are unaware that New Zealand is home to a freshwater crayfish, koura. Even fewer know that it is the basis of one of the world's most fabulous dishes — Sauce Nantua. Their particular northern home is Annecy, a medieval lakeside town high in the Haute Savoie. The problem is getting the crayfish. If you can get them, make a bechamel sauce, stir in about 300 ml of cream, and a few mushrooms stewed in butter, then add the shelled crayfish tails. Some recipes call for the addition of truffles but that seems to me an unnecessary refinement — and besides, where would you get the truffles? It's a superb sauce to serve with a boiled chicken done in white wine stock.

These crayfish must once have been relatively plentiful in England. There's a soup recipe in Hannah Glasse's *Art of Cookery* which calls for 200 of the things.

Baked Flounders

I agree with 'Hopeful' at least on one thing, and that is that flounders aren't a patch on sole. But they're not to be sneered at, and continue to be relatively cheap and plentiful. Most people fry them, but that destroys their delicacy. They're better baked.

4 or 5 fresh prepared flounder
30 g butter
100 ml dry white wine
100 ml fish stock
a little lemon juice
sprig of fresh dill or fennel
salt and pepper

Lay the fish on foil in a baking dish, and season and add the other ingredients, but go easy on the lemon juice. Fold over the foil and bake in a hot oven preheated to 200°C for about 10 minutes or so. Garnish with lemon wedges and serve.

All of the fish excoriated for their absence had their New Zealand equivalents. They were not on sale only because there was little demand for them in a predominantly meat-eating country.

Attempts to introduce a range of seafood delicacies beyond the salmon were failures. These included lobsters and oysters. This latter is not the oddity it seems: the oyster beds off Bluff were not discovered until late in the century, although small local beds had been enjoyed throughout the country from the outset. In 1857, while living in Auckland with her clergyman brother Humphrey, Eliza Jones discovered, to her delight, an oyster bed less than 100 metres from her harbourside garden: 'As we were both very fond of them, Humphrey soon procured the proper knives for opening them. We often used to go down to the rocks to feast on oysters, taking with us a supply of bread and butter with vinegar and pepper.'[36] She discovered later that many others enjoyed the same pleasures, and oyster picnics were an institution around the Hauraki Gulf. The strictures of 'Hopeful' notwithstanding, crayfish were also harvested and eaten with enthusiasm, as were other delicacies. Lady Barker vividly described an eel hunt, and although the fish themselves made her shudder, she greatly enjoyed the eel pie prepared by her shepherd, who claimed that he had learned the secret of making this dish without it becoming impossibly oily from his Maori acquaintance.[37] Alas, the eel pie is not now seen in New Zealand, and eating eel, freshwater or sea, smoked or fresh, seems, at least among most European settlers, to have disappeared with the end of the nineteenth century. Perhaps it came to suffer from the general bad reputation of fishy foods, particularly among those of working-class origin. Of the fish dishes widely eaten by the poorer classes in Britain, only fish and chips appears to have survived the immigrant experience. There is no record of when this dish first made its appearance in New Zealand.[38]

Perhaps the least heralded introduction was also one of the happiest and most successful — that of the bee. For without bees we would have not only no honey but no fruit either. And while we cannot say when fish and chips came to New Zealand, we can date the arrival of the first honey bee precisely, to 13 March 1839, when the Reverend Mr Bumby carefully carried two straw skeps ashore at the Hokianga, and his sister established hives of these New South Wales immigrants at Mungunga. Mrs Hobson brought more in 1840, and they were introduced at Nelson in 1842 by a Mrs Allum. It should not surprise that these initiatives were made by women: keeping a hive of bees was a common task of women cottagers and those who kept kitchen gardens in the nineteenth century. Soon the bees were everywhere and wild hives became commonplace in the bush, with reports of well over 100 kilograms of honey from a single tree.[39] In 1881 Adela Stewart, pioneering south of Auckland, took the opportunity of a visit by sea to Tauranga to bring back the gift of a swarm of wild bees to start her own honey production.[40] On another occasion she recorded taking custody of 21 swarms of bees over a period of just two months. Interestingly, the New Zealand bees had to be supplemented by bumblebees, because the smaller honey bees proved unable to pollinate the red clover crucial to the developing pastoral industry. After several failed attempts, 48 bumblebees arrived at Lyttelton on the *Tongariro* in November 1884, and quickly settled in. They were spread to Wellington in 1888 and to Auckland in 1890, and are now to be found everywhere.

WILLIAM DAVIDSON AND THE VOYAGE OF THE *Dunedin*

What, more than any other thing, confirmed nineteenth-century New Zealanders as mutton and dairyfood eaters was the development of the frozen meat and dairy trades in sheep carcasses, and in butter and in cheese in the later part of the century. For this tradition we have to thank William Soltau Davidson. Davidson, who was born in Canada in 1846, came from a Scottish banking and commercial family with international connections to what would today be called agribusiness, although it was then in its infancy.[41] He came to New Zealand while still in his early twenties to work for the large-scale sheepfarming enterprise which later became the New Zealand and Australian Land Company (NZALC), one of nineteenth-century New Zealand's largest landholding businesses. Davidson learned this business from the bottom, starting as a shepherd, but by the time he was 31 he was the manager of an organisation owning hundreds of thousands of acres and running many thousands of sheep. In the late 1870s New Zealand entered what has become known to economic historians as 'the long depression'; it ruined many budding entrepreneurs, particularly those in the land business.[42] But the NZALC survived. The reason for this was simple. Unlike his fellow property managers, most of whom were urban-based land speculators, Davidson managed his estates for long-term business development and profitability as farming enterprises.

By the 1880s New Zealand, for four decades seen as an opportunity for London investors, had ceased to be an attractive proposition. In 1878 the Glasgow Bank failed in criminal circumstances, and a number of New Zealand companies, including those Davidson was managing, were caught in its backwash. It was the end of an era in New Zealand's economic history. New Zealand's international credit collapsed, precipitating a political crisis which brought the Liberals to power in 1890, and this new political culture was paralleled by a new economy which was based on New Zealand's role in international agribusiness. From now on New Zealand was to be a society based on food. This was Davidson's achievement.

New Zealand always has the same economic problem. Its main object as an economy is the production of agricultural products in sufficient quantity to trade in these internationally and thus underpin the domestic economy. By the 1880s the two principal New Zealand exports were failing to deliver that underpinning. One of these, gold, was purely exploitative and was running out. The other, wool, was in a depressed market. To break out of that loop and survive, New Zealand had to find a new product to deal in.

Davidson understood this. Because of his family and commercial connections he was aware of successful experiments in both the Argentine and Australia in exporting chilled and frozen sheep carcasses to Britain, where there was a ready market for what was essentially low-cost and low-quality food protein for consumption by the industrial workers. It was a market already successfully exploited by the canning industry. But he was also aware of both the potential that the same chilling techniques had for the longer-term export of cheese, butter and fruit, and the experiments being carried out by one of his subordinate managers, Thomas Brydone, with the quality production of dairy produce on a mass basis. By combining all of these aspects he was able to invent a whole new reason for New Zealand to exist.

It was not enough in itself. He had also to spend time in London organising landing, storage, transport, and marketing plant and facilities, but by the time he was done, he had created an agribusiness structure which was to last for nearly a century. This had several important and

fundamental consequences for New Zealand. It made it viable economically, and made it a suitable field once more for investment capital, without which the Liberals would have been unable to pursue their land policies — essentially making the family dairy farm the central instrument of agricultural production — and the structures of cooperative dairy production and meat processing which were erected on the same foundation. In 1881 New Zealand exported 250 tonnes of cheese and butter, and no meat at all. By 1895 we were exporting over 50,000 tonnes of meat, and 6650 tonnes of cheese and butter annually. In 1896 butter and cheese accounted for 4 percent of New Zealand's total exports by value; by 1913 this had risen to 17 percent. Frozen meat, in the space of 33 years to 1913, had risen from nothing to 19 percent of total exports. Between 1896 and 1913 wool, which was still the country's most significant export commodity, fell from 47 percent to 35 percent of the total.[43] New Zealand had ceased to be primarily a cloth-based agricultural exporting economy and had become food based.

This fundamental structural change also reinforced and confirmed the developing nature of the New Zealand diet as it existed until well after the Second World War. It has been noted that the cuisine which came to New Zealand with the immigrants in the nineteenth century predisposed them to eat certain things prepared in certain ways. Influences canvassed have included the tradition of food use and cooking they inherited both in the immediate and the longer term. This was combined with social ambitions which also predisposed them to eat quantities of meat protein, eggs and dairy produce, in combination with the fruit and vegetables they had introduced and which, initially at least, they largely grew themselves for domestic consumption. Their cultural predisposition was to ignore any indigenous food traditions they found, and to eschew readily available large-scale alternative sources of protein such as fish. The domestic technology of the day and their experience of colonial life predisposed them, as shall be seen, to a certain style of cooking and hospitality-based food preparation. Sheepmeat and dairy products suited these developments very well.

When William Davidson farewelled the *Dunedin* in 1882 with its first successful cargo of chilled mutton, he was not only changing the direction of a New Zealand economy in the doldrums. He was also creating and confirming a domestic cuisine which was to last as long as the food-trading nexus he had invented, and which he was soon to manage into full-blown existence. Like many cultural phenomena it was neither anticipated nor planned for, but can be seen in retrospect as the logical consequence of the pattern of settlement of New Zealand after 1840, the configuration of the cultural baggage which the immigrants had brought with them, and what they made of it here.

The food culture this created bears some similarities to that of Australia, Canada and the United States, but it was also unique. Some of the reasons for this have already been canvassed, but there were others, and to these it is now convenient to turn.

5

MR SHACKLOCK AND MRS BEETON

THE GREAT BRITISH DIASPORA to New Zealand over the four decades from 1840 coincides more or less with what the principal historian of nineteenth- and early twentieth-century technology has called 'the mechanisation of the hearth'.[1] From time immemorial food had been cooked mainly, although not exclusively, over an open fire. This does not imply that the techniques in use were simple or unsophisticated. On the contrary, highly skilled cooks, aided by such devices as clockwork spits, reflecting ovens (a sometimes elaborate, highly polished tinned and open-sided box which sat on the hearth and in which meat could be roasted),[2] and brick ovens built into the sides of fireplaces were perfectly able to produce dishes of considerable complexity. These were largely, of course, for the wealthy. Just how complicated and sophisticated they could be is clear from a study of the inventories of kitchen equipment discovered during the restoration of the seventeenth-century Ham House near London.[3] These include numerous specialist cooking devices for roasting apples, catching dripping, and roasting larks on the spit. The poor, as they had always done, mainly cooked directly over open hearth fires or, as has been noted, in the new industrial cities of the nineteenth century, bought cheap, mass-produced food ready-prepared from vendors.

THE ARRIVAL OF THE KITCHEN RANGE

From the early mid-nineteenth century all of this changed, and there was a veritable revolution in food preparation. That this happened is in

Spitted Meats

I'd like to offer you a recipe for larks on a spit, but where would I get the birds? They still eat such small birds in Italy. If you go to the mercarto centrale in Florence, for example, you can purchase boxes of plucked and drawn sparrows (imported from China) for spit grilling in the traditional manner. Richard Boston claims, in his *Anatomy of Laughter*, to have encountered a menu in Florence which offered not only larks *in* the spit but also tarts of the house at pleasure. Well, if he says so . . . Fractured English of this sort has a certain surreal grandeur.

Traditionally a spit would rest on two iron dogs on either side of the hearth, and was turned by two small children. Bird spits were long and thin, and often had spikes on them to hold the small birds in place as they turned. A long pan was set underneath to catch the drippings and these were either made into a gravy or were used to fry small meat items, or the pan was used as a handy place to make a Yorkshire pudding. There's an interesting description of pre-stove cooking techniques in Dorothy Hartley's *Food in England*, first published in 1954. With the growing appreciation of Middle Eastern food and the invention of the rotisserie oven, spit cooking is making a comeback.

large part a tribute to the inventiveness of Benjamin Thompson, Count von Rumford (1753–1814), colonial American by nurture, British officer and Bavarian statesman by profession, and physicist and inventor by inclination. To Rumford we owe what is now our archetypal kitchen appliance, the domestic stove. This implement is now so taken for granted as essential to the equipment of a kitchen that we find it hard to imagine a culinary world in which it did not exist. But until Rumford came along there were few stoves in the world.

This is not to say that he was its sole inventor. The fecund imagination of Benjamin Franklin, among others, had in the mid-eighteenth century already come up with the idea of an iron box for cooking. He produced no archetype, but a number of those others had experimented with what became known as the 'Pennsylvania oven'. This was a cast-iron box with a hinged front that opened out to give access to an enclosed cooking space, usually heated by lighting a fire above it and sometimes beneath it as well. Rumford may have been familiar with these fire boxes from his youth. He may also have known of a London patent of 1780 in the name of a Thomas Robinson which describes something very like the later kitchen range.[4] Contemporary or slightly earlier French illustrations of kitchens based around a brick 'stewing stove' suggest other inventors at work.

But these were the unique kitchen appliances of a few innovators. Rumford took the concept and made it universal by adapting it on an economical and affordable basis to mass catering in a Munich workhouse around 1800. His stove supplied not only an enclosed baking space but also a flat and continuously hot surface for heating pots. The heat he supplied from existing fires by an ingenious arrangement of flues which fed the heat around the cooking surfaces without directly playing upon them. This also allowed for a considerable innovation — the control of the oven temperatures. Other institutions quickly took up such a useful device, and from there it was a short step to adapting the technology to the household. Here the inventors added a long grate and an ash chest, so that the new stove could be located in the space previously occupied by a hearth. By the 1840s these 'kitchen ranges', as they were known, were in common use in Europe and the Americas.

The initial novelty of the iron range in Britain even in the mid-century is clear from the way in which the cooking techniques involved were handled in the cooking manuals of the period. As late as 1845 Eliza Acton, for example, found it necessary to dwell at length on the subject.[5] Use of a domestic oven, which she denominated 'baking' to distinguish it from roasting which was still carried out with a spit over an open fire, enjoyed a number of advantages over more traditional cooking methods, she thought. She excoriated those who persisted with the use of an open fire despite its manifest disadvantages. 'In a vast number of English kitchens the cookery fails from the hurried manner in which it is conducted, and from the excess of heat produced by the enormous coal fires kept constantly burning there at all seasons without which ignorant servants imagine no dinner can be properly cooked.'[6] Her description of common cooking techniques also hints at the drawbacks associated with the centuries-old practice of using the public baker's oven for the same purpose:

> The improved construction of the ovens connected with all modern cooking stoves, gives great facility at the present day for home baking even in very small establishments; and without this convenience it is impossible for justice to be done to the person who conducts the cookery; and many and great disadvantages attend the sending to a public oven; and it is very discouraging to a servant who has prepared her dishes with nicety and skill, to have them injured by the negligence of other persons.

Acton went on to explain the best technique to be used. In essence she described what we would now call 'slow cooking', i.e. the cooking of meat largely in its own juices over quite long periods in a well-sealed container at fairly low temperatures. Interestingly, she also recommended it for uses we now find curious, such as the cooking of rice, of soup and even of fish wrapped in buttered paper (for which she also recommended the Dutch oven).

That the invention of the stove implied very significant changes in the cuisine itself is clear from the appearance of large numbers of recipes for baked meats in Acton's own cooking manual, a category almost entirely absent from works such as that of Hannah Glasse a century earlier.[7] The convenience of the new stoves to a smaller household is hard to exaggerate, and probably explains their rapid acceptance and popularity both in Europe and in new colonies such as New Zealand.

Slow Cooked Rice

We have all but given up the technique of slow cooking some foods such as fish or soup. But Stella Attenbury who ran a country house hotel for many years, found it a very useful technique — as her book, *Leave It To Cook*, illustrates.

This is a rather unusual recipe for a risotto cooked by this method. I don't much care for it myself, but it's an instance of how food might sometimes have tasted in the nineteenth century.

20 g butter
1 large onion, sliced
half a dozen tomatoes, skinned and chopped
100 g good-quality rice (patna is best)
300 ml chicken stock
a little grated parmesan
salt and pepper

Melt the butter in an iron casserole and cook the onion until transparent. Add the tomatoes and work this into a sauce, then add the rice, stock and seasoning. Bring this quickly to a simmer, take off the stove and put it in the oven preheated to 100°C. Leave it to cook, testing it from time to time until it is done, and sprinkle on the cheese just before serving.

IMPROVED PATENT KITCHEN RANGE,

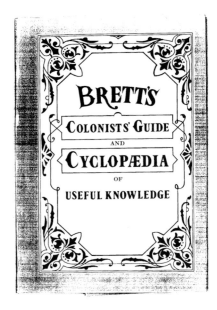

Camp-oven Stew

A camp oven is best suited to stew-type dishes such as the following, variations on which appear in a number of nineteenth-century collections of New Zealand recipes, both printed and in manuscript.

2 large onions, chopped
2 stalks celery, chopped
a dozen or so large mushrooms, sliced
some dripping
about 800 g potatoes, peeled and sliced
6 good-sized lamb neck chops
6 lamb kidneys, cored and sliced
salt and pepper

Fry the onion, celery and mushrooms in the dripping until soft. Remove, leaving the drainings in the camp oven. Put about half the potatoes in the bottom of the oven, then the chops, kidneys and vegetables, seasoning as you go. Cover with the rest of the potatoes, and add enough water just to cover. Put on the oven lid and either bake this all day in an oven at 100°C or, if you are doing the genuine thing, bake in the hot ashes of the hut fire while you're away chasing a deer or whatever. Among variable additions I have seen are peeled, cored and chopped apples, or oysters.

The cooking technologies in use in New Zealand changed as the century progressed. Edward Jerningham Wakefield, describing life on a whaling station in the early 1840s, said of the cooking and dining arrangements:

> A huge chimney nearly fills one end of the house — and generally swarms with natives, iron pots and kettles, favourite dogs, and joints of the whale's backbone, which serve as stools. A view of some fine hams, bacon and fish, repays the exertion of peering through the wood smoke up the chimney . . . The harness-cask (for salt meat), flour keg, and water butt stand on one side, and a neat dresser, shining with bright tin dishes, and a few glasses and articles of crockery on the other side of the door.[8]

Such scenes became rarer as open-fire cooking was replaced by the range, which came to New Zealand with European settlers from the 1860s. Before long it had taken on its characteristic form as the ubiquitous coal range. This provided the heat source for most domestic cooking from the middle to late nineteenth century to well into the twentieth. In more isolated parts of the country coal ranges were still quite common in the 1970s.

In light of this, it is interesting that *Brett's Colonists' Guide*, as late as 1883, was advising against the installation of the coal range in the kitchen fireplace on the grounds of safety (from fire). Instead, the editor, Thomson Leys, advocated 'a brick oven made in the old style, out of doors, entirely separated from the dwelling house . . . [and] superior to a range in the kitchen. In such an oven everything will be baked just right, above and below, through and through.'[9] He included detailed instructions for its construction. From this it is clear that Leys had not had much practical kitchen experience. Given the inconvenience which his design would have entailed for a busy housewife, who would be required to tramp back and forth in all weathers between kitchen and outdoors, it is unlikely that many householders took his advice. He did not even take his own. The plans for small cottages included in the same guidebook provide space for a kitchen range!

But alongside the coal range there continued to exist a range of technologies and cooking techniques, particularly in remote or newly settled areas. These included especially the camp oven. This is often imagined to have been specific to the antipodes, but it had been in use

Girdle or Griddle Scones

The spelling of the name of this implement
is optional. It was heated over a fire or over
one of the apertures of a coal range with the
cover removed. If a little flour is sprinkled
on and it takes a few seconds to brown, then
it is at about the right temperature. This is a
very traditional Scots recipe.

1 cup flour
1 tsp baking powder
pinch of salt
1 tbsp butter
milk to mix

Sift the dry ingredients and rub in the butter.
Add enough milk to make a stiffish dough.
Roll out to about ½ an inch thickness and a
round shape; cut into 8 but keep the shape.
Cook on a hot greased griddle 5 minutes on
each side.

for centuries in Europe, where it was known more generally as a 'Dutch oven'. It is essentially a lidded, cast-iron pot to be stood in the ashes of the hearth, available in a variety of sizes, and with a depression in the lid into which embers can be piled to give an even, all-around heat. This served for all sorts of purposes, including the baking of bread. It is still sometimes used as a casserole. Workers like musterers and shepherds who are required to live, for part of the year at least, in the remote back country, or those who tramp the hills for recreation, staying overnight in huts, continue to swear by the camp oven. Skill in its use is an accomplishment not to be sneered at.

Less usually in use was the iron griddle. This was common in certain areas of Britain, notably Scotland, and travelled to New Zealand with other cultural artefacts of the kitchen. It was a refinement on the flat stone set into the hearth and used for baking bannocks and oatcakes in many Scottish cottages. In essence it was a flat iron plate suspended by its handle from a hook over the fireplace like a kettle. It could be used for thin pancakes, or for thicker muffins or griddle scones.[10] The gas stove had been invented quite early in the piece — the chef Soyer was using one at the Reform Club in the 1830s — and had been available for domestic use since 1855, but was too expensive at £35 to be generally adopted. In 1873 it was introduced into Australia, by which time its price had fallen significantly to £4.[11] But by then coal ranges had come so universally into use in the antipodes that there was little motivation to replace them with gas stoves. They relied, in any event, on a regular supply of domestic gas, and this did not become available in most places (and not at all in the country) until the end of the century or later.

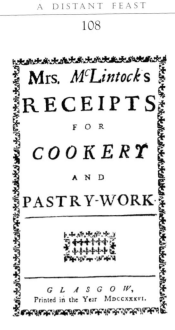

Mrs. McLintock's
RECEIPTS
FOR
COOKERY
AND
PASTRY-WORK.

GLASGOW,
Printed in the Year MDCCXXXVI.

Camp-oven Bread

Making bread in a camp oven is a useful accomplishment and is relatively easy with a bit of practice. The use of baking powder as an alternative to yeast first became widespread in Britain in the 1850s. Essentially, baking powder is a combination of cream of tartar (tartaric acid) and baking soda (sodium bicarbonate), an acid and an alkali. When mixed with water or milk, they liberate carbonic acid gas which aerates the bread mix in the same way that yeast does, but the mixture needs to go into the oven as soon as possible after mixing while the gas is still trapped and the dough risen. Some people say that buttermilk is the best liquid to use with baking powder. Elizabeth David has quite a lot to say on the subject in her *English Bread and Yeast Cookery*.

4 cups flour
pinch of salt
1 tsp sugar
4 tsp baking powder
milk to mix

Sieve all the dry ingredients and mix to a soft dough with enough milk for the purpose. Knead it lightly on some flour, and form it into an oval ball. Cut it into quarters and bake either in an ordinary oven preheated to 220°C for about 20 minutes, or in a camp oven until it is done. Instructions for camp oven cooking are never exact. It all depends on the heat of the embers, and one has to learn to use one's judgement.

The gas stove aside, it is clear from many contemporary accounts that these several alternative technologies (including those which would not have looked out of place in the whaling settlements of the early decades of the century) were in use in New Zealand throughout the nineteenth century. In *The Otago of Our Mothers*, the writer Eileen Soper[12] remarked on the skills involved in juggling heavy iron utensils on bars and hooks over an open fire, and on the difficulty of keeping these clean in such circumstances, otherwise 'a housewife suffered many disappointments when it came to serving a meal'. And in a reminiscence of cooking for her father and brother in a bush clearing on the Northern Wairoa river around the turn of the century, May McDermott described the nikau shanty in which they lived as having 'a huge fireplace, almost the full length of the room, up in the chimney of which were hung huge lengths of fencing wire with a hook bent on the bottom on which our cooking vessels were hung — mostly billies and the camp ovens.'[13] McDermott had been taught to cook using such techniques by her mother and had no difficulty in taking over this role once her father had introduced her to the secrets of yeast and of soda breadmaking. Soper also referred to the use of the camp oven and a variety of the Pennsylvania oven, 'an iron box with a door, which had the ordinary fire built on its top, and was heated with an extra fire underneath when required for baking or roasting. Flues at the back led away the smoke.'[14]

The sheer hard work of chopping the wood consumed daily by such fires no doubt helped to ensure that coal ranges soon came to predominate in domestic cooking. The local manufacture of such ranges, which began within just a few years of the establishment of British rule in 1840, attests to the convenience and popularity of this type of cooker. The best known of all these manufacturers is probably Henry Shacklock, an iron moulder who emigrated from the Midlands to Dunedin in 1862 at the age of 23. By 1871 he had set up his own business, mainly for jobbing work such as the making of agricultural implements. But Shacklock was also an inventor.

The British ranges then available in New Zealand had to be built into the fireplace by a skilled bricklayer. This was expensive. Their freestanding American counterparts, on the other hand, performed poorly on lignite, the local coal. Shacklock reconciled these difficulties. The stove he designed in 1873 did not need a brick surround, and drew well on lignite coal. He also invented a method for mass producing its easily assembled components, and thoroughly mechanised the production process. But perhaps most important of all, he called upon the insights of his wife Elizabeth to ensure that the standard stove he made from 1882 onwards was one that was genuinely convenient to the needs of his women customers. The stove which emerged from this rigorous process weighed about 760 kilograms, cost £6 (about three week's wages for a highly skilled worker), and could deliver 310 litres of boiling water in an hour or less.[15] This last must have been a particular boon, ensuring that the Shacklock *Orion* quickly became popular, and the mainstay of Henry Shacklock's business. By 1900 he was employing 40 men, a large workforce for the period,[16] and his range, or a variant of it from a lesser known manufacturer, was a standard item in the great majority of New Zealand domestic kitchens.

THE COMING OF THE COOKERY BOOK

But the creation and development of a new technology was not enough in itself to generate the new approach to food which lies at the root of the nineteenth-century New Zealand cuisine. Those unused to using such techniques or indeed to preparing their own food economically at all needed further assistance.

Manuals describing the methods for preparing food are some of the oldest of all surviving items in writing. The oldest so far known dates from the paleo-Babylonian culture of southern Mesopotamia, probably from about the seventeenth century before the Christian era, and includes a soup made from salt meat, onion, leek and garlic which would not have been a surprise to nineteenth-century steerage emigrants on their way to New Zealand.[17] The best known is the *De re coquinaria* of Apicius, who may or may not have been a Roman of the second century.[18] Other manuals, such as the famous *Life of Luxury* by the Sicilian Greek Archestratus, and works on cakes, on breadmaking and even on the giving of cookery lessons (by Parmenon of Rhodes, who possibly ran a cooking school), are to be found referred to throughout the *Deipnosophists* of Athenaeus.[19] They reappear in the medieval period in an ever-increasing stream until by the eighteenth century they had become a flood, and are the source of much of our information on the European tradition in food brought to New Zealand by our nineteenth-century forebears.

The World's Oldest Recipes

You'll find these in Yale Oriental Studies Babylonian Tablets XI, 26 and 27. If you don't have these immediately to hand, or your Babylonian cuneiform isn't all that hot, try J. Wilkins, D. Harvey and M. Dobson, *Food in Antiquity*, in the item by Jean Bottero, 'The Most Ancient Recipes of All'. These make use of recipes for quite a number of bouillons which make use of two herbs or flavourings called variously *samidu* and *suhutinnu* which can't be translated. There is also a recipe for what might be a wild duck or an earlier variety of goose, which calls for the drawing of the bird and the retention of innards and gizzard. Now read on:

> **In a scoured cauldron place bird's gizzard and entrails [presumably with water]. After sufficient cooking remove the meat and wash it in fresh water. Then wash well a large pot and add water, milk, and heat. Wipe birds dry, and put them in the pot with the cooked entrails and gizzard. Sprinkle with salt and add fat with the nerves removed, aromatic herbs as you choose and rue. Add onions leeks and garlic and simmer until cooked.**

Also to be added was the mysterious *samidu*. This was eaten with a sort of semolina cake into which pickle of fish or grasshoppers had been kneaded. The birds were set in a pre-cooked pastry case, and some of the cooking liquid was added with more crushed leeks and garlic. A lid was put on, and then it was taken to the table to be served. Sometimes birds cooked in this way would be garnished with a sort of cereal porridge not unlike the English frumenty.

A Typical
Eighteenth-century Recipe

Unless one was already skilled in cooking it would be difficult to use a recipe book such as Hannah Glasse's *Art of Cookery Made Plain and Easy*. This recipe is headed 'A German Way of Dressing Fowls':

> Take a turkey or fowl, stuff the breast with what forcemeat you like, and fill the body with roasted chestnuts peeled; roast it, and have some more roasted chestnuts peeled, put them in half a pint of good gravy, with a little piece of butter rolled in flour; boil these together with some small turnips and sausages cut in slices, and fry'd or broiled. Garnish with chestnuts.

This contains only one quantity, no times, and no temperatures. Such manuals nevertheless have their uses and their charms. Glasse heads one of her chapters: 'Read this chapter and you will find out how expensive a French cook's sauce is.'

A Garden Soup

Eighteenth- and early nineteenth-century cooks were innovative in what they put in their soup, and used some items we wouldn't normally think of.

> 250 g shin of beef, and some beef or veal bones with a little meat still on them
> 2 onions
> salt
> a dozen peppercorns and 3 or 4 cloves
> 1 tsp ground mace

Make a strong stock from these items by simmering for about 4 hours. Cool, skim and strain, and chop up the shin and return to the stock. Now add a chopped lettuce, some sorrel, some spinach, some chopped spring onions and some chopped cooked asparagus stalks. (Use tinned if you like, in which case also add the liquid.) Correct the seasoning and add finely chopped parsley and thyme. Simmer this for about 30 minutes and serve.

But prior to the nineteenth century cookery books were mostly manuals for the already expert. They quite often contained incomplete lists of ingredients, and no quantities for those which were included. Those for whom they were written were generally already capable and experienced cooks who needed an *aide-mémoire* only, and who, when consulting a recipe, might be expected already to understand what was required of them. This tradition died hard. As late as the 1870s Lady Barker, bewildered by instructions to 'fold in the eggs', was still complaining about their uselessness to the amateur:

> I want to lodge a formal complaint against all cookery books. They are not in the least use in the world until you know how to cook and then you can do without them. Somebody ought to write a cookery book which would tell an unhappy beginner whether the water in which she proposes to put her potatoes is to be hot or cold; how long such water is to boil; how she is to know whether the potatoes are done enough; how to dry them after they have boiled, and similar things which make all the difference in the world.[20]

This is a *cri de coeur* which has echoed down the centuries, but Lady Barker, going on to confess that she learned in due course not only to boil potatoes but also to bake bread and passable cakes of which she was proud, was already several decades out of time with her complaint. By this time the cookery book for the novice was well established and had come into its own.

The origin of these publications had rather less to do with the needs of cooks and rather more with the belief, widespread among middle-class social reformers, that the poor were underfed because of their own ignorance and profligacy, not the inadequacy of their income or facilities. If only they could be induced to spend their money wisely (and especially not on alcohol, tobacco and such morally reprehensible pastimes as gambling), then they and their families would be perfectly well off, nay more than comfortable. The busybody givers of such moral advice to others about how they might best conduct their lives appear, like the poor themselves, always to be with us. In the nineteenth century one of their favourite nostrums was the publication of cookery books to show how it could be done. Never mind, as one social historian of food has remarked, that the cost price of a small oven was 30s, and that the working-class housewife did not have the wherewithal to buy in bulk, had no adequate water supply, and had to contribute her time to the extra earnings which made survival possible at all.[21] The busybodies would see to it that she would learn to cook frugally despite herself.

As it happened and notwithstanding their motivation, quite a lot of useful handbooks for food preparation by those on modest incomes were published as a result. They were as much books on cottage housekeeping as cooking books. One of the most interesting of these was *Cottage Comforts* (1820) by Esther Hewlett, a clergyman's widow and the author of about 30 more or less morally uplifting tracts of one sort or another.[22] Despite this unpromising provenance, the book is informed by a sympathy for the poor which suggests some first-hand experience (although a section on paying wages would indicate that she was more interested in the plight of the struggling lower middle class than the poor as such). Her recipes, embedded in helpful sections on equipping a cottage and bringing up children, are straightforward and unpretentious. There was much attention paid to the nourishing nature of soups, a favourite in such publications as the century advanced.[23]

How far Mrs Hewlett's advice was heeded is hard to say. She was very down on such extravagances as buttered toast, beer and tobacco, but spoke up for tea, and sought to encourage the consumption of porridge in England, on the grounds that royalty gave it to their children — although her prospective readers, no doubt more conscious of its regular appearance on the workhouse menu, were probably not impressed. What makes her book so interesting is that Hewlett was one of the first of all food writers to begin with advice on nutrition, a science then in its infancy and of doubtful value (scientists continued to believe that uncooked fruit and vegetables were bad for the health until well into the century).[24] But it was the beginning of a new approach.

William Cobbett was also an early writer in this field. His *Cottage Economy* predates Hewlett by a couple of years, but is rather more concerned with brewing, baking and stock raising. Cobbett appreciated that the problem was not food but the pattern of landholding, and sought to make labourers into self-sufficient and intensive smallholders. But he also appreciated that this was a political problem, and so concentrated on that field of endeavour.[25] As far as Cobbett was concerned, if a smallholder retained his interests in common grazing and his rights to

Poor Man's Pie

Among those full of advice for the poor was Martha Gordon, the author of *Cooking For Working Men's Wives*, but many of these earnest reformers forgot that those for whom they wrote either had no oven or could not afford the fuel to go in it. This Poor Man's Pie would have been filling but not much else. Some recipes for the poor in 'helpful' books of advice had obviously not been tried by their authors. Even the chef Charles Francatelli in his *Plain Cookery for the Working Classes* gave some recipes which, when tried, simply don't work. How the poor must have hated being patronised in this way.

75 g tapioca
100 g dripping
2 or 3 sliced onions
1½ kg potatoes, sliced
salt and pepper
225 g flour
1 tsp baking powder

Soak the tapioca for an hour in cold water. Put a little of the dripping at the bottom of a pie dish; mix the onion, tapioca and potato, and season well. Put it in the pie dish and make a lid from the remaining dripping, the flour and baking powder. Roll this out and fit, and bake the pie at 200°C for about an hour or a little more.

Cobbett's Bread

William Cobbett was particularly incensed
that potatoes had replaced bread as the staple
of the poor cottagers, and in his *Cottage
Economy* he gave directions for making what
he called 'household bread'. This recipe
requires a bushel (about 36 litres dry weight)
of flour mixed with half a pint of yeast and a
pint of warm water. This is mixed to 'a thin
batter' and is then covered in a layer of flour
and left to rise. A pound of salt should then
be added, and it should be kneaded
thoroughly ('the fists must go heartily into it,'
he says) and the whole formed into a stiff or
tough dough. This should then be shaped into
loaves and cooked for about 3 hours.

When I first encountered this recipe my
thought was that Cobbett had never been
near a bread trough in his life, but when I put
it together and filled in the gaps in the
instructions from my own knowledge, I found
(apart from the salt) that it made a reasonable
loaf of bread. The baking time is an indication
of the contemporary technology, usually a
cooling baker's oven.

Soyer's Mushrooms

Soyer was an innovative cook who was always
looking for new ways to prepare surprise
dishes. One of the most interesting of these,
from his *Gastronomic Regenerator*, is for
meringue mushrooms to be served at the very
end of a meal.

> 3 egg whites
> ½ cup caster sugar
> 90 g cooking chocolate
> 1 cup cream
> more sugar
> 2 tbsp brandy

Whip 2 of the egg whites until stiff, then add
the caster sugar and whip again until it is well
absorbed. Pipe this mixture as 8 discs and 8
'stalks' about ½ an inch high onto a baking
sheet, grate the chocolate over the discs, and
bake at 200°C until they are set. This may take
some time; they will need to be checked at
intervals. Now very carefully pry the caps and
stalks off the sheet, make a small hole in the
underside of the cap to take the stalk, paint
this with a little of the remaining white, and fit
the two together. Let them set for 30 minutes.
When you are ready to serve them, whip the
cream, remaining egg white, brandy and sugar
until stiff, and pile it in a dish with the
'mushrooms' in the centre.

mastage, along with access to a little land to till and to grow fruit trees
and bushes, then he might keep chickens and a pig, and he and his family
would have more than sufficient to eat. There is a philosophical line
from Paine to Henry George which passes through Cobbett, and the
influence of this on subsequent popular feeling about the sort of life and
economy many emigrants were seeking was to have a significant outcome
in the patterns of food production which developed in the antipodes.[26]

None of this was much use to town workers, crammed into tenement
slums in the developing cities. Succour in the form of advice on how
best to undertake their catering came from an unexpected quarter —
the French chef Alexis Soyer (1809–1858). Dismissed from his position
with a Paris restaurant because of his probably inadvertent associations
with the revolution of 1830, and blackballed from his profession, Soyer
came to London, where after a short period as a private chef to various
aristocrats he was appointed to head the kitchens at the Reform Club, a
position he held for the next 14 years. Not only was he an excellent and
innovative chef, but he was also a culinary inventor, with three improved
stoves, a coffee pot, carving scissors, several varieties of sauces, a beef
extract and, most popular of all, a hangover cure to his credit.[27]

Unlike many others who serve the interests of the wealthy, he appears
to have been possessed of a social conscience. He did sterling practical
service during both the Irish potato famine (in which he ran a soup
kitchen in Dublin) and the Crimean war, when he travelled to Scutari
at his own expense and re-organised the entire military catering
establishment. A good case can be made, indeed, that in making one
simple change to the military diet he saved more lives than Florence
Nightingale. Discovering that the daily meat ration for the sick was served
to the men in a lump, and the liquid in the cauldrons in which it had
been boiled was poured away, he reversed this order, discarding the meat
and adding vegetables to what became a very nutritious broth. Many
soldiers who had previously and literally been starving because they could
not swallow or digest the meat now recovered.[28]

But Soyer's most significant contribution to the improvement of the
eating habits of the nation was a series of small publications dealing
with food for the poor. These included particularly *The Poor Man's
Regenerator* (1848) and *A Shilling Cookery for the People* (1854). Soyer
was friendly with a number of medical men who were increasingly turning

their attention to nutrition, and appears to have been particularly familiar with the work of one of the century's most interesting eccentrics, Dr William Kitchener, whose *The Cook's Oracle* (first published 1817 and still in print in 1840) was one of the earliest and most successful cookbooks of the first half of the nineteenth century.[29] Soyer's books reflected Kitchener's nutritional concerns, and the importance he ascribed to food in daily life. '[T]he morals of the people greatly depend on their food,' Soyer remarked in the *Shilling Cookery*, 'and wherever the home of an individual, in whatever class of society he may move, is made comfortable and happy, the more moral and religious will be that person.' His intention was to ensure that the poor had 'quick, nutritious, wholesome and economical' food. But unlike most of the writers on this theme, he placed immense emphasis on variety and the use of the meats and vegetables of the season when they were most likely to be cheaply available. He also went out of his way to encourage the poor to use many more vegetables (such as pumpkins, widely eaten in France but not in Britain), and highlighted the value of these as a possible and filling substitute for meat. He also stressed the importance of how food looked. If it looked attractive, then no matter how unusual the ingredients, people would be more inclined to sample and acquire a taste for it. This seems to us to be common sense, but it was a revolutionary proposition for the poor in the nineteenth century.

A recent analysis of the content and nutritional value of Soyer's dishes compared to those contained in other cooking books he wrote for the wealthy has established that they differed little from these, except in the cost of the main ingredients.[30] It is not surprising, therefore, that his book was an enormous success and had many imitators. It became, indeed, almost *de rigueur* for chefs of well-known establishments to follow his example, as did Soyer's successor at the Reform, Charles Francatelli, with his *Plain Cookery for the Working Classes* (1861). Most importantly, from our point of view, this genre carried over into the numerous books of advice to intending emigrants, which along with chapters on what to take on the journey and related questions, almost always contained a section on recipes which could be used in the new land.[31]

It should also be noted that it was not only the working class who were felt to be in need of culinary advice and counsel. As the newly emergent urban middle class burgeoned, many a new young wife found

Poor Man's Soup

Soyer was also famous for inventing a soup, widely copied, which would nourish the poor in the soup kitchens of his day at very little cost. This is an adaptation from his *Poor Man's Regenerator*.

  50 g dripping
  100 g meat diced
  100 g each chopped onions, turnips,
    leeks and celery
  350 g wholemeal flour
  250 g pearl barley
  salt, brown sugar and water

Soyer mixed all these ingredients and added 5 litres (!) of hot water. He brought it to the boil and simmered it gently for 3 hours before serving. It could be made even more economical, he remarked, by using the green leaves of the celery and the green part of the leek, both usually discarded, and even the peelings of vegetables. His soup, he also claimed, had been tasted by 'members of parliament, and several ladies who have lately visited my kitchen department and who have considered it very good and nourishing'. He had particularly omitted spices because these 'flattered the appetite, irritated the stomach, and made it crave for more food'. I daresay the 'several ladies' would not care to eat this soup every day, no matter how nourishing they found it, but beggars, literally, couldn't be choosers.

Potato Balls Ragout

Unlike Cobbett, Dr Kitchener was an enthusiastic proponent of the potato, and included a number of recipes for its use in his *Cook's Oracle*. This dish, he remarked, is an agreeable vegetable relish to be served with meat, but it can also be eaten on its own for supper.

  2 tbsp butter
  1 cup cooked ham, finely diced
  1 large onion, chopped
  2 egg yolks
  900 g potatoes, boiled and well mashed
  salt, pepper and a grating of nutmeg
  brown bread crumbs
  a little clarified butter for frying

The butter, ham, onion, egg yolks, potato and seasonings should be thoroughly mixed, rolled into small balls, and coated with the crumbs. They should then be fried in the butter until brown. They can be made in advance and reheated in the oven just before serving.

**Francatelli's Lamb Chops in a Sauce
with Quenelles**

You need up to 8 good-quality lamb frying
chops for this dish. These can be grilled in
advance. For the quenelles:

**4 thick slices white bread with crusts
removed
4 tbsp of butter
60 ml dry white wine
3 egg yolks
salt and pepper**

Soak the bread in tepid water for about
20 minutes, then squeeze out gently but
thoroughly. Put it in a small pan with the
melted butter and wine, and cook it gently,
stirring, until it becomes a paste and begins
to come away from the pan. Take it off the
heat, stir in the yolks and season well, and
when it has cooled enough to handle make it
into small balls with a teaspoon. Put these on
a baking dish and cool them in the
refrigerator for a couple of hours.

For the sauce:

**2 tbsp butter
200 g small white onions, peeled
120 g mushrooms, chopped
60 ml red wine
salt, pepper and nutmeg
1 tsp sugar
a small quantity of brown stock**

Melt the butter and fry the little onions until
browned. Remove, and gently fry the
mushrooms. Pour off any excess butter and
add the pre-grilled chops, the onions, wine,
seasoning and sugar. Simmer gently for about
20 minutes. Remove the chops and keep
warm, add the stock and quenells to the pan,
and cook for about 5 minutes or a little more.
Spoon and pour this over the grilled cutlets
and serve.

Francatelli suggests serving this with a dish of
creamed salsify, a longish root vegetable rather
like a parsnip which is no longer much eaten
in England, and seems not to have been
introduced into New Zealand, but which is
still common in southern Europe.

herself running a household and expected to manage many matters
previously unknown to her, including a cook and a table. She was not
short of willing advisers. The prize for these is usually awarded to Isabella
Beeton, but Mrs Beeton's reputation as an innovator is unjustified; the
plaudits belong to Eliza Acton.

Acton, who has been quoted in respect of the baking of meats in the
newly fangled domestic oven, published her *Modern Cookery for Private
Families* in 1845. 'It cannot be denied,' she said in her introduction, 'that
an improved system of domestic cookery, and a better knowledge of its
first principles, are still much needed in this country.'[32] Although her
reputation as a writer initially rested on her poetry, her publishers thought
that a book about food would be of greater interest to the reading public
than a book of her verse. How right they were. Her book is interesting
for several reasons. The first is that it stands at the threshold of change
in food preparation. As her many recipes bear witness, many items
prepared for centuries in the home kitchen — preserved and bottled
items, ready-dressed meat, a wide range of foreign fruits and vegetables,
and even bread — could now be bought from food suppliers, although as
Acton lived most of her life in Tonbridge and Hampstead it is hard to
say how typical this was.

Modern Cookery was the first cookery book in English not only to
list the ingredients of the recipes but also to give quantities and the
process to be followed in meticulous detail. It includes as well a number
of French and Jewish recipes which were presumably current at the time,
and it contains numerous incidental details which suggest that the writer,
unusually for a Victorian gentlewoman, had practical experience of what
she wrote. With Eliza Acton, the modern cookery book as we know it
arrived. But its principal claim to an unheralded fame was the action of
the far more famous Mrs Beeton in lifting Acton's recipes from the latter's
publication almost verbatim and without acknowledgement.

Mrs Beeton may perhaps be excused for this. She was not by profession
a cook but a magazine editor who, through her *Domestic Magazine*, sought
to educate her women readers in the domestic and culinary fields, among
many others. She wrote her culinary columns herself, but borrowed all
her recipes from elsewhere (with one self-confessed exception, a 'useful
soup for benevolent purposes'). Ultimately she founded two further
women's magazines (one of which still survives as *Harpers & Queen*),

and it was her experience in this context of the general ignorance of young middle-class wives which led her to compile her famous *Book of Household Management*, published in 1861 and almost continually in print since.[33]

The many imitators her magazine example spawned are of particular significance. These showed publishers that there was a tremendous market for books specialising in cookery. By the end of the 1860s the publishing boom in this genre was in full swing and has never since abated. By the end of the century the most common dictionaries, compendia and manuals in use, published in the main by Cassells and by Warnes, were, in the words of Elizabeth David, 'to be found in every literate household in the land'. Not a few had found their way to new lands in the trunks and baggage of both steerage and cabin passengers. In New Zealand they provided the foundation for a tradition of cookery publishing which has never diminished, and found a role in the origins of our cuisine. In so doing they joined the other great food innovation of the nineteenth century, the industrialisation of the manufacture and preservation of food for retail sale.

MANUFACTURED FOOD

War is a major spur to innovation. Napoleon coined the tag that 'an army marches on its stomach', and it was indeed the French who first did something about this, by inventing food preservation processes to feed the mass armies of a new European era. There is, of course, nothing new about food preservation. Since human food-gathering began, periodic or seasonal gluts of particular items, and particularly fish and meat which spoil rapidly, have been subjected to preservation techniques of one sort or another. Cooking is itself the most universal example, but there are many others. The fireplace with its hams hanging in the chimney for smoking was a standard in kitchens for centuries, and both salt and wind-dry preservation are ancient techniques. So is potting with a layer of fat to preserve what is beneath.[34] Other techniques, such as the burying of fish, are less well known.[35] European trade with other nations had added crystallisation with sugar to more traditional techniques in the sixteenth century — this included not only fruits but some root vegetables and herbs, of which angelica is the only remaining common instance.[36]

Eliza Acton's Beefsteak Pudding

Almost all of the hundreds of recipes in Acton's *Modern Cookery* are worth the exploration, although her original ingredients are a little too rich in fats and salt for late twentieth-century taste. Her recipes have been adapted to that taste by Elizabeth Ray in *The Best of Eliza Acton*. This recipe is fairly typical of the basic Victorian fare.

450 g flour
200 g suet
300 ml water
400 g rump steak
salt and pepper

The flour, suet and salt should be mixed to a firm dough with some water. This should be used to line a pudding basin, reserving some for the top. Fill with the steak, seasoning and some more water. Fit and seal the top crust, and steam in a pudding bowl for about 3 hours. All sorts of additional things can be put in the filling — chopped heart, kidneys, stock and/or red wine instead of the water, and even a few oysters. Acton also suggests making the same pudding with chopped partridge meat. First catch your partridge. A wild duck would also respond well to this recipe.

Mrs Beeton's Beef à la Mode

If steak pudding was one archetypal dish, beef à la mode was another. No Victorian cookery book, post Acton, would dare to miss it out. This is Mrs Beeton's version.

2 cloves
a dozen black peppercorns
3 allspice berries
2 sprigs parsley and a sprig thyme, finely chopped
1 crumbled bay leaf

a little red-wine vinegar
half a dozen rashers rindless bacon
a piece of rump steak (Mrs Beeton calls it thick flank or top rump), about 2 kg
60 g butter
1 onion, sliced
2 sticks of celery, sliced
a carrot and turnip, chopped
100 ml port wine
salt and pepper

Pound the cloves, peppercorns and allspice finely, then mix with the parsley, thyme and bay. Add the vinegar, and make sure that the bacon strips are well rubbed with the mixture. Rub the remainder of the mixture into the meat, season well, and roll and tie neatly with the bacon tied on the outside. Brown the onion in the melted butter in a deep iron casserole, add the other vegetables and the rolled meat, pour on the wine and about 200 ml of water, bring to the boil, lower the heat, and simmer gently for about an hour and a half, turning a couple of times. The meat can then be removed and a sauce made of the strained, skimmed liquid with some *beurre manie* (small balls of butter into which a small quantity of flour has been rubbed).

Dr Kitchener gives a slightly different recipe for the same dish in his *Cook's Oracle*. He claimed to have perused 180 cookbooks in pursuit of the perfect recipe for beef à la mode. The one he eventually chose was for a cut he calls the 'mouse-buttock or clod of beef', unknown to me or my butcher. He attributes the distinctive flavour of this beef dish to the combination of allspice and bay, and the very slow cooking (3 hours) he recommends, using a reflecting Dutch oven.

But the French scientists of the Napoleonic era added something new when they made the interesting discovery that cooked food kept in a receptacle from which all air had been excluded, and which remained airtight, would be unspoiled. The food scientist Nicholas Apert was first in the field, using glass bottles as receptacles to preserve meat, fruit, vegetables and even milk. These were adopted by the French navy in 1806.[37] But bottles were fragile to transport, especially for military purposes, and an Englishman, Bryan Donkin, quickly realised that iron coated with tin would be a much more practical container. In 1812, after numerous failed experiments, he produced a workable patent which allowed mass production, and he was quick to obtain contracts from both the army and navy. By 1818 he was selling nearly 50,000 pounds weight of food in 25,000 tins annually to the navy alone. This included a wide variety of foodstuffs, but mainly corned beef, boiled beef and mutton, carrots and a range of soups.[38]

The outbreak of peace in 1815 did nothing to halt this development, which was quickly adapted for civilian supply to cities where the daily provision of fresh meat had always been a problem. But until the middle of the century and the discoveries of Pasteur, the canning of meat and other foodstuffs was a dodgy business, not well regarded by the public who were suspicious of both what they were getting and the state it might be in when they opened the tin. This was not helped by a government enquiry in 1852 which revealed that many of their suspicions were well founded. It took another two decades, the perfection of the technology, and a leap in the price of fresh meat caused by a cattle epidemic between 1863 and 1867 to popularise tinned food.

About the same time an Australian meat-canning operation which had been in business since 1847 began exporting in bulk to Britain. The product produced was not very appetising, and was subsequently described by one of its consumers as 'a large lump of coarse grained lean meat inclined to separate into coarse fibres, a large lump of unpleasant looking fat on one side of it — and an irregular hollow partly filled with watery fluid'.[39] But it sold at about half the price of butchers' meat, which may explain why the trade grew from £16,000 in 1866 to £22 million in 1871. Over the next decade America also joined the trade, exporting both beef and pork. By the end of the century, tinned food was a basic item in European diet. Truly, as George Orwell was later to remark, the First

World War would not have been possible without the invention of tinned food.

The other great industrial food innovation of the nineteenth century was the production of bread in large factories in mechanical ovens using industrially milled flour. As with many other techniques, that for the milling of wheat and the baking of bread had not changed for centuries. Grain of whatever variety, but increasingly wheat, was either ground domestically in a quern (a small hand mill, essentially one stone inside another), or was taken to a local water or wind mill which might be more or less a monopoly of the local landowner.[40] Householders then made their bread and either baked it themselves in a wall oven built into the side of their fireplace or, more usually, took it to the village baker to be baked. It was possible to buy bread ready-baked in the larger towns, but this was a very small-scale local operation. Cheating on weight by bakers was a centuries-old problem which had led to the detailed regulation of the business through what was known as the Assize of Bread, although this was deregulated (along with much else) in the 1830s.[41]

In the nineteenth century the whole basis of bread manufacture was transformed. Wheat milled between stones mixes the various ingredients of the grain inseparably. Although the quality of any particular grain could be improved by sieving out the larger crushed ingredients (an expensive hand process until the automatic mechanical sieve or boulter was introduced in the seventeenth century), the populace by and large ate the same variety of flour if they used the same grain. The wealthy might eat whiter bread, i.e. made from finer or sieved flour, but differentiation was largely on the basis of the grain used. The rich ate wheaten bread, the poor barley.

In the 1830s steam power was applied to rollers which were set further apart than millstones.[42] This enabled a mill to separate the ingredients of the grain over several millings rather than mixing them together in one milling. These ingredients could be removed or re-added at will. The result was the creation of a wide range of flours.[43] Within a short time techniques had been developed for cleaning, whitening and bleaching (effectively sterilising) flour. This created the basis for the industrialisation of bread production.

Mechanical mixing, forced fermentation, standard measuring of bulk ingredients, steam-heated ovens through which the bread moved on

Breads and Flours

'Browne breade made of the coursest of wheat having in it much branne, filleth the belly with excrements,' says an anonymous fourteenth-century source quoted by Dorothy Hartley in *Food in England*, 'and besides that it is good for labourers, I have known such as have been used to fine bread, when they have been costive, by eating brown bread and butter have been made soluble.' I doubt they asked the labourers what they thought. Those who could not afford wheaten flour used a cheaper grain or other substitute — the use of potatoes for this purpose is well known. Perhaps lesser known is the use of rice. Anne Cobbett gives the following recipe in *The English Housekeeper* (1851).

To a quarter pound of wheaten flour allow one pound of rice; the latter first boiled in four times its weight of water till it becomes a perfect pulp, then mix by degrees, the rice with the flour, and sufficient yeast for the quantity of bread, knead, and set it to rise.

From my own experiments with this you will need 150 g flour, strengthened with 1 tbsp gluten flour, to about 400 g rice, boiled until mushy and all the water absorbed. To this should be added about 20 g yeast creamed in a little hot water, and 1 tsp salt. You'll have to use your judgement as to how much additional water to add (if any) to make a stiffish dough. It needs to rise and be knocked down once, or twice if you have the time and energy, and then rounded into a ball and left to rise finally on a baking tray. The kneaded and risen loaf can be baked at an initial 200°C, reducing to 160°C, over about 45 minutes.

conveyors, and artificial cooling ensured that by the 1880s the bulk of bread came from large industrial plants. Home baking of bread became an act of almost self-conscious archaism in large towns, particularly among those of modest means. The introduction of sodas to replace yeast in 'self-raising' flours made this process of industrialisation even less dependent on rogue nature than previously, although the discoveries of Pasteur ensured that where yeast continued in use it could now be manufactured artificially, and to a reliable and consistent standard.

By the middle of the nineteenth century many of the food items which, for centuries, had had to be made from their basic ingredients in the domestic household were available from local retailers who had obtained them from bulk industrial producers. These included not only tinned meat and bread, but also cakes and cake powders, egg powder, factory-produced cheeses, tinned and dried milk, vegetables and soups, and a wide range of jams, pickles and sauces.[44] By the 1870s many staple items such as flour and pulses were also imported. There was considerable specialisation in the larger towns into grocers, butchers (of various types), fishmongers, greengrocers, and so forth. In the big cities particularly, competition ensured that prices were kept relatively low compared to the home-manufactured equivalent, while the convenience of having made ingredients readily available without personal labour cemented the popularity of industrial food products. The domestic economy was revolutionised as a result. This was not, however, without its costs.

ADULTERATION AND NUTRITION

The industrialisation of food production also meant that consumers, who had previously known what went into the food ingredients they ate because they made them themselves, lost direct control of many of the things they put in their mouths. Industrialisation presented the food manufacturers with many opportunities to add ingredients which did not occur naturally to their products. Sometimes the temptation to turn a quick profit overrode consideration for the health and even the lives of their customers. The horrifying story of food adulteration in the nineteenth century, and the steps taken to control what could or could not be included in retailed food items, has been often told and can be briefly summarised.[45]

The first phase of this battle on behalf of consumers was mainly to do with the burgeoning chemical industry. Manufacturers seized with enthusiasm on any substance which appeared to show promise of preserving or colouring or flavouring their food products more effectively or cheaply. There was nothing new about this, but as science advanced the chemists added many more possibilities to the repertoire. The practices in question were, indeed, so widespread that Eliza Acton thought it necessary to caution her readers particularly against using a brass container to boil gherkins in vinegar — a technique very widely used and even recommended to give the vegetables a brilliant green colour, but which was poisonous.[46] This development was not assisted by the prevailing economic orthodoxy which eschewed any controls in the interests of vigorous trade and innovation on the basis that the market was the best regulator. The deaths which resulted from *Coculus indicus* in the beer, verdigris in the tea, arsenic in the confectionery (it coloured sweets an attractive red) and various fatal diseases in the dirty water used to adulterate milk were justified as regrettable side products of the market settling down. The chemist Frederick Accum, who was the first to lift the lid on many of these practices, was not popular with industrialists, and he was eventually driven out of the country for his trouble. Nevertheless, his work and that of many others meant that the worst excesses were curbed. From the middle of the century consumers were much less likely to commit inadvertent suicide from the mere act of eating what they thought was food.

This did not put a stop to adulteration. The field of battle now shifted to retail fraud. A popular ditty which runs 'Little bags of sugar/ Little grains of sand/ Make the artful grocer/ The richest in the land' tells its own story. Arthur Hassall, a London medical man, led the campaign for food items at the grocer actually being what they purported to be, instead of being, surprisingly often and in quite large measure, something else entirely. Hassall's interest began when, intrigued by the wide range of coffee prices in London, he investigated the content of what he purchased as 'coffee' by analysing the ingredients. He found 31 out of 34 samples adulterated. Outraged but fascinated, he investigated the contents of dozens of foods between 1851 and 1855, publishing his results monthly in *The Lancet* as he went. He found charred dog biscuit and burnt sugar in the coffee; chalk, bone dust and alum in the flour; flour in the mustard;

Boiled Mutton and Caper Sauce

By the later decades of the century, cooks were turning increasingly to pre-packaged or prepared items for their dishes. Those who manufactured such items were quick to encourage this trend by publishing cookbooks which featured their products. One of these was the *Defiance Book of Cookery Recipes*, published in 1905 by a North Island dairy company, from which this recipe is taken.

a middle neck of mutton
stock
2 carrots and an onion
salt and pepper
1 tbsp Defiance dried milk
1 tbsp flour
30 g Defiance butter
1 tbsp capers

Plunge the mutton into boiling stock to which have been added the vegetables, salt and a handful of peppercorns. Simmer until cooked (half an hour to the kilo). Mix the dried milk to a paste with a little water, and stir in 150 ml of boiling water. Make a roux with the flour and butter, and stir in the milk mixture and a ladle of the cooking liquor from the meat. Simmer gently for about 15 minutes or until it thickens, stir in the capers towards the end. Serve in a sauceboat with the meat.

dried leaves of every description in the tea; and sand and worse in the sugar. His conclusion was

> that the adulteration of articles of consumption had been reduced to a system, to an art, and almost to a science; that it was universally practised, that adulteration was the rule and purity the exception, that everything that could be cheapened by admixture was so, and that the articles thus debased were sold as genuine and often with the most high-flown names and with assertions of unblushing falsehood.[47]

When he began naming names, the fury of the manufacturers knew no bounds, but Hassall was entertained rather than intimidated by this reaction (which he described as a commotion greater than the firing of a gun into a rookery). Popular pressure arising from his articles forced a parliamentary enquiry and a series of laws, culminating in that of 1875, which established the principles that the ingredients of a foodstuff should be recorded on the label, that food should be what it purported to be, and that the responsibility for ensuring this lay with the seller, not with the buyer.

The campaigns of Accum, Hassall and many others were greatly assisted by the development of knowledge concerning nutrition during the course of the nineteenth century. This was largely the work of one man, the German chemist Liebig, who in the course of his work with organic chemistry and oxidation was the first to understand the relationship between physiology and botany. To him may fairly be ascribed the discovery of the food chain. More particularly he was the first to appreciate the fundamental importance of protein and the key role it plays in maintaining the health of organisms, including humans. (He did not himself discover protein — that honour belongs to the Dutch chemist Mulder.)

In one sense there was nothing new about this. Ever since Galen in the second-century, European science had known about the relationship between food and health, but this relationship had been formulated in terms of the classical doctrine of humours, a form of sympathetic magic masquerading as science.[48] The achievement of the nineteenth-century organic chemists was to break humanity out of that centuries-old conceptual loop.[49] By the middle of the nineteenth century it was widely recognised, at least among scientists, that a healthy human being needed a balanced diet which incorporated not only a certain number of calories every day but also a balanced quantum of protein, carbohydrates (such as fats, sugar and starch), amino acids and certain minerals. This, in its turn, led directly to the discovery of vitamins. By the latter part of the nineteenth century most medical practitioners knew about the relationship between meat, vegetables, fruit and bread or potatoes, and the combinations of foods which would keep an individual healthy. Such knowledge was further disseminated by the decision in Britain at least to include instruction in domestic economy (for girls only) in the education syllabus in 1876.[50] That such knowledge gradually filtered out into the populace at large is clear from a comparison of the recipes of the early cookbook writers with their end-of-the-century counterparts. The unbelievable quantities of fats such as suets contained in some of Acton's recipes have, by the time of the early women's journals of colonial New Zealand, been reduced to levels which we would now find much more palatable.

The cuisine which came to New Zealand with the nineteenth-century European immigrants reflected the techniques and scientific developments which made that century the most significant period of change in the history of food since Neolithic times. It was a cuisine fashioned by the cooking techniques appropriate to a stove technology (baking, roasting, and slow but thorough cooking). It took such aids as cookery books and the ready availability, at least in the towns, of many pre-made ingredients and some staples (such as bread) for granted. Underlying that was a knowledge, however limited, of the science of nutrition which permitted the notion of food as fuel to become a primary perception among those whose responsibilities in the new land included educating the young, and particularly young women, in the practical skills they required to live successfully in their new land.

We should not be surprised, therefore, that the food of nineteenth-century New Zealand (and indeed our food until well into the twentieth century) reflected these fundamental influences, and that it was, at worst, replete with overcooked meat and over-cooked vegetables, and characterised by a fascination with the variety of cakes and biscuits which could be produced from an oven. That it was a standardised cuisine reliant on a very few main dishes should not surprise either. Nor, finally, should we be surprised that it was underlaid with a plethora of cookery books

Nineteenth-century New Zealand Cookery Books

New Zealand seems to have been no more immune to the nineteenth-century explosion of cookery books than any other English-speaking nation. While not many have survived in present-day collections, the various provenances of those which have, speak the origins of our indigenous culinary publishing tradition. There are those produced to advertise and familiarise a food product by demonstrating its practical utility. There is the *Defiance Book of Cookery Recipes*, published in Wellington in 1905, complete with testimonials from satisfied users of the produce in question — a proprietary milk powder and brand of butter for which *J. Nathan and Company* held the agency. Handbooks for the intending settler abound, and most include recipes of one description or another; the best known of these is *Brett's Colonists' Guide*, already cited in these pages.

Then, as now, all sorts of sporting bodies published their cookery book as a fund-raising activity. Some of these are handsome productions, notably *Tetaka Kai Recipes*, published by the *Napier Rowing Club* in 1906. Others are straight commercial productions. These must have fulfilled a genuine need. Whitcombe & Tombs' *Colonial Everyday Cookery* boasted of its '930 carefully selected and tested recipes' and was into its fifth edition by the time it appeared in the bibliographies in 1908. But best of all are those books which were plainly a labour of love, produced by those who loved good food. I have no inkling of who was the Mrs Murdoch who, in Napier in 1887, produced her 80 pages of *Dainties*, but God bless her anyway.

which placed more than the necessary emphasis on plain and wholesome food as the basis of good health.

Our experience was not entirely unique in these regards. The Australian Richard Twopenny, writing in his *Town Life in Australia* in 1883, remarked:

> Generally speaking food in Australia is cheaper than in England but poorer in quality . . . Of course, meat is the staple of life [but] vegetables are for the most part despised, though the thoroughly old English dish of greens remains in favour, and potatoes are largely eaten.[51]

He could easily have been speaking of New Zealand at the same period. In fact, the only truly surprising thing about food in nineteenth-century New Zealand, is that, despite its drabness and other manifest faults, it was at the centre of a lively and colourful social life at all levels of society.

6

THE RISE OF THE
NEW ZEALAND SCONE

IN 1951 THE SCOTTISH HUMOROUS WRITER Eric Linklater visited New Zealand. His observations were tart if superficial, and one of the aspects of contemporary life which arrested his attention was the standard of food available. He was not very complimentary:

> The natural quality of the food is so good that it deserves both skill and reverence in the kitchen. What lordly dishes a French housewife would make of it! But the New Zealanders, like the Scots, think that baking is the better part of cookery, and spend their ingenuity, exhaust their interest, on cakes, and pastries and ebullient, vast cream sponges. Soup is neglected, meat mishandled. I have seen their admirable mutton brought upon the table in such a miserable shape that the hogget — so they call a sheep of uncertain age — appeared to have been killed by a bomb, and the fragments of its carcass incinerated in the resultant fire.[1]

Leaving aside his unwarranted slur upon the Scots kitchen, it is important to be aware that Linklater arrived in New Zealand more or less at the point at which our nineteenth-century-oriented culture was at its peak (or nadir, depending on your point of view). What he was describing was real enough, but he had little appreciation of the origins of this culture and so his understanding of his experience was fundamentally flawed.

No doubt in those days meat did sometimes arrive at the table in the condition he rightly excoriates, but there was no universal rule which demanded it, and his misunderstanding of the tradition of baking was palpable, as was his subsequent strained humour at the expense of those who did not value fish. There were very good reasons for this state of affairs, some of which have been canvassed. But what he was also describing was one of the most important traditions to have acclimatised itself to the New Zealand environment — the culinary fruits of egalitarianism.

Managing without Mary Jane

The nineteenth century has yet another unique distinction not so far discussed in this analysis. Although the employment category 'servant' continued to be the numerically greatest of all British occupations (as late as the census of 1891 there were 1.5 million domestic servants in England and Wales, 15.8 percent of the workforce, and 4.9 percent of the population),[2] this was the first century in the whole of human history in which the wealthy had to begin to learn to make do without domestic servants. This unwelcome social innovation, which had already entrenched itself in the United States, first struck the English in those new colonies in which there was no significant indigenous population to fill the role. New Zealand was a particular case in point. Maori people did not take naturally to the notion of serving others in a subordinate capacity, as the 20-year-old Wesleyan missionary wife Eliza White discovered in 1832:

> A day of much trial and vexation, the Native boys so very insulting, I
> could not bear it. We leave all that is dear to us for their sake and they do
> all they can to irritate and make us angry . . . the conduct of our domestic

natives causes me to indulge an angry spirit, and this brings darkness and heaviness in my mind.[3]

Her tribulations had hardly begun. A month later one of her Maori women servants ran off, with the encouragement of her parents, stealing some clothing in the process and notwithstanding that she had been taught the useful skill of preserving fruit. White settlers in New Zealand very quickly gave up on Maori as a primary source of domestic servitors.

But it came as an even bigger shock to those colonists wealthy enough to employ servants to discover that the working-class immigrants to whom they looked for their cooks and housemaids had not come to the new country to serve them. They had, in particular, not come to a new country to find themselves in an occupation they may well have emigrated to escape. They had better things to do establishing themselves by their own efforts in a comfortable subsistence in their new land. Those who had been used to servants as a fact of existence, and who had been able to pick and choose, suddenly found that they could barely get them at all. It is hard for us, living in a society in which a domestic servant is a curiosity, to appreciate what this meant to those for whom servants had been considered a necessity.

Servants had long occupied an important place in European households. In earlier centuries those filling the role had often been related to the family they served by blood kinship or marriage. Even when they were not, they could occupy a position in the household which went far beyond anything we would recognise as a contract of employment, into a much more comprehensive nexus of social relationships, the meanings of which are still the subject of hot debate among social historians.[4]

Some household servants were also highly skilled members of a team of servitors whose skills granted them a relatively high status both in the household and in the broader community. In medieval times, for instance, those responsible for serving bread or carving meat in a large domestic establishment performed important ceremonial and hospitality functions; in royal households they might even be of noble birth. Carving in particular demanded considerable knowledge, the ability to follow elaborate rituals, the dexterity to use some quite complicated equipment, and familiarity with an esoteric specialist vocabulary. Mutton or beef

Preserving Fruit

One of the things which most delighted the new settlers, particularly those of modest means, was the ready availability of seasonal fruit and vegetable surpluses. The preservation of these for later use became a central aspect of the New Zealand domestic economy in the nineteenth century. Mostly the method used was what became known as the 'open pan method'. This entails making a medium syrup (1 cup of sugar to 2 or 3 of water), and cooking the fruit carefully in this until it is tender. This is then lifted out with a sterilised spoon and conveyed to sterilised jars. The jars are filled to the top with the boiling hot fruit and syrup, and the air bubbles worked out with a sterilised knife. Sterilised patent seals and screw caps are then screwed tight.

Other methods include a cold pack and water-bath system. The Whitcombe & Tombs cookbook mentions additional methods using boiling water to cook the items and their preservation under a thick layer of beef or mutton fat, and the use of salicylic acid for preserving raw fruit in syrup. It also gives a recipe for crystallising fruit:

Make a syrup of one pound of sugar to one quart of water. Boil the fruit in this syrup as for preserving. Drain it. Sprinkle with crystalised sugar and dry slowly either in the oven (with the door open) or in a hot sun. Some soak the fruit before boiling for twelve to twentyfour hours in lime water (one dessertspoon of lime to one quart of water).

This skill in home preserving of fruit has become a lost art almost within the compass of a single post-war generation. It largely lingers now as a conscious antiquarianism.

might be carved, but capons and rabbits were 'unlaced', crayfish were 'departed' and pheasants 'allayed'.[5] Stewards and butlers, who commanded whole households or even estates, were always persons of consequence. So too were some cooks.[6] But these were the exceptions.

Most of the routine kitchen and domestic work of the household, much of it physically heavy, was done by young women and boys. This continued to be the case down the centuries. As late as 1851 the British census records that 66 percent of female domestics were under the age of 24 and nearly half were under 19.[7] There were few labour-saving household appliances to take the elbow grease out of this heavy work, and most of those who employed servants did not see why there should be. Domestic service mainly entailed long hours of drudgery, and its low status meant that only the young finding their way into the workforce for the first time, or those with no other options, were prepared to do it. For young women, with little or no education, the choice was effectively between industrial work in the cities, farm work in the countryside, or service. Many women took the last course because they thought the work would be lighter and more varied, and the opportunities for advancement and an independent life much greater.[8] This was sometimes but not always the case. The hours, for instance, were usually very long. As late as 1914 an official investigation showed that the ordinary working day of a servant was from six in the morning until ten at night, with few breaks, and no opportunity to leave the house except on the one free day allowed each week.[9]

The incorporation of servants within the household social nexus, if not within the kin group, survived, particularly in rural areas, well into the nineteenth century. But increasingly from the eighteenth century, as strictly contractual arrangements replaced the social, the relationship between master and servant became purely monetary.[10] It was also a demeaning and humiliating one for the servant who lived in constant personal contact with a social superior who treated her or him as inferior as a matter of course. Some took to the role well enough and made a life of it, but given the choice most preferred not to do it at all. If they were to avoid it, emigration was often the only other choice.

In New Zealand servants were in such desperately short supply that there was a concerted drive to find young women who might fit the bill in Britain and to bring them to New Zealand in batches. Between 1861

and 1864 nearly 1500 arrived in this way at Lyttelton alone.[11] Other provinces strove similarly to attract servant girls. But as soon as the young women found themselves in a situation where they might do other and better-paid work, or were much in potential demand as marriage partners, they tended to turn their noses up at domestic service. As the better-off colonists were quick to discover, a competent cook in particular who could be induced to stay was a rare treasure indeed; and the relative demand for servants' skills encouraged in them an independent attitude which was not always welcome to their prospective employers. Martha Adams for one was scandalised when she asked a servant her name shortly after her arrival in Nelson in 1850 and was told tartly that it was 'Miss Sarah'.[12]

And Jessie Campbell, writing to her sister Isabella from Wanganui in 1843, could hardly have been more disgruntled:

> Servants are a great curse here. I have a young girl from Arbroath whom I brought down here with me, altho' inexperienced I thought she would be obedient. Once here she found out her own value. I can assure you that I have enough to do with her, she neither can nor will work, the best I can say of her is that she is kind to the children.[13]

Others were more sanguine in their approach to the realities of housekeeping in the antipodes. Lady Barker took it all with her usual aplomb. After remarking on the difficulty of getting any sort of a servant who was aware of even the most basic of domestic duties (and 'as for a women knowing how to cook, that seems the very last accomplishment they acquire'),[14] she retailed her experiences with gusto. On one occasion, a new cook having unaccountably failed to arrive, she sought the assistance of a newly engaged housemaid, who

> professed her willingness to supply her place, but on trial being made of her abilities, she proved to be quite as inexperienced as I was, and to every dish I proposed she should attempt, the unvarying answer was 'the missus did all that where I come from.' During the first days after her arrival her chief employment was examining the various knick knacks about the drawing room.

In due course the cook did arrive, and notwithstanding a propensity to poke the fire with the toasting fork, was sufficiently accomplished to be able both to roast mutton and bake bread. Eventually Barker decided to

Veal Cutlets

Lady Barker's various cooks did not have the assistance of the later *New Zealand Graphic and Ladies Home Journal* which, along with its reports on European diplomatic news, regularly published a recipe column with careful instructions for various homely dishes. This from the issue of Saturday 9 July 1892:

> Veal cutlets should be cut from the neck in the same shape as mutton cutlets — as many cutlets as there are guests; but let them be very small. They must be prettily larded on one side like a sweetbread; braise them — don't fry them — in the same manner until quite tender; glaze lightly and salamander to the colour of old gold. Have ready boiled a pint of green peas (young ones if you can afford them, but peas are capitally preserved nowadays). Put them in a stewpan with two pats of butter and a little salt, and if your guests are accustomed to Continental cookery a teaspoonful of powdered sugar. When boiling finish with a liaison of one yolk of egg and a teaspoonful of cream; pour into the dish and dress the cutlets in an oval ring. You may have a little mould of mashed potato if you like in the middle.

A salamander, now virtually unheard of, was once standard kitchen equipment. It is best described as a red-hot blowtorch for giving a final browning or glaze to a dish, and was kept in the fire or fed with gas for the purpose.

Traditional Rhubarb Pie

Mrs Beeton gives this recipe and includes a number of variations with gooseberries, redcurrants and raspberries, all of which would have been found in a nineteenth-century immigrant garden.

350 g plain flour
90 g each butter and lard
tsp salt
700 g rhubarb, cut into 2 cm lengths
150 g sugar
a little milk

Make a shortcrust pastry from the flour, salt, and butter and lard rubbed well in with enough cold water to mix to a smooth, stiff dough. Line a pie dish with two-thirds of the pastry and fill with the rhubarb, sprinkling the sugar liberally as you go. Roll out the remaining pastry and cover, sealing well. Make a small hole in the centre, and decorate and glaze with the milk. Bake in a preheated oven at 200°C for 20 minutes, then lower the heat to 160°C and give it 20 minutes more. The pastry should be golden-brown. Serve hot or cold.

cut her losses, and to learn to cook for herself, which she did very successfully.

Some of the new settlers even discovered that they preferred this arrangement. Maria Richmond soon began doing without servants altogether. 'I am afraid I have the soul of a maid of all work,' she wrote in a letter to her English friend Margaret Taylor in 1853, describing an entertainment for a visiting party of 13, ' . . . [But] when my pantry shelves are scrubbed and it contains as it will tomorrow afternoon a round of boiled beef, a roast leg of pork, a rhubarb pie, fifteen large loaves, and eight pounds of fresh butter ready for the Sunday bush party, I feel as self satisfied and proud as a mortal can.'[15]

The views of those who were prepared to continue to perform the role of servant in the new colony have rarely survived, but show some appreciation of the position in which they found themselves. Mary Hunter, writing home from Auckland in 1867, described how she was now to take up a dressmaking apprenticeship, because 'I am tired of being at service', although 12s a week was available for such work — a good wage when the other perquisites such as meals and accommodation were taken into account. 'Servants do not work half as hard here as they do at home,' she went on, 'such a thing would never be thought of as a woman going out to work in the fields, and as for milking cows, that is a man's job, and the women in general would be afraid of spoiling their fingers.'[16]

Anthony Trollope, visiting in 1872, summed up the situation succinctly:

The one great complaint made by the ladies arises from the dearth of maid servants. Sometimes no domestic servant can be had at all for love or money, and the mistress of the house with her daughters, if she has any, is constrained to cook the dinner and make the beds. Sometimes a lass who knows nothing will consent to come into a house and be taught to do housework at the rate of forty pounds per annum, with a special proviso that she is to be allowed to go out two evenings a week to learn choral singing in the music hall. By more than two or three ladies my sympathy was demanded on account of these sufferings, and I was asked whether or not a country must not be in a bad way in which the ordinary comfort of female attendance could not be had when it was wanted. Of course, I sympathised . . . but I could not help suggesting that the maid servant's side of the question is quite as important as the mistress's. The truth is that in such a town as Christchurch a girl of twenty or twenty three can earn from thirty to forty pounds a year and a comfortable home with no oppressive hard work; and if she be well conducted and of decent appearance she is sure to get a husband who can keep a house over her head. For such persons New Zealand is a paradise.[17]

One historian claims that about 10 percent of all women over 15 years of age in the South Island were wage-earning domestics in 1871, although he does not cite his source, and this may be an over-estimate.[18] The official statistics of New Zealand put the proportion of domestic servants in the total population at about 3 percent for the three censuses to 1867; even as a proportion of the workforce, this amounts to nowhere near the equivalent English figure, and represents a much smaller number than those employed in such areas as agriculture, mining and labouring.[19] Notwithstanding Trollope's remarks, wages were not very good. A male cook on a country station and a female cook in Auckland could both earn about 20s a week with full board in 1898. This was about the same as the rate for a farm labourer, and significantly less than a grocer's or draper's assistant (although these last did not receive board).[20] Domestic service was never popular nor much valued, and by the turn of the century it had all but vanished, especially in urban areas.

This had a significant effect on the development of the cuisine. Busy housewives, including the middle classes, put to doing much of their own domestic work, including the cooking, had no time for elaborate meals, except perhaps on social occasions. Domestic cooking was

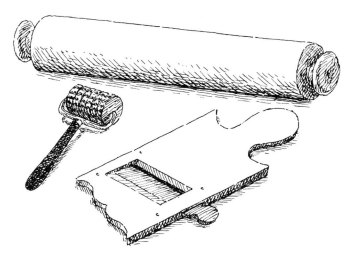

Rich Butter Sponge

The sudden availability of virtually limitless eggs and butter, and a continuously hot oven in the range, must have been an encouragement to endless cake-making and the entertainment involved in eating it in quantities afterwards.

    3 large eggs
    120 g caster sugar
    90 g butter
    75 g flour
    15 g cornflour

Whisk the eggs and sugar for about 10 minutes in a double boiler, but don't let the mixture boil. Mix in the melted butter and sieve in the dry ingredients with a pinch of salt. Fold this together lightly but well, and pour into a shallow baking tin lined with greaseproof paper. Bake at 160°C for about 45 minutes. This cake is best served cut into fingers and iced.

therefore greatly simplified compared to its class equivalents in Britain. In combination with the egalitarian ethos of the colony, it also ensured a relative homogeneity in catering throughout all strata. The farmers' ordinary came to be the standard by which all private family cooking was judged: plain food in abundance. But alongside this, there developed a tradition of social cooking which had no equivalent in the English cuisine (although it was an adaptation of it), and which seems to have been unique to colonial societies such as Australia and New Zealand.

ABUNDANCE AND HOSPITALITY AT LARGE

This tradition was remarkably long-lived. Eric Linklater, as has already been remarked, drew attention to it and its basis in the skills of baking sweet confections. A moment's thought establishes that it must, necessarily, have grown out of the nature of the standard cooking technology and a colonial tradition of extending casual hospitality even to strangers. The former because the oven was there and available for use so it might as well be used to bake a cake or similar, especially if the ingredients — eggs, butter, flour, sugar — were staples and readily available. The latter because nineteenth-century New Zealand was a society in which people might be expected to be often on the move, and thus not in a position to feed themselves easily. They were likely to arrive without warning, and expecting hospitality, on the doorsteps of those who were.

    This tradition developed early and linked easily to a similar and pre-existing custom in Maori society. The appreciative comments of Edward Markham and others on the hospitality readily extended to them by Maori have been noted. It extended well beyond the point at which British sovereignty was established in 1840 and organised colonisation began. The explorer Charles Money recounted how, after spending some exhausting weeks in the bush, he was invited to attend a tangi at Kaiapoi in the 1860s. He and his companions spent three days there:

> and were treated with as much hospitality as any civilised people could
> have shewn towards a few ragged, hungry adventurers like ourselves. The
> old chief in particular was profuse in his generosity. He went into the bush
> to obtain honey for us; he made his women prepare huge masses of potatoes
> and salt ka-ka (the New Zealand parrot), and when we left, after buying

thirty pounds of his flour from him, he went out in the morning in his canoe and brought in a gigantic basket of eels (over two hundred) which he gave to us.[21]

Money and his friends took a few of these with them, and returned the chief's compliment by helping him to split the balance open for drying. He commented, presumably from prior experience, that dried eel 'were almost as good eating as the celebrated Finnan haddock'.

This tradition of Maori hospitality to strangers overlapped easily with a similar practice at the early whaling stations on which Jerningham Wakefield commented in *Adventure in New Zealand*:

> Should a stranger visit the settlement on his travels, he is met by a hearty welcome. The best of eating and drinking is placed before him; and the steward and women are ordered to attend to him while the boats are away; and the best bunk is prepared for him at night.[22]

The opening up of the country to exploration by Europeans and the uncertainty of provisioning which this often entailed extended and amplified this tradition of casual hospitality almost into a code. C. Warren Adams, in his 1853 account of his experience in the Canterbury settlement, summed this up succinctly. After spending several days semi-lost in the bush, he and a companion found their way out and

> were received by Mr Keale, the owner of the little reed-built hut or 'warri' with that warm hospitality which is amongst the most amiable characteristics of these colonies. It is true that he had only potatoes to offer us, the fare upon which he had for some time subsisted; but, in our famished condition, we held them to be luxuries, and took advantage of the temporary absence of our host to devour them before they were half cooked.[23]

By the latter part of the century, a failure of such hospitality in extremis was regarded as deeply shocking. Lady Barker recorded at length a case involving an itinerant worker turned away from shelter on a stormy night and sent on to her own property 25 miles distant. Her account makes it clear that she was highly critical of those responsible for this lapse.[24]

By the last decades of the century, as many rural workers were left with no option but to go 'on the swag' in search of work, economic necessity had added considerable point to this practice of casual

Beefsteak Pie

Anne Cobbett gives this recipe in her
English Housekeeper (1851). Presumably the
filling described was to be baked in a
covered crust, and the catsup, noted without
instruction, was to be poured in to taste.
This is an example of the traditional
inclusion of oysters with beef which survives
now in the so-called 'carpet bag steak'.

**Cut small steaks from the rump. Season
and roll up as olives, or lay them flat, fat
and lean mixed, seasoned with salt,
pepper and spices. Then put in half a
pint of gravy, or half a pint of water, and
a tablespoon of vinegar. If you have no
gravy a piece of kidney will enrich the
gravy of the beef, and is a valuable
addition to a meat pie. Forcemeat in
layers between the slices of beef, or in
small balls, makes this much richer; if
to be eaten cold, suet must not be used:
some cooks put in a few large oysters
also. Walnut or mushroom catsup. A
good gravy may be poured into the pie
when baked.**

hospitality to travellers. Although some of the more censorious members
of the community insisted that these men were workshy and were taking
advantage of the hospitality tradition, there was no suggestion that they
should be refused. Mrs Robert Wilson, in her account of her experiences
in New Zealand as wife of one of the principal engineers for the Vogel
railways schemes, spoke of the situation thus:

> Sundowners walk from station to station during the day, sleeping under a
> haystack until sunset, make their appearance at the hour before the 'whares'
> or huts provided for them, and demand from the owners supper and shelter,
> which are generally granted . . . At Springfield, as well as at all large stations
> a man is employed solely to prepare meals for these casual though
> unavoidable visitors. The owner of a small property told me that one night
> when only he and his sister were at their lonely homestead, eighty of these
> uninvited guests made their appearance; and of course asked for food and
> lodging, which he was fortunately able to supply.[25]

And she went on to point out that even at 6d a head this added up to £4
and was a considerable expense. It is understandable that in such
circumstances the emphasis was on cheap food in quantity — bread, tea,
cold roast or boiled mutton. It also had its hazards. Adela Stewart fed
two swaggers one evening and found that when she came to her larder
the following morning they had made away with a beefsteak pie, a cold
roast and half a loaf of bread. She later taxed them with this, and was
sceptical of their denials, but she made nothing of it ('I believe they had
been out of work for some time and were really hungry') and fed them
breakfast of bacon and eggs as well.[26]

That people from any station in life could turn up in large numbers
and expect to be fed is also clear from a number of accounts. Marianne
Williams, writing from Paihia to her friend Charlotte Brown in Tauranga
in 1842, recalled the day 'Mr and Mrs Butt arrived and the Bishop's
party came down from Waimate to meet them and Capt and Mrs Bateman
came over to see them and Mrs Burrows and Mrs Baker called and Mrs
Mair. Is this not the place to see company?'[27] All of these visitors had to
be fed, and Mrs Williams had that day 32 European visitors to various
sessions of tea and 27 to dinner. Twenty years later, Mary Hobhouse,
wife to the Bishop of Nelson, found herself hostess to the General Synod
of the Church of England in New Zealand. She had two girls and a

housekeeper in poor health to look after what must have been a rather daunting group, and she 'trembled as I saw in my imagination an encamped host of clergy beside our own house full to the brim to be cooked for and washed-up for.'[28] When she enquired how she was to feed this group, the Bishop airily suggested that some tea, sugar, a sack of flour and some bacon be got in, and they be fed on pancakes which they could cook for themselves. This unhelpful suggestion was ignored, and she produced instead the much more suitable roast beef and apple pie.

Catering for these larger gatherings could at least be planned for in most circumstances. On several occasions Adela Stewart gave dance parties for very large groups. In 1881, for instance, anxious to introduce a young English visitor to some of the local bachelors:

> we spent an extra busy day roasting lamb, chicken etc. and making all sorts of good sweets, and having invited over fifty people, most of them arrived in drays, on horseback or on foot, one afternoon for early dinner, followed by tennis and quoits, high tea on the wide verandah, dressing in every available room for the dance that followed, with supper at midnight, soup at 2, broke up after 3, when the majority rode away, leaving nineteen in the house for breakfast, followed by a picnic on the river bank.[29]

This was a custom of some standing, it seems. Two decades earlier Lady Barker had written: 'We are always eating in this country, so you will not be surprised to hear that there was yet another meal to be disposed of before we separated to dress in all sorts of nooks and corners.'[30]

Although accounts of the giving of dances are mostly to be found in the reminiscences of the wealthier settlers, this was an activity by no means confined to them. On the contrary, it was an effective indicator of the developing egalitarian spirit of the colony. May McDermott, speaking of her early life near Dargaville, described her first dance:

> They were mostly young people, bushmen's wives, that had come to join their husbands, perhaps with one or two children, may be more, but they all came carrying their children in front of them on horseback and rugs to put the babies to bed on the floor . . . The ladies brought lots of food to eat and the men boiled water for tea in a kerosene tin in the yard. The music was grand. I don't think there is any music better to dance to than the accordion and the men knew all the music, even for the different sets of the Lancers, the D'Alberts and Quadrilles. It was a lovely dance.[31]

Lamb Roasted and Boiled

The editor of *Brett's Guide*, Thomas Leys, has good advice for cooking lamb. It should be cooked very fresh.

> **It should be roasted at a brisk fire and done thoroughly, so that no red blood shows (this remark is applicable to all white meats). A leg of lamb will occupy about an hour and a half in roasting: a fore-quarter, half an hour longer; a raised loin and saddle also about two hours. Serve with a little gravy and mint sauce.**

Boiled lamb, on the other hand, should be put into boiling water and, when it comes to the boil again, moved to the side of the stove where it can simmer gently for an hour and a quarter for each five pounds of lamb. It is best served, he says, with melted butter poured over, and garnished with boiled carrots and cauliflower tufts.

Leys goes on to advise those who are entertaining on the right way to dress the table:

> **See that the linen is spotlessly white; a piece of bread cut thick, or a French roll, should be placed under the folds of the table napkin allotted to each guest. The table should be decorated with vases of flowers, or what is more popular, with fancy pots containing a strawberry plant, orange or other fruit tree in full bearing, ferns in pots etc.**

For an ordinary small cottage dinner he recommends fish, roast meat and fowl, game or some savoury pie, followed by pudding, tarts, blancmange and cheese, concluding with dessert and coffee. Heaven knows what he would have recommended for a banquet.

Stewed Opossum

Eating opossum stew was not unusual among
country folk following the regrettably
successful introduction of the animal in
1858; it is not uncommon today. It is more
than likely that May McDermott ate
opossum stew at country dance suppers.

After skinning and cleaning the animal, and
removing the fatty gland from under its tail, it
should be cut into joints and browned in a
little lard. It should then be simmered in
water to cover for about an hour, with plenty
of cut-up vegetables and seasoning to taste.
The meat should then be removed, and the
cooking liquid strained and kept simmering.
In another pot make a flour and butter roux,
and return sufficient of the strained liquid to
make a thickish sauce. Return the opossum to
the sauce and simmer gently for a further
hour. At this point the dish is very good
cooked in a camp oven.

Sweet Lamb Pie

Many of New Zealand's nineteenth-century
immigrants brought traditional recipes with
them from 'the old country'. This lamb pie is
from Westmorland.

　shortcrust pastry
　200 g minced lamb mixed with 100 g
　　minced lamb fat
　150 g apples, peeled, cored and grated
　125 g each raisins, currants and sultanas
　50 g candied peel, chopped
　combined juice of an orange and a lemon
　50 g chopped blanched almonds
　a jigger of rum
　salt and pepper
　¼ tsp each nutmeg, cinnamon and mace

Roll out enough pastry to cover the bottom of
a pie plate. Mix all the remaining ingredients
thoroughly, and fill the pie plate, mounding
up towards the centre. Cover with more
pastry, seal well and glaze. This should be
baked at 200°C for about 30 minutes, and can
be eaten cold. It would have done very well at
one of Adela Stewart's picnics, especially at
the Christmas season.

Such occasions could also be fraught with unexpected hazards, especially
in rural areas in which the men well outnumbered the ladies of dancing
age or inclination. Lady Barker recounted how, during a stay with friends
at a bachelor establishment, she surprised eight bearded men solemnly
practising quadrilles to a large music box, and sharing both the male and
female roles, presumably to be in fettle for the next social gathering. She
also told of a large dance at which there were only five female partners
available, and described their exhausted state when the gathering finally
broke up in the early hours.

Regular picnics were also a key feature of group entertaining in
nineteenth-century New Zealand. Most urban workers had at least one
a year, usually on Labour Day, and based on either their workplace or
their union. They also featured largely in Adela Stewart's life; her bi-
annual picnics at Waihi Beach became locally famous, and impromptus
might also be held to celebrate particular events, or in association with
athletic contests or other outdoor sports. In 1882, a month of rain meant
a mammoth wash on the first fine day, and to celebrate its completion a
moonlight picnic was called for and 'we set to work to make all sorts
cakes, pies and sausage rolls . . . then after early dinner we started, a
party of thirty in carts and on horseback, to the beautiful Waihi Beach
spring, where the boys lit a fire, boiled water in billies, made tea and
feasted.'

Other impromptus were less relaxing. On one notable occasion Adela
Stewart found herself entertaining the redoubtable Te Kooti, recently
pardoned by the government of past depredations in the interests of
opening up the Waikato to further settlement, and more than 100 of his
followers, some of whom were heavily armed. This she took in her stride
by refusing them beer and offering them the alternative of tea, which
they accepted enthusiastically before going on their way. Shearing too
brought the need for much cooking, as did the visit of a piano tuner who
spent three days and was fed lavishly. More bothersome was the sending
away of the iron stove for nine days for repairs, during which time Stewart,
instructed by a local tinker who also repaired her cauldrons, fell back on
the trusty camp oven which supplied her with the dinner for a surprise
visitation. On her menu for that occasion was sheep's head broth, cutlets
with tomato sauce, boiled mutton with caper sauce, vegetables, jelly,
stewed peaches and cream, followed by coffee and music.

New arrivals in New Zealand were often astonished by the generosity of total strangers in not only entertaining them but also pressing produce on them when they left. Eliza Jones wrote in her journal of a week-long excursion with friends around the Hauraki Gulf in 1858. On their fifth day, having been feasted by local Maori on watermelons the previous day, the party happened unexpectedly on a neat cottage with climbing roses. It required only a remark to the owner on the thriving nature of the cottage garden for Eliza to find herself instantly loaded with sage, beans, thyme and onions, together with fresh-made bread and butter, eggs and a large portion of cake.[32] This was not, as she discovered to her evident pleasure, the exception but the rule.

Naturally, the ceremonies of European family and community life continued to be kept up in New Zealand, despite the seasonal discrepancies. Weddings and Christmas in particular were celebrated with an abundance of food. Lady Barker wrote with great charm and enthusiasm of a Christmas feast she gave for her shearers and shepherds in her large wash-house, suitably decorated with ferns and flags for the occasion. As was customary the catering was as lavish as she could make it:

> For two days before the great day I had been working hard, studying recipes for pies and puddings, and scouring the country in search of delicacies. Every lady was most kind, knowing that our poor, exposed garden was backward; I had sacks of green peas, bushels of young potatoes, and baskets of strawberries and cherries sent to me from all round the country; I made poor Frederick ride twenty miles to get me a sirloin of beef, and to my great joy two beautiful young geese arrived as a present only the day before. It is a point of honour to have as little mutton as possible on these occasions, as the great treat is the complete change of fare. I only ventured to introduce it very much disguised as curry or in pies.[33]

Weddings too were celebrated with an abundance of food. The letter of an otherwise unidentified Mrs Smith in Auckland describes the marriage in 1852 of Bishop Selwyn's ward Anne Hector to the Rev. William Hihill. After recalling the ceremony itself, she gave an account of the wedding breakfast (to which over 100 guests, many of them Maori, sat down); the five bridesmaids cut the cake and there was an abundance of meat, plum pudding, bread and vegetables.[34]

Rich Fruit Cake

The making of a rich cake for a ceremonial occasion such as a wedding or Christmas is one of the few nineteenth-century culinary cultural traditions to have survived into the present, and has roots in the medieval practice of adding fruit to meat dishes. Even this is becoming rarer as our culture changes. Nevertheless, it is a habit which, in common with such archaisms as blacking your shoes every day, ought to be preserved.

500 g sugar
500g butter
10 eggs
1 kg flour
2 tsp baking powder
500 g each currants, sultanas and raisins
120 g each mixed peel and ground almonds
100 ml brandy or port

Cream the butter and sugar and then add the eggs one by one, the sifted dry ingredients, and the fruit, peel, almonds and brandy. Ensure that this is mixed well and turn into a well-buttered or lined tin or tins. Bake at 160°C for about 4 hours or until a skewer comes away clean. Such cakes are usually covered with marzipan and iced with a plain white icing, then decorated with piping and other confectioner's items. My mother always kept a small tin of decorations to do her annual Christmas cake. If you have been sentimental enough to keep some threepences, watch out for your teeth.

Date Cake

When I was a child no afternoon tea was complete without a cake or loaf with preserved dates in it. Often it would be thickly spread with fresh butter too.

  125 g butter
  125 g sugar
  a drop or two of lemon essence
  2 eggs
  250 g flour
  1 tsp baking powder
  a little milk
  125 g stoned dates, chopped

Cream the butter and sugar and add the essence. Beat the eggs well in, and then thoroughly stir in the dried ingredients, adding the milk to make sure it is not too dry. Lastly, add the dates. Bake in a greased tin for 50 minutes at 180°C.

Ginger Kisses

One of the great New Zealand institutions which has now all but disappeared is the formal afternoon tea, which gave a housewife the opportunity to display both her baking skills and her moral rectitude, as exemplified by her 'well-filled tins'. Who now has the time or the inclination for such a thing? Generations of New Zealanders have grown to adulthood without sampling a Neenish Tart, a Ginger Kiss, or worst deprivation of all, a Lamington.

  2 tbsp butter
  125 g sugar
  1 tbsp golden syrup
  2 eggs
  250 g flour
  1 tsp baking powder
  1 tsp each cinnamon and ground ginger

Cream the butter, sugar and golden syrup, then beat in the eggs, and mix the dry ingredients in thoroughly. Grease a baking try and cover with spaced dessert spoonfuls. Bake these at 200°C for about 10 minutes. Leave to cool. These are then traditionally put together as two halves with a cream filling. The *Edmonds Cookbook* suggests a very rich variety of this made of butter, condensed milk, crystallised cherries and chopped walnuts. This, I confess, I never encountered in my own childhood.

Inevitably, the gold-mining communities added their own unique contribution to the tradition of entertainment hospitality. The opening of a new mining work of some sort — a giant wheel, a water race, a dam or a steam engine — was invariably marked by a day off and an outing with lashings of good food. In line with the egalitarian spirit of the goldfields, all were welcome, even a Supreme Court judge. The principal historian of the West Coast goldfields recounts the opening of a new race at Kaniere in 1866 complete with Judge Gresson as principal speaker and a number of ladies of various descriptions to grace the occasion. The party was 'laden with hampers', and His Honour proposed a toast to loud cheers and the popping of champagne corks.[35]

The tradition of good eating which arose from the available abundance and which very quickly formed the basis of New Zealand's food culture in the nineteenth century, combined with the custom of unquestioned offering of liberal, not to say lavish, quantities of food to visitors and strangers, created a tradition which placed the emphasis on bulk and quantity in eating. This could be a significant drain on resources. Adela Stewart (admittedly an exceptional case but not so very exceptional) spoke of having to bake bread every day, of purchasing a ton of flour at a time, and of not unusually using up 100 pounds of it in a week.[36] This was also a community which did not simply adopt a very different attitude to the effects of carbohydrates and fats on the human body from what we do now, but which actively promoted their consumption. 'The consumption of fat in some shape or another is necessary to our existence,' opines *Brett's Colonists' Guide*,[37] which urged its regular consumption as an important basis for health. The author particularly recommended butter as the form of fatty matter least likely to disagree with the stomach.

LADIES A PLATE

Today we have begun to find it odd to encounter someone who regularly bakes and stores sweet foods against the unexpected arrival of visitors. But the hospitality and baking culture has deep roots in the soil of our colonial experience, and it continued to subsist well within contemporary memory, at least a century and a half after its genesis. A recent work on change and continuity in the lives of New Zealand women contains copious references to it. 'You spent your day baking,' says one, recollecting her early married life, 'Friday afternoon, or Saturday.' The key remained hospitality. 'If people came you offered food . . . You always cooked extra . . . You never cooked just for the people that were present when you started cooking, so that if ever someone else came, there was enough . . . so you'd put in the potatoes for all the people that were present and always what was called one for the pot.' Another recalled:

> The first thing that you did was you offered someone refreshment of some sorts. Or, even if you'd just finished eating, you asked them if they'd eaten. And if we'd eaten then we prepared something for them. And if we had people staying who were from the town — relatives that were called 'townies' — then they were always given meat and eggs when they left.[38]

For obvious reasons this tradition survived longer in the country than in urban areas, although ironically at the one time of the year when a significant call on the tradition might have been expected, during lambing, it could not be offered because the coal range was in use to keep newborn but motherless lambs warm until a foster parent could be found. There is also evidence in this account of the competitive and display activities which subsequently developed from the tradition. This involved showing baking and preserves at Agricultural and Pastoral fairs: 'Some families showed,' remembered one interviewee, 'and others didn't. My grandmother and mother and aunt would only have "shown" in the rural district where they lived.' She explained that it would have taken tremendous confidence to show display food outside the immediate district. Other women recalled individuals who were famous for their sponge cakes, and who guarded the secret of their success jealously, always refusing to give an accurate recipe.

The tradition lives on. One of those contributing to the same collection bridges the gap to our fat-conscious world with the comment: 'I've just filled my tins. My husband likes it but I try to avoid it because I think I've put on a bit of weight since we came to [this place] . . . but he'll make himself a cup of tea, he always does, and mostly he'll go and get himself a bun, and have a look in the tins.'[39] But to establish itself, this tradition had initially to struggle against the culture of those who had expected to maintain the same social distinctions in the new colony as they had enjoyed 'at home'.

Lamingtons

Make a sponge sandwich cake from 3 eggs, 125 g sugar, 25 g cornflour, 50 g flour and 1 tsp baking powder, well creamed and mixed together, and baked for 15 minutes at 180°C in a sandwich tin. When this has cooled, cut it into squares and dip in a chocolate icing made from 2 tbsp butter, 2 tbsp cocoa, 6 tbsp boiling water, 300 g icing sugar and a drop or two of vanilla essence, all well mixed together. While still wet, roll in grated coconut and leave to dry.

PLAYING AT LADIES

Many of the new colonists, including those who had come out in the cabin, expected that life would be different in their new communities, and were inclined to poke fun at those who hoped that the same pretensions to gentility could continue to apply in the new environment. Warren Adams, although himself relatively comfortably off and resident in Christchurch, most socially conscious of all the new settlements, was contemptuous of some of his fellow settlers, one of whom had gone to considerable trouble and expense to bring two carriages with him. He laughed at those gentlemen who had brought 'handsome and well-furnished gun and dressing cases' and those ladies who 'had not forgotten a full supply of kid gloves and evening dresses'.[40] They should have no expectation, he thought, of continuing their usual social habits in the new colony. Others, however, were determined to go on much as before and tried to continue such practices as the leaving of cards on suitable visitors; they usually waxed indignant when others refused or failed to play this game and behaved in ways they considered socially inappropriate.

In 1843 Maria Kemp, sister of the missionary John Wilson and wife of the government interpreter, wrote to her friend Charlotte Brown at Tauranga that she had been hurt to return to her home following her honeymoon to find that few of her cards had been returned by the missionary community. Perhaps their attitude was understandable. Apparently without irony she remarked in the same letter: 'I don't like Kororareka much — there is no society — at least not for people who are at all particular, so my husband has not introduced me to any.'[41] She was particularly dismissive of Marianne Williams, whom she described as wanting in etiquette and delicacy in sending messages across the bay to say that she would call as soon as demands on her hospitality allowed.

Others took a more realistic view of the inappropriateness of trying to maintain such petty visiting distinctions in the new circumstances. Mary Hobhouse, writing to a friend in 1860, shrewdly drew attention to the foolishness of these pretensions in a place where 'you see your acquaintances here stripped of all accessories, and deriving no borrowed charm from possession or connections'.[42] Attempts to maintain some sort of gentility often foundered on necessity. When Margaret Herring was entertained to a formal dinner in 1861 by Hannah Barton, wife of one of the principal landowners in the Hutt Valley, she recalled with amusement its 'half style and half dilapidation . . . On the table for instance silver sugar basin and rusty iron salt spoons, silver table spoons and common brassy looking forks and old tin teapot. Yet her hospitality is most genuine.'[43] Herring was sufficiently aware to note that this rough-and-ready approach arose from the lack of servants and the intrusion of other, more basic farm-building priorities, and accorded it little importance. And when Lucy Johnson, daughter of a wealthy Hawke's Bay landowner who moved in the 'best' colonial circles all her life, wrote to her sister Ellen in 1877, she made a comedy of the panic which had ensued when unexpected society guests turned up, she had only a curry to give them for dinner, and her cook chose this moment to give notice on the spot.[44]

Attempts to combine the traditions of egalitarian hospitality and social formality could be unintentionally charming even at the highest level. In 1886 the Governor, Lord Onslow, visited Nelson and held an 'at home'. But the invitation was issued in the *Evening Mail*, causing a great to-do over who might and who might not go. Emily Harris, a member of Nelson 'society' but living in straitened circumstances, decided that her poverty should be no bar; wearing the only good dress the family possessed, she attended and had a fine time. She wrote in her diary:

> It was more like a garden party than a formal call . . . Most of my friends were there and I enjoyed it very much . . . I often think how very different our position here is to that of persons in England with a small income. There, unless they had a great many relations, they would only know two or three families. Here there are always more than fifty families where we can call — all people better off than we are . . . I do not say that we are the better off for knowing so many people, but it is pleasant.[45]

No doubt, if they did call, they would have been fed without question.

British social traditions appear to have been maintained in two areas only, those of the society ball and of formal dining, particularly at the official level. Charlotte Godley described one society ball in Christchurch in 1852 as 'a "got-up" ball with a committee of gentlemen to arrange everything, and four Lady Patronesses to decide upon who should be asked in doubtful cases, and so on.'[46] She thought it quite successful,

A Boiled Ox Tongue

1 large ox tongue, pickled, and smoked or not, as you prefer
a light chicken or veal stock
bouquet garni
a peeled onion stuck with 2 or 3 cloves
sliced carrot and celery
a few peppercorns

If the tongue has been pickled, soak it for a few hours to get most of the salt out. Cover it with fresh water, bring it to the boil and skim. Drain and refresh the water and add the vegetables and peppercorns. Cover well and simmer gently for 3 or 4 hours. When it is cooked, let it cool and peel off the skin.

This can be eaten cold, decorated with an aspic jelly (which would probably have been the case for the formal dinner described). It was sometimes skinned hot (never mind the cook's fingers) and then served with a hot Madeira sauce.

Wild Duck with Liver Stuffing

If you are not prepared to shoot your own ducks, cultivate friends who are. But be prepared to pluck and draw them yourself. Ducks, especially wild ones, can be tricky. Sometimes they taste strongly of fish. They can also dry out in the cooking unless you watch them carefully.

300 g poultry livers
half a dozen rashers rindless bacon
1 large onion, chopped
1 clove of garlic
1 egg
500 ml chicken stock
flour, salt and pepper
2 dressed ducks

Mince the livers, bacon, chopped onion and garlic. Bind with the egg and season well. Stuff the two ducks with this, sprinkle the exteriors with salt and pepper (and drizzle over a little oil or melted butter if you like). Roast these at 190°C for about an hour. They can then be served cold, or hot with a sauce made by thickening the dripping with a little flour and simmering gently with the stock.

Cabinet Pudding

This was a standard Victorian dessert for formal occasions. There are two versions, hot and cold. For a formal banquet the cold version given here would be more usual.

4 lemons
150 g sugar
4 cloves
a piece of cinnamon stick
50 g gelatine
whites and crushed shells of 2 eggs

These ingredients are used to make a jelly as follows. Pare the zest from the lemon and squeeze the juice, making this up to about 250 ml with water. Combine with the other ingredients in a pot, and heat, whisking constantly. Do not boil but keep up the whisking until a crust begins to form on the top of the liquid, then simmer for 5 minutes. Turn off the heat and let the contents settle, then strain through a fine jelly bag into a bowl. Have to hand the following ingredients:

a dozen sponge fingers
2 eggs and an extra yolk (kept from the jelly-making)
a little caster sugar
350 ml milk
some ratafia (coconut) biscuits, crumbled
glace cherries and angelica, chopped
20 g gelatine
lemon essence
150 ml cream

Pour half the liquid jelly into a soufflé dish or mould. Let it set. Chill the balance. Line the mould sides with the sponge fingers, trimming them so they fit well. Beat the eggs and sugar in the bowl and stir in the milk brought almost to boiling point. Cook this custard mixture in a double boiler to thicken, then remove from the heat and beat in the ratafia crumbs and the cherries and angelica. Soften the gelatine in a little water, then stir into the custard and bring back to warm in the boiler until the gelatine is well combined. Flavour with a few drops of the essence. Whip the cream and fold into this mixture when cooled a little, then pour over the jelly and sponge in the mould. Leave to set in a cool place. When ready to serve, chop the reserved jelly, and turn out the pudding onto it as a bed.

As you will note, many Victorian dishes presumed a kitchen staff with the time and energy to go through what is a fairly complicated process to get a result. This may explain why desserts such as this are no longer commonplace.

although one or two 'suitable' people thought it a great nonsense and declined to come. She also thought the supper and wine insufficient and bad, and served in unsuitable circumstances; there was, she inferred, a lack of proper ballrooms in the better class of residence (these tended to appear later in the century).

The guests and premises of society and official dinners were, perhaps, easier to control. Early instances of the genre are notable for their astonishing plenitude rather than their elegance. A dinner given for Governor George Grey and nearly 200 of the more prominent settlers in the Hutt Valley in July 1851 featured a bill of fare which included three rounds of beef, six large pieces of pressed beef, six boiled legs of mutton, two saddles of mutton, four hams, four tongues, five geese, 12 ducks, three turkeys, three sucking pigs, four chickens, 12 fowls, three pigeon pies, six beef steak pies, six apple tarts, four raspberry tarts, 18 plum puddings, a cake, six dishes of custard, 18 dishes of assorted fruits, four and a half dozen loaves of bread and two cheeses. The diners washed this down with 51 gallons of ale, 36 dozen bottles of ginger beer, three and three-quarter dozen bottles of sherry, 18 of port, and two gallons of brandy.[47] Such a menu owes more perhaps to the bucolic gourmandising culture of late Georgian England than to the reign of Victoria.

But by the time Grey returned for his second governorship in the 1860s, a much more genteel tradition of upper-class dining had become established. When the Mayor and council of Dunedin entertained him to a 'complimentary dejeuner' at the Otago Hotel, they were able to offer him a choice of galantines of veal, a turkey in aspic, boar's head, and a raised pigeon pie among a total of 16 main courses, and the same for desserts (including apples Chantilly and Charlotte à la Russe), finishing up with a 'mayonaise' of lobster.[48] Similarly, in November 1875 the members of the Wellington Council gave a dinner for their mayor, W. S. Moorhouse. This little repast comprised oysters, 'soups à la Reine' and asparagus, boiled kahawai and 'filets' of trevally, 'entres' of calves head, lamb cutlets and larded sweetbreads, a boiled turkey with oyster sauce and a roast duck Provençale, joints of roast lamb and a York ham, anchovy toast, six desserts (including a Nesselrode and Cabinet puddings, and a Bavarian creme), and a cheese soufflé by way of a savoury to tidy it all away.[49] This was not untypical. The previous year Charles Hartman's colleagues gave a dinner to mark his departure as manager of the New

Zealand Steam Shipping Company. This too commenced with oysters and two soups (one of them mock turtle) and proceeded through a fish course, four entrées including lobster, 10 removes or principal courses, eight desserts and a macaroni cheese.[50] (Serving a 'savoury', usually but not always cheese-based, at the end of a meal was common practice in Victorian times.)

The principal historian of the nineteenth-century South Island landholding gentry remarks that 'these large well-bred households ate prodigiously' and cites a dinner on the Mount Algidus property which featured chicken, pork, turkey, mutton, blue duck and beef. He goes on to quote Lady Barker on the subject of 'ordinary station fare' at a meal with began with a thick mutton broth, moved on to pickled lambs' tongues, and finished with a Devonshire junket and cream.[51]

But somehow the two traditions, those of the fake genteel and of democratic abundance, seem to have been unable to avoid collapsing in on one another. Possibly the classic instance of this was the banquet organised by that inveterate social climber Walter Buller to welcome home Colonial Treasurer Joseph Ward in 1895. This feast was so extreme in its sumptuousness that William Pember Reeves, casting an ironic eye over the menu, was said to have remarked that it should perhaps be renamed 'the Buller gorge'.[52] It is a pity the menu for this dinner seems not to have survived, although one given by the Lyttelton Harbour Board in January 1883 to mark the opening of a new dock has. Grandly displayed in crimson and gilt on white card, this features seven courses of 33 dishes, and a choice of 25 wines and liqueurs, including several vintage clarets and a choice of three champagnes.[53] Clearly, local government was the place to be.

'ONE OF THE MOST PREPOSTEROUS FARCES EVER PERPETRATED'

It is easy enough to laugh at and dismiss the pretensions of a Walter Buller, always desperate for the company of what he perceived to be the 'best' people and hoping that he might be mistaken for one of them. But not many years after his notable celebration for Ward, the tradition of lavish egalitarian hospitality found itself confronted by a much more formidable foe in the form of social and political conservatism masquerading as science.

For some time there had been an agitation to have the skills of cooking included in the technical school curriculum. This eventually happened in 1908, when Wanganui Girls' College decided to introduce a course in domestic economy, or housewifery as the principal insisted on calling it. With the vigorous encouragement of George Hogben, the Director of Education, this example was quickly followed elsewhere.[54] This was appropriate as far as it went, but there were others who were determined that it was going to go much further.

In 1906 John Studholme, a wealthy Canterbury landowner, had approached the University of New Zealand and offered to endow a school of home science at what was then Canterbury College of the university.[55] His motives were curious, to say the least. Impelled by his experience as a young man working in the charitable settlements based on Toynbee Hall in the east end of London, and horrified by what he perceived to be a regrettable conflict between capital and labour in New Zealand over their share in the profits of industry, he suggested that these conflicts could be resolved if working-class housewives were taught that food could be supplied cheaply and nutritiously, thereby making money go further and avoiding demands for higher wages. What was needed, he thought, was a university school to lead the way, creating a cadre of trained professional women who could proselytise his message throughout the community. As is often the case, because Studholme was wealthy, and was prepared to put up the money, and because his views suited those looking for a way around worker insistence on a better sharing of the fruits of their endeavours, this notion was taken more seriously than it deserved. The matter went as far as steps being taken to engage a professor, before Canterbury College decided enough was enough and the idea lapsed.

Sorry to say it was taken up again two years later by two Dunedin medical luminaries, Drs F. C. Batchelor and Truby King. Their motives were, if anything, even more reactionary than those of Studholme. Both were bitterly opposed to the higher education of women, the latter describing it as 'one of the most preposterous farces ever perpetrated'. Once women had reached puberty, the two good doctors thought, they should concern themselves with efficient domestic management and the raising of healthy children, not with frippery attempts at an education suited only to men. They therefore supported Studholme's proposal as a suitable activity for women who, if they insisted on proceeding to higher education, should direct themselves to something useful, and they encouraged Studholme to redirect his offer of endowment to the university college in Otago.

There it received a warmer welcome, and the school was established in 1909, although not without some opposition from the university senate which expressed scepticism about the appropriateness of this subject to a university. Their doubts are easy enough to appreciate. The proposed curriculum leading to both a diploma and a degree in its own right emphasised chemistry (but in its particular application to food, theories of cooking, laundry work and housewifery), the management of household affairs, practical cooking, needlework and dressmaking, household pests and how to deal with them, and hygiene. Students also studied biology because, as an early historian of the university expressed it, this enabled women 'to understand some of the problems in heredity in natural selection so essential to the well-being of the race'.[56] This last was a response to the views of Truby King, whose notions concerning the need to preserve the purity of what is now seen to be a non-existent 'British race' were well known and widely accepted at the time.

In due course the school rose above the philosophical limitations of its curriculum and gave rise to the Otago University home-science degree, which became a proper qualification in its own right rather than a second-class training in suitable skills for women. But its early history indicates that alongside the tradition of good eating and hospitality for all which had impelled the developing New Zealand cuisine, there developed a joyless other, in which food was seen as fuel rather than as one of the more enjoyable and fundamental aspects of human life. That it was able to gain some sort of grip may be attributable to another dimension of the New Zealand character — that unlovely object, the Puritan conscience. But if its application to the hearty enjoyment of food was never other than an irritant, its application to the enjoyment of drink turned out to be dire.

7

THE DEMON DRINK

IN 1830, 10 YEARS PRIOR TO the signing of the Treaty of Waitangi, the English radical reformer, the Rev. Sydney Smith, issued a report on the state of the English nation: 'Everybody is drunk. Those who are not singing are sprawling. The sovereign people are in a beastly state.'[1] His point of reference was the Beer Act (a reform he had supported and regretted) which deregulated the sale of beer with the intention of discouraging the excessive consumption of other alcoholic drinks, and in particular the widespread tippling of gin which had developed in England in the eighteenth century.

Distilling was not itself new. It had been known for centuries, and French brandy was widely imported (and smuggled) into Britain, but the process had been used as much to produce medicines and other tonic substances as intoxicating drinks. However, in the seventeenth century the Dutch, perhaps because they felt they had enough water to be going along with, began to flavour their distilled drinks with juniper and orange, initially as a health measure. This Dutch habit of taking tonic gin or genevers became fashionable in England, for obvious reasons, during the reign of William III. From the aristocracy it spread to all classes, especially when its distillation was deregulated and the excise on it greatly reduced. By the time of Hogarth's famous Gin Lane prints, it had become so abused that the reform later regretted by Smith was thought desirable to try to wean the English away from it. Alas, that was no cure because it was addressing the wrong problem. England had initially coped with the social breakdown occasioned by the industrial revolution by drowning the sorrows of its workers in a sea of gin. Freeing up the sale of beer simply substituted one remedy for distress for another. In fact, the Beer Act led,

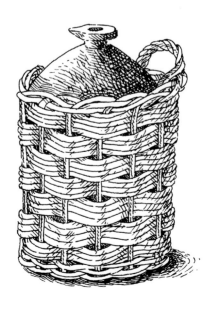

by one calculation, to the establishment of well over 100,000 unregulated beer shops.[2] All the reformers had succeeded in doing was replacing one form of tippling with a cheaper substitute.

By 1853 the situation had become bad enough for an official enquiry to be launched. This heard evidence that many beer shops were centres of crime and vice. They opened early in the morning for the sake of poachers, and their customers, especially but not exclusively in rural areas, were largely thieves, receivers and prostitutes.[3] Nevertheless, when it was suggested in 1856 that something should be done about this, and that closing on Sundays would be a good place to begin, the London mob rioted, and pelted wealthy churchgoers with stones and mud for several Sundays. This is understandable. The rich could always drink at home, and this was not an option available to the poor.

In fact the response to the suggestion that there should be some sort of regulation imposed on drinking was so violent that there were no further attempts at regulation for a generation, and the only limits on consumption, even by small children, were the depth of the drinker's purse or their falling down insensible. Drunk for a penny, dead drunk for tuppence, straw free was the cry. The English trade in alcoholic drinks was not regulated until 1871 when midnight closing hours were imposed and a minimum drinking age of 16 introduced. At the same time steps were taken to make the adulteration of beer — commonly spiked with logwood, tobacco, strychnine, various salts of aluminium, zinc and lead, iron filings and even fish entrails to give it a good head — subject to a fine. This was not before time. The chemist John Mitchell had analysed 200 samples of beer in 1855 and had found not a single one to be pure.[4] Some brewers even went so far as to adulterate the beer with that most dangerous of all nineteenth-century substances — water.

The state of the water was one of the reasons for the popularity of alcoholic drinks. No one in industrial England drank the water if they could help it. It was filthy beyond belief. In 1827 an anonymous pamphleteer wrote of London's water:

> The water taken up from the river Thames between Chelsea Hospital and London Bridge for the use of the inhabitants of the Metropolis, being charged with the contents of more than 130 common sewers, the drainings from the dunghills and lay-stalls, the refuse of hospitals, slaughter houses, colour, lead, gas and soap works, drug mills and manufactures, and with

Apricot Tart

The Rev. Sydney Smith (1771–1845) was not only a social reformer but also a noted gourmet with a particular penchant for apricot tart, according to Jane Grigson, who includes this recipe in her *Food with the Famous*.

125 g butter
175 g caster sugar
800 g apricots, halved
puff pastry
2 tbsp sliced almonds

Melt the butter and stir in the sugar, then mix in the apricot halves, turning them over and over until they are well coated. Line a 25 cm baking tin with puff pastry, arrange the apricots in this with the juice from the pan and sprinkle on the almonds. Bake at 220°C for about 30 minutes but don't let it brown too quickly. Serve cold or warm with cream.

Sydney Smith once said of a friend that his idea of heaven was eating pâté de foie gras to the sound of trumpets, and that fine religious feeling could best be evinced by sending strawberries to a clergyman.

all sorts of animal and vegetable substances, rendering the said water offensive and destructive to health, ought no longer to be taken up [by the companies which had the monopoly of supply] from so foul a source.[5]

In the circumstances this was a relatively mild conclusion. London was an extreme case, but not much, and even the water in the wells of rural Britain was liable to be unsafe. It should be recollected that the premature death of Prince Albert was from a water-borne disease, probably typhus or cholera, and he would not by any means have drunk the worst water in England. At least the process of brewing was an attempt, however feeble, to clean it, and the alcohol went some way to sterilising it.

This may help to explain why, when the new beer control legislation came into force in the 1870s, there was widespread outrage and further rioting. It probably also contributed to the fall of the Gladstone government. But this public fury was not entirely driven by the need to leave the water to those fish which could survive in it. Care for sobriety was not widespread in nineteenth-century Britain, and this was an attitude which came to the antipodes with the European colonists.

Interestingly, the preferred tipple in New South Wales and New Zealand, given our subsequent reputation as beer drinkers, was initially not beer but rum. This drink had long been produced in the West Indies. A mid seventeenth-century account of Barbados remarks: 'The chief fuddling they make in the island is rumbullion, alias kill devil, and this is made of sugar cones distilled, a hot, hellish and terrible liquor.'[6] For many years it was known only as a local drink, but by the end of the eighteenth century and the early nineteenth it had spread widely in the Pacific region — one of the more peculiar outcomes of the American War of Independence and, eventually, the abolition of the African slave trade.

New England traded with the West Indies, supplying from the ample forests of North America the barrel staves and hoops which were the cargo containers of their day. The West Indies produced mainly sugar, and so the traders brought back large quantities of molasses in return. This was then distilled, and the spirit was shipped to Europe, and to Africa where it was traded for slaves who were also traded with the West Indies.[7] Strictly speaking this was illegal under the terms of the Navigation Acts, but the merchants of New England paid these little heed. Quite a number of those who signed the Declaration of

Independence, notably Samuel Adams and John Hancock, were wealthy rum smugglers. Their fellow smuggler Paul Revere had several for the road before embarking on his famous ride from the home of Isaac Hull, another rebel against the Crown and a well-known distiller.

The British sea blockades of the War of Independence and later of the war of 1812, and ultimately the policing at sea of the British anti-slavery Acts, made the circular trade with Africa and the West Indies too hazardous for other than the boldest of American traders, and they turned instead to the south Pacific, although some were still prepared to take the risks for the high profits involved. It is interesting to note that Salem shipped 860,000 gallons of rum to East Africa between 1832 and 1864.[8] But a new trade with China soon developed, and this encouraged the American clippers down into the south seas in search of sandalwood and seal pelts, two of the commodities the Chinese demanded. It was this alteration in trading patterns which brought the Yankee whalers first to Hawaii and then to Kororareka in the 1830s, but they had also traded regularly between Cape Colony and the convict settlements in New South Wales almost from their establishment.[9]

One of the trade items they had in abundance was rum. They had so much of it, indeed, that they used it as a form of currency at home in the newly independent United States. There, as elsewhere, considerable ingenuity and much imagination was expended in inventing new ways to drink it. Such drinks as 'black strap' (rum mixed with molasses), 'flip' (a mixture of rum, beer and sugar heated with a poker) and a 'yard of flannel' (a mixture of rum, cider, cream, beaten eggs and spice) became the order of the day. Still the good people of New England could not use up their surplus rum, and besides, it was becoming a social problem at home. Early nineteenth-century New England was almost as drunken as Hogarth's England. Finding a market for rum in Australia must have been a godsend to the New England shippers who, like the Irish girl who feared that her beautiful red velvet dress was dragging her down to Satan and who disposed of it by giving it to her sister, exported their social problem elsewhere.[10]

The new convict colony was desperate for supplies of every description, and when in 1793 the trader *Hope* insisted that the 7500 gallons of rum it carried must be purchased at high prices as a precondition of unloading any other cargo, the masters of Sydney bowed to the

Peabody Punch

This recipe for a rum punch is attributed to the Salem merchant Joseph Peabody (1757–1844). It is obviously conducive to a long life. It comes from *Food, Drink and Recipes of Early New England*.

3 bottles of good rum
1 bottle of good port wine
½ bottle of Bordeaux
¼ glass of Grenadine
a small jar of guava jelly
a pot of strong tea
the juice of a dozen oranges, a dozen limes and 2 lemons

These should all be mixed together after dissolving the guava jelly in the hot strained tea. We don't all have a pot of guava jelly to hand, so quince or redcurrant will do instead. Just before serving chilled in a punch bowl, mix in 2 bottles of dry ginger ale.

Hot Milk Punch and Sherry Cobbler

One tablespoon of sugar, two tablespoons of hot water, one wine glass of Cognac brandy, half a wine glass of St Croix rum, fill up with hot milk, and grate a little nutmeg over it for a Hot Milk Punch, recommends *Brett's Colonists' Guide*; alternatively, it recommends a Sherry Cobbler comprising a wine glass of sherry, a tablespoon of sugar and two slices of orange. This should be shaken well with ice and decorated with the fruit of the season.

All in all the *Brett's* editor recommends 16 different extremely potent alcoholic drinks, including a lethal-sounding gin cocktail made of bitters, a wine glass of gin, some curacao, and a lemon peel, served over ice. These he blames on a Mr James Keefe, 'a well known authority on the subject in America'.

inevitable. From that point rum appears to have become central to life in New South Wales.[11] Certainly the first European Australian immigrants took to it with much more than mere enthusiasm. A recent major historian of convict Australia says outright that 'Colonial Sydney was a drunken society from top to bottom. Men and women drank with a desperate, addicted, quarrelsome, singlemindedness.' By 1817, in a population of 20,000, 'nearly all the men and most of the women were addicted to alcohol. In Australia, especially between 1790 and 1820 rum became an obsession.'[12] This may be an exaggeration, but New South Wales certainly seems to have been an outstandingly drunk place in an outstandingly drunk period of European history.

Before long it was also being imported from Bengal, and 'rum' became a generic term for any distilled intoxicant, including arrack (distilled from dates) and *aguardiente*, a fiery spirit produced in Brazil. Rum became central to the economy and culture of New South Wales, and a major element in the currency. The deeply addicted preferred it laced with tobacco juice. Free colonists were ruined by it, being apparently willing to lose their farms and livelihoods to get even small quantities of it. The local authorities captured a monopoly in it and made fortunes from it. And as for the rest, 'the dis-spirited, indolent convicts cannot be excited to exertions without it,' lamented Samuel Marsden, chaplain to the settlement.[13] Others claimed that the problem was the opposite; once they had it they could not be induced to work either. Even Governor Macquarie, sent out to settle the colony down after the so-called 'rum rebellion' of 1807, never completely succeeded in stamping out drunkenness. Most likely rum simply supplied a solace to men and women in despair at being dumped down in this place at the ends of the earth — a place from which most of them knew they would never return, and where they were treated with exemplary and barbarous physical and emotional cruelty.

Whatever the reason for it, the thirst for rum came to New Zealand with the shore sealers and whalers, and others who came to live around the Bay of Islands a little later. Certainly it is a matter of record that when Wellers of Sydney established a whaling station at Otago in 1831 the originating stores included, along with six cases of muskets and over 100 barrels of gunpowder, a pipe of gin and two puncheons of rum.[14] Extant popular songs of the period speak of the regular visits of 'the

Wellerman' bringing 'sugar, tea, and rum' and the payment of wages partly in liquor.[15] Edward Markham, never a one to let a discreditable tale pass, wrote of his visit to the Bay of Islands in 1834 that:

> All the sawyers on the river came down and the cask of spirits was brought on shore. What a scene of drinking and fighting for two days. Eighteen Irish devils not a bit more civilised than the New Zealanders who were holding lighted raupo on the beach that they might fight by the light.[16]

The Maori too, after initially rejecting it as waipiro (stinking water), had acquired a taste for it 'and like now to get drunk if they can'. It is significant that when there was controversy at Waitangi over the translation of the Treaty by Henry Williams in 1840 it was to a long-standing grog seller that the objectors turned.[17] Such men were substantial merchant figures in the early New Zealand Pakeha community.

The habit of drinking as a matter of course, if not to excess, survived both the imposition of British sovereignty and the strictures of the missionaries. The traveller George Chamier remarked that 'in those early days of universal boon companionship and unsophisticated manners all good men and true drank together. It was considered a mean thing to drink alone; it was considered a meaner thing not to drink at all.'[18] Another traveller, David Kennedy, said similarly:

> Mr Black meets Mr White, whom he has not seen for a whole week and the consequence is a couple of 'drinks'. Jones has something particular to say to Robinson about the weather — they step 'across the road'. Smith settles an account with Brown and two 'nips' of brandy are immediately called for. 'Nobblers' act in many cases as the receipt stamps of business.[19]

And Samuel Butler remarked of colonial workers: 'Some good hands are very improvident, and will for the most part spend their money in drinking a very short time after they have earned it. They will come back possibly with a dead horse to work off — that is, a debt at the accommodation house — and will work hard for another year to have another drinking bout at the end of it.'[20]

But he was very careful to make it clear that this was not a problem confined to workers only. 'Whether men are rich or poor,' he went on to say, 'there seems to be far greater tendency towards drink here than at home; and sheep farmers, as soon as they get things pretty straight and can afford to leave off working themselves, are apt to turn drunkards, unless they have a taste for intellectual employments.' We should recollect too the dinner (noted in chapter 6) given for Governor George Grey by the Hutt Valley farmers in 1851, and the astonishing amounts of alcohol consumed on what was presumably an entirely respectable occasion.

The phenomenon we are dealing with here is not just drunkenness. It is, instead, the inseparability of alcohol and both private and public social behaviour which came to this country with the first European settlers, and which has been with us ever since. In a very entertaining account of the celebration of the first anniversary of the settlement of Port Nicholson, Brad Patterson notes the appearance of alcohol at both the socially exclusive and popular celebrations.[21] Of the latter and its sporting contests he remarks: 'Fuelled by the fine fare and libations generously provided by the mercantile sponsors, the corporates of the day, spectators witnessed a number of well contested events.' The day concluded with a 'popular' ball in a store on Te Aro beach, attended by some of the 'better class' of settlers who 'consumed more than their share of the imported Scottish salmon and smoked oysters laid on; as well as making inroads into the brandy and French wines ranged alongside the porter'. Similarly, at their own exclusive entertainment two nights previously, the same group had dined on 'a really elegant cold dinner'[22] and had made heavy inroads into the liquor provided.

Any public event might be marked by a celebration, in which eating and drinking to excess seems inevitably to have played a part. In 1849, Wellington celebrated the Queen's birthday with a race meeting at which, one of the spectators commented ironically, 'many a reeling and reeking wretch among the white civilisers of the savage, fell a victim to the rum-booths'.[23] No public dinner was suffered to pass without its

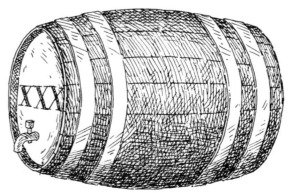

innumerable toasts, and early political events seem to have been notorious for the drunken scenes they occasioned. Of the general elections in the Auckland of the 1850s, William Swainson wrote that 'every election was attended with a fair amount of drunkenness and bribery, falsehood and fraudulent personation'.[24] In 1858 legislation was passed making it illegal to provide meat, drink or entertainment in exchange for votes. This was ineffective and had to be repeated in 1881. In 1876 Captain George Read had his election for the East Coast cancelled following allegations that his agent had gone around the hotels and distributed cards which could be redeemed for liquor after a vote had been cast for Read — a fact publicly ascertainable in the days before the secret ballot when votes were entered in a register which was open for public inspection.[25] The same laws forbade the holding of election meetings in public bars and the playing of bands on election day in support of any candidate; politics in early New Zealand seems to have been a colourful as well as a drunken business.

The statistics suggest that during the first part of the century at least, New Zealand was the same sort of rather drunk place as New South Wales and New England had been a little earlier. One researcher has noted that charges for public drunkenness far outnumbered all others in the nineteenth-century period following the signing of the Treaty. There were more than 15,000 such cases in Auckland courts alone between 1845 and 1870.[26] Even as late as 1890 public order offences, usually fighting or creating a disturbance, and almost invariably associated with alcohol consumption, accounted for 75.2 percent of all convictions for males and 81.6 percent for women, although it should be noted in fairness that overall conviction rates were by then declining.[27]

There was a widespread contemporary tendency to blame bad elements, and especially gold miners for this pattern, but although miners were probably more likely to offend than some others, this reflected the nature of their occupation and community rather than any inherent wickedness. Nevertheless, they were not by any means exempt from the general tendency to tipple to excess. In 1867 alone Hokitika (the main port) saw the import of some 625,000 litres of beer, 586,000 litres of spirits and 214,000 litres of wine. This did not, as the major West Coast goldfields historian has remarked, 'make for sobriety'.[28]

The accommodation houses mentioned by Butler constituted

Stuffed Bullock's Heart

Bullock's heart seems to have been quite a popular item in the nineteenth century. *Brett's Colonists' Guide* gives five recipes for its use: roasted, roiled, stewed, baked whole, and a rather interesting pie in which the heart is diced and combined with an equal quantity of pork, then baked in a crust. Your butcher may regard you oddly when you order this ingredient (as you are bound to have to do), but plough on regardless.

1 ox heart
125 g fresh breadcrumbs
60 g suet
1 tbsp chopped parsley
1 tsp dried marjoram
grated zest of a lemon
an egg yolk
a little grated nutmeg and salt and
   pepper to taste
200 ml red wine

Make a stuffing with the breadcrumbs and the other ingredients, except the wine, and then stuff the heart cavities with this. Preheat an oven to 230°C and bake the heart, covered, for a few minutes, then reduce the heat to 180°C and bake for another 45 minutes or so. Then add the wine and bake a further 10 minutes. Remove and slice, and serve with the cooking juices poured over.

Herb Beer

Beers were made of any ingredients that were to hand in nineteenth-century rural England, including beetroot, nettles, treacle, honey and barley. This one is made of common garden herbs.

a bundle of fresh herbs (including
   parsley, thyme, sage and mint)
25 g hops
8 litres water
900 g sugar
15 g yeast

Boil the herbs, hops and water for about an hour. Strain onto the sugar to dissolve, and when it is cool add the yeast. Let it stand for about 24 hours, then strain again and bottle it. It should be ready in a few days but improves with keeping.

something of a social problem too. It is significant that one of the first pieces of wages protection legislation passed in New Zealand forbade the payment of wages in any hotel bar-room. Often they were little more than drinking dens for the local workers who had nowhere else to go on social occasions or when their day's work was done. Eliza Stack, visiting the Waikato in 1858, recorded:

> We went to bed, but not to sleep. In the first place my bedroom door would not shut, and as it opened upon a passage where stood a row of beer barrels which seemed to possess an irresistible attraction to a number of half-drunken men who were continually tumbling over them and indulging in loud and not always proper remarks, I barricaded my door with chairs as best I could, fearing that at any moment the men might come into the room.[29]

And Lady Barker, intent on keeping the local farm labourers and shepherds out of such places, provided a special annual Christmas meal for them during her years in the Canterbury back country.

It should not, of course, be assumed that every accommodation house was a low bar. Both Anthony Trollope and Sarah Courage (the latter with her husband), travelling in the South Island during the later part of the century, commented favourably on them. At an accommodation house at Kaiapoi, the Courages ate heartily of bullock's heart, colonial goose and a ham, and Sarah admired the ale-quaffing locals ('a more cheery and hearty set of people we never saw.')[30] Nevertheless, that the inevitable consumption of alcohol on festive occasions could have its sordid side is clear from the description by 'Hopeful' of a Christmas spent in a boarding house in Christchurch in the eighties. During Christmas week:

> numbers of 'up-country' young men came flocking in, and servant girls and a few shop girls and that class. We all met at table three times a day, there was plenty of food, such as it was, large joints for dinner, boiled or baked, vegetables and plain puddings or tarts, and at six o'clock the remains of the cold joints were sent in cut in thick slices and were most unappetising . . . On Christmas Eve I saw the novel scene of the ordinary washing jug of the bedroom used to fetch beer in, two or three of these were sent for in the course of the evening . . . As soon as I appeared on Christmas morning, I saw several young men were already boozy and looking excited and standing 'shout' for the girls.[31]

When she returned from church, having declined several invitations to drink, she noted with disgust that some of her fellow boarders were so intoxicated that they could not appear for dinner at two o'clock.

Her mention of beer but not other drinks is interesting. From the 1870s the widespread consumption of rum and other hard liquor appears to have declined and to have been replaced, although not exclusively, by beer. Overall, the consumption of alcohol fell between 1870 and 1890 from 23.6 litres to 11.8 litres a head. By the end of the century this had fallen again to about 8 litres a head.[32] This compares to an astonishing calculation of 45 litres in 1840.[33] But over the same period the consumption of beer rose markedly. This decline in overall alcohol consumption is usually attributed to the vigorous prohibition movement, which was in its heyday between 1880 and the First World War. This undoubtedly had its effect. Equally relevant may have been a general decline in real earnings during the 'long depression', when many workers gave up a luxury they could no longer afford, and the arrival of large numbers of rural labouring immigrants whose preferred drink, when their income allowed (which was not often), had been beer. This, of course, contained a much lower content of alcohol than rum or other spirits.

Possibly the early immigrant working men, freed at last from the constraints of poverty in their new land, seized the opportunity to drink deeper than they had ever had an opportunity to do before, until the novelty wore off and harder times sounded a tocsin of memory in their subconscious. And it may simply have been that habitual drunkenness became socially less acceptable as the century progressed and the community became more law-abiding, and more inclined to worry about what the neighbours might think. John Barr, an 1852 immigrant to New Zealand, for many years composed light and occasional verse which captured the social mores of the time. In one of these, 'Rise Oot Your Bed', a wife rails at her husband for his excessive drinking and declares that she 'never kent a drunken man/ That e'er cam muckle thrift/ . . . It taks it a' I weel I wat/ To gar the twa ends meet.'[34] Those adversely affected were simply unwilling to put up with habitual boozing.

There was also something of a move in New Zealand from the 1870s to emulate the English example and regulate alcohol consumption; in 1873 the first Licensing Act came into force.[35] This allowed some control over local licensing by elected committees, and may have helped put a

Beer Flip

This drink, as well as being thought suitable for winter evenings, was traditionally taken by bell-ringers before a long peal. Eight yolks of egg were beaten with sugar, orange juice and spices. A quart of strong (i.e. dark) beer was then heated in a tankard and poured into the beaten yolks, then poured back again from a height to cause a froth. The beaten whites of the egg were then folded in and the whole drunk while still hot.

Wassail Bowl

This was a drink traditionally taken during the apple wassailing, a curious ceremony during which a shotgun was fired through the branches of the orchard trees to ward off evil spirits. This recipe, which is given by Dorothy Hartley in her *Food in England*, is taken from a manuscript recipe of 1722 attributed to the household of Sir Catkin Wynne.

450 g brown sugar
500 ml hot beer
grating of nutmeg
small piece of preserved ginger, sliced
4 glasses sherry

Mix this well and allow to cool. Add 3 litres of cold beer and spread a little yeast on a slice of toast, sink this in the beer, and let it stand for a few hours. It should then be strained and kept bottled for a few days before being served in a punch bowl with hot roasted apples floating in it.

Hop Beer

Adela Stewart doesn't give her recipe for hop beer. This is from *The Farmhouse Kitchen* by Mary Norwak.

450 g malt extract
25 g hops
4.5 litres water
25 g yeast

Boil the malt, hops and water for about an hour and a half, adding water to top up as you go. Strain through muslin, and when cool add the yeast and leave for three days. Siphon it off and bottle with a lump of sugar in each bottle. Use crown caps (a home-brewing store should be able to help), and used beer bottles. This should be ready in about a week, but it's better for the keeping.

Stewart does give her recipe for peach wine, which calls for 50 kg of peaches and 10 gallons of water left in a tub for a week. Then, after straining, she added 15 kg of sugar. She left this to ferment in a barrel for about two weeks, put in a tight bung and kept it in the cellar for a year or two. It made, she said, 'an excellent sherry like wine'.

Ginger Beer

My father always made ginger beer when I was a child by feeding and drawing off from a plant. This was always rather exciting, because if he used too much yeast the corks might 'blow'. It was always stored in the wash-house just in case.

10 g fresh yeast
2 tsp ground ginger
2 tsp sugar
400 ml water

Mix these ingredients together and leave for 24 hours, then 'feed' daily for 7 days with 1 tsp of ginger and 1 tsp of sugar. Strain, and reserve both the solid and the liquid. If you want to keep going, halve the solid, add the 400 ml of water and start again. Mix the liquid with 3 litres of cold water, the juice of 2 lemons, and 675 g of sugar dissolved in a litre of boiling water. This should be bottled and kept for at least a week before using. My father used to cork it and sometimes tie down the corks with string but that isn't advisable. I prefer to use crown tops on large beer bottles. Take care opening it.

The next four recipes are from my father and grandmother. I've seen similar versions in many books since. The raspberry vinegar, for instance, is very similar to one found in Lydia Child's *The Frugal Housewife* published in Boston in 1832, and almost precisely the same recipe appears in *Tetaka Kai*, published by the Napier Rowing Club in 1906. They are obviously part of a generalised lore.

Lemonade Syrup

juice of 6 lemons
1 kg white sugar
1 tsp lemon essence
2 tsp tartaric or citric acid
1 litre boiling water

Put the lemon juice and the dry ingredients in a bowl, and pour over the boiling water and stir until dissolved. Bottle when cool, dilute with cold water to taste, and serve over ice.

Lemon Barley Water

This was much drunk in the fields during harvest as a refresher.

100 g pearl barley
2 lemons
a little sugar
1 litre boiling water

Rinse the barley and put it in a saucepan with the water, the grated zest and juice of the lemon, and the sugar to taste. Boil for about 5 minutes and strain. Cool and chill to serve.

Raspberry Vinegar

This is a very refreshing summer drink and much pleasanter than its ingredients suggest. Most berry fruits can be used in the same way.

1 kg fresh raspberries
1 litre good-quality white wine vinegar
1 kg white sugar

Crush the raspberries well in a bowl and cover with the vinegar. Seal the bowl top with plastic or muslin, and leave for a week. Strain into a saucepan and add the sugar, and heat slowly until this is dissolved, then boil rapidly and skim. Bottle when cool and serve diluted to taste.

stop to the worst abuses by limiting hours of consumption and the number of outlets. New Zealand from this point seems to have become predominantly a beer-drinking society and, popular tradition notwithstanding, a relatively sober one. In 1897, 486 people were sent to prison for drunkenness, a progressive decline from 1038 a decade previously. New Zealanders drank just under 6 million gallons (about 27 million litres) of beer in the former year, which is not a great deal by present standards — about 100 ml each day. We drink far more today as a matter of course than our ancestors did 100 years ago. Between 1938 and 1968 consumption doubled, and to 1987 it increased a further 21 percent.[36] While we may have deserved our reputation as a hard-drinking nation before 1870, we seem to have sobered up considerably over the next three decades, although the rate of conviction for drunken behaviour stands out by comparison with other societies for which there are figures available.

In England there had long been a tradition of drinking flavoured beers. These usually involved the incorporation of sage or other herbs and spices, and sometimes fruit in ale. In winter these were often drunk hot as a 'purl' or 'mum'. In apple-producing districts, cider was widely produced, and other fruit wines were often home brewed, depending on the locality and the surplus of fruit available. Only the cider tradition seems to have transplanted to New Zealand to any significant extent, although settlers in many remote districts were expected to and did brew their own beer. Adela Stewart recorded in her reminiscences that in 1884 'with so many young men constantly coming and going, we began to see that it was desirable to provide them with something a little stronger than tea, so I started hop beer and kept it up without intermission for twenty two years'.[37] She also recorded using a surplus of peaches to make fruit wine in 1889 and gave her own recipe for this, but such contemporary references are relatively rare.

It should also be noted alongside this that the agricultural immigrants in particular introduced a parallel tradition of the home manufacture of non-alcoholic drinks, usually syrups and vinegars made with fruit and sugar. Nor should we forget that George Grey's settler celebrants in 1851 consumed 36 dozen bottles of ginger beer along with their spirits and ale.

The grape vine also made an early appearance. Marsden had commented in 1819 in his report to the Church Missionary Society that

Three Drinks for Summer from Tetaka Kai

The recipe book published by the Napier Rowing Club in 1906 gives these three summer drinks under a general heading. The first is for a Claret Cup which requires that 2 bottles of claret be mixed with 2 of soda water, 1 of lemonade, a wine glass of maraschino, and a sprig of borage, with as much cold water as suits the taste of the drinkers.

Rather less alcoholic (in fact not alcoholic at all) is a recipe for Fruit Salts which combines 8 oz (225 g) of icing sugar with 4 oz (125 g) each of tartaric acid, cream of tartar, carbonate of soda (possibly the anonymous author means bicarbonate of soda), and Epsom salts, with 1 oz (25 g) of magnesia. This was to be thoroughly combined and kept well corked and dry in a glass bottle, to be used as one teaspoon in a glass of water.

But surely the most curious of the three drinks is Chilli Beer, contributed by a Mrs C.L. Margoliouth of Wai Tiro. To make this oddity, boil 23 chillis (why precisely 23?) in 4 gallons (18 litres) of water for 20 minutes. This is then strained onto 2½lb (about 1 kg) of sugar and 2 oz (50 g) of cream of tartar. Eight quarts (19 litres) of cold water, 2 tsp of essence of lemon, and 3 tbsp of brewer's yeast are then added, and the resulting liquid is bottled and capped. After 5 days it is ready to drink. I confess to not having tried this last, so anyone who does is on their own.

he thought grapes would do well in New Zealand.[38] Their first use for the production of wine is usually attributed to James Busby in 1838, and grape vines were freely available for transplanting through nurserymen in Nelson as early as 1850. Many of the plantings were, of course, for the fruit alone, but some were for wine. Nor did European settlers wait for their own land to produce. Wines as an accompaniment to food were imported from the outset. By 1897 New Zealanders were drinking about 500,000 litres of wine annually, the great bulk of it imported, although some local vineyards produced wine of a sufficient standard to win prizes in Philadelphia in 1876 and Sydney in 1880. As this level of consumption and as the 214,000 litres landed at Hokitika in 1867 appears to show, not all of the hoi polloi were drinking beer, but wine was largely the tipple of the 'gentry', a pattern reinforced by a curious prohibition preventing wine from being sold in quantities of less than two gallons (9 litres), which would have put its purchase beyond the pockets of most working people. Committees of parliament recommended the development of a local wine industry in both 1880 and 1895, but despite such official encouragement the full development of the New Zealand wine industry had to wait another century.

Most of the wine consumed in this country in the last century was in the form of port and sherry imported from Europe, but other wines were certainly available. The extraordinary variety of wines offered at the official banquet to mark the opening of the new Lyttelton dock in 1883 has already been referred to. They included a white burgundy, two white Bordeaux, five hocks, four chateau bottled clarets (three of those specific vintages) and three French champagnes. And by the end of the century about half of the imports into New Zealand were coming from Australia in the form of light table or fortified dessert wine.

The other great mainstay of thirsty colonial New Zealand was tea. Common belief may have it that alcohol fuelled the early development of New Zealand, but tea is also well in the running for this title. A schedule of major goods imported into the country from Australia in 1830 already contains tea,[39] and it has been noted that it formed, along with rum and sugar, one of the items of payment in truck for sealing and whaling gangs.[40] By 1870 New Zealand's tea imports were worth £128,046 a year. For comparison this was about three times the value of the agricultural machinery imported the same year.

Looked at dispassionately, tea, an infusion of the leaves of a plant, is an odd thing for anyone to consume.[41] It seems first to have reached England in small quantities from China through the East India Company in 1664, and was sold as a luxury and curiosity. Its high price confined its use to the wealthy, particularly after it became subject to an excise duty of 2s a gallon from 1670.[42] But its use began to be more and more widespread as it became progressively cheaper, until by the beginning of the nineteenth century it had become a necessity with all classes. One writer has claimed that the amounts of tea drunk by labourers and their families was 'astounding'.[43] It was sufficiently widely smuggled to make the excise on it meaningless and it had been abolished at the end of the eighteenth century. Parson James Woodforde, source of much culinary information in this period, confided to his diary in 1777: 'Andrews the Smuggler brought me this night about 11 o'clock a bag of Hyson tea 6 pound weight. He frightened us a little by whistling under the parlour window just as we were going to bed.'[44] No doubt the appeal of tea lay not only in its warming and stimulating properties but also in the fact that boiling water was needed to make it. This meant it was much safer to drink than water direct from the pump.

Descriptive household budgets for working-class homes produced by English social reformers during the nineteenth century rarely included beer but they almost always included tea. In 1863, for example, even the poorest families were consuming about two ounces of tea per family per week.[45] Interestingly, the development of tea drinking among workers and their families was a bone of political contention. Radicals speaking on behalf of working people deplored the decline in beer drinking and its replacement by tea drinking. William Cobbett in particular was savage in his condemnation of the decline of home brewing, a once widespread practice which was hurried to its demise by a precipitate leap in the malt tax from 10s a quarter in 1791 to nearly 40s 12 years later. A labourer, he thought, speaking as an employer himself, 'well lined with meat and beer is worth two or three creatures swelled out with warm water under the name of tea'.[46] There were several squabbles on the subject in parliament, where one of tea's advocates, Robert Peel, defended it as the national beverage and a 'moral refreshment'. Cobbett poured scorn on this categorisation, and described tea and temperance advocates as 'despicable drivelling quacks'.

Later in the century, further point was added to this criticism when it became apparent that tea was widely adulterated. In 1855 a House of Commons committee had taken widespread samples of tea leaves on general sale and found not only that used tea was dried and resold, but also that it was commonly contaminated with Prussian blue, turmeric, lime sulphate, iron filings and graphite, to name only the commonest additives. Some substances sold as tea contained no tea whatsoever, being made of common hedgerow leaves treated to resemble tea.[47]

Some of these practices seem to have come to New Zealand with the early immigrants. There were regular complaints that the tea was full of dust and that the packers were including what were known as 'sweepings' — the spilled leaves swept up from the floor of the packing shed and put back in the filling hopper. In 1882 a Tea Examination Act was passed. This made the selling of pure tea a legal requirement, and by the end of the century tea purchased in New Zealand could usually be relied upon to be what it said it was.

Lady Barker was loud in her praises of the drinking of tea as an alternative to beer, and described its consumption during a rural picnic among working men:

> Over another fire a little way to leeward, hung the bushmen's kettle on an iron tripod, and so, as soon as it boiled my little teapot was filled before Domville threw in his great fistful of tea. I had brought a tiny phial of cream in the pocket of my saddle, but the men thought it spoiled the flavour of the tea, which they always drink '*neat*' as they call it. The Temperance Society could draw many interesting statistics from the amount of hard work which is done in New Zealand on tea . . . and at the end of a year or two of tea and water-drinking, their bright eyes and splendid physical condition showed plainly enough which was the best kind of beverage to work, and work hard too, upon.[48]

This was undoubtedly an exaggeration; these men were in good fettle because they ate better than they had in England — a point which they politely pressed upon their hostess, but which she seems to have misunderstood. Her great fear was that they were giving up the habit of tea drinking for beer. Instead, it was spirits, not tea, that those who drank were giving up for beer.

There had been a brief flurry in the 1880s when the liquor interest had tried to argue that tea was itself a dangerous stimulant and that using it excessively was bad for the drinker's health. Beer, it was claimed, built up the blood and contributed to strength and energy, whereas tea thinned the blood and weakened the body. This ridiculous view was even endorsed by Richard Seddon, who claimed in 1882 that the temperance movement was urging the drinking of a substance more poisonous than beer if taken to excess.[49] But Seddon was well known for his animosity towards prohibitionists, and in particular towards their leader Robert Stout, so it is hard to say whether he really believed this or was posturing. No one else of any note seems to have given this view much credence, and it died a natural death as a result.

In the event, not even the association of tea with prohibition could dent its popularity, and it continued to be drunk everywhere through the nineteenth century both as a social and hospitality custom and as an accompaniment to food. Those travelling in the bush marked the end of their day by 'boiling the billy'. Those who called unexpectedly were invariably offered a cup of tea along with any available food. Drinking cold tea from a bottle as a refresher during heavy physical work was commonplace among working men until well into the twentieth century, particularly among those working in dusty conditions such as mines. In the light of this popularity, it is perhaps surprising that despite the suitability of some parts of the country (especially the west coast of the South Island) for growing tea, New Zealand has never developed its own tea industry. This was probably because no one could match the low cost of the imported product, particularly after the reduction of the duty payable in 1882 and again in 1900.[50]

Coffee, although drunk in New Zealand in the nineteenth century, usually in a form mixed with chicory — not then regarded as an adulterant but as a flavour enhancer — never enjoyed the popularity it did in the United States. It was certainly more expensive and more highly taxed than tea and this may partly account for its use only by a small minority. But even after 1900, when the duty was removed from raw beans, this made little difference. Tea, beer and wine were the typical hospitality drinks of New Zealand during most of the period of the development of our nineteenth-century cuisine.

Bavaroise au Café

The Victorians used coffee as a flavouring as well as a drink. Claudia Roden gives this very nineteenth-century recipe in her 1977 book, *Coffee*.

500 ml milk
5 heaped tbsp ground pale coffee
5 egg yolks
120 g caster sugar
1 sachet gelatine
250 ml cream
3 tbsp cognac

Bring the milk to the boil, infuse the coffee in it for about 20 minutes, and strain. Whisk the eggs and sugar in a bowl, and then slowly beat in the eggs. Transfer to a double boiler and allow to thicken to a custard. Remove from the heat and stir in the gelatine dissolved in a little hot water. Leave to cool while you beat the cream until stiff, and then fold this into the custard with the cognac. Mould and allow to set before serving.

This can be served with a chocolate sauce made by dissolving together over low heat 120 g of bitter chocolate, 250 ml of cream and a jigger or two of dark rum.

CONCLUSION:
OUR CHANGING DINNER

THE WORLD OF FOOD described in the previous pages is rapidly disappearing. To those born after 1970 it is increasingly as remote as the nineteenth century which gave rise to it. But this does not mean it is no longer relevant. On the contrary, those who live in any culture must be aware of where they have come from if they are to make sense of what is happening to them now.

The food tradition our forebears brought to New Zealand had been hallowed by literally millennia of responses to an annual cycle in a particular place in which food was not only of prime significance but also central to survival. It is hardly surprising, therefore, that the tradition that situation created lay at the heart of European and, more particularly in our case, English and Scottish life. It is similarly unsurprising that it travelled with our immigrant forebears to their new land. But the very act of emigration began a process which, ultimately, led to the disintegration of that tradition. The reasons for this have been teased out the preceding chapters. The reversal of the seasons, and an agriculture of fertile abundance based on readily available land, rendered the agricultural survival strategies developed over centuries (and which, because of their importance, had been erected into a coherent culture) first redundant, then irrelevant, and finally meaningless.

This process, however, was paralleled by another. No person or group can live without a culture and those who are denied it, for whatever reason, will re-invent it in another form. That is what happens in all immigrant societies — a process both inevitable and fascinating to untangle and often unexpected in its results. In our case, the newcomers took the abundance they found was now possible, and married it to the traditions they had brought with them. This produced a food culture based on their aspiration to rise in the world, and on what they knew of the food habits of those whose status they were pursuing. Within a very short time they had invented a culture based on a wide choice of meats, fruits and vegetables, and characterised by plenty and hospitality. That it ignored the available pre-European food culture (also unique and well adapted to its environment) was their loss, as was their determination, though they lived in a sea-girt environment with bounteous fish available, to eat fish, if at all, only as a secondary supplement to a thoroughly carnivorous diet. Deploring or sneering at these cultural innovations, as some subsequent food writers have done, is to miss the point. The point is, rather, to know what and why.

It is the second of these — the whys — which allows us to understand the changes which have happened in our food tradition over the last three decades, and more specifically why the tradition brought and created here has all but vanished in less than two generations. That all things change is one of the world's few continuities. But why so sudden and so complete? As always, the basis of change can be found in the origins and nature of the thing which has been changed.

The forces which drove our ancestors to emigrate are also the forces which have changed what they created. It is just that these events are separated by more than a century. Technology and the internationalisation of the food market which were important components in the genesis of our food tradition are also the things which are destroying it.

A food tradition based on seasonal dearth becomes doubly meaningless in a world in which not only the seasons are reversed and plenty available, but also in which whatever is wanted can be had by simply bringing it from somewhere else, and in quantities which ensure that it remains as freely available as if it had been produced locally in its season. However absurd it may be to import apples from California and pork from Canada when we produce both of these items in quantity ourselves and have plenty of other commodities to eat when these are seasonally unavailable, this is the way we live now. The question, as it was for our predecessors, becomes: what should we make of the opportunities this affords us?

We do not make the best of them. If they were asked at random to characterise the changes in our eating habits over the last two or three decades, most New Zealanders would be either puzzled by the question — because they would not recognise the incremental changes which have occurred as adding up to much — or they would speak of the mushroom growth of restaurants and cafés, the habit of dining out and the widespread variety of cuisine now available. These are, of course, manifestations of the way we live now, but they are not that way in itself; rather they are the symptoms of that way as they affect what have come to be appropriately known as 'the chattering classes'.

But for most New Zealanders these pleasant and regularly available experiences are *terra incognita*. Most do not eat out regularly at fashionable cafés; and do not sample the delights of properly and lovingly prepared Venetian or Catalan or Provençal traditional food. Even the new amalgams of European high cuisine and the Asian tradition so much discussed among fashionable food consumers are unknown to most. The fact is that when the majority of New Zealanders dine out, they eat at a fast-food outlet, where what they swallow has been carefully designed to appeal crudely to certain tastes in artificially created ways, bears no relationship to either a food tradition of any sort or to the principles of nutrition, and in ingredients and quantity is designed primarily to be profitable to its franchise holder. Conversely, when they eat in, what they eat has been so highly processed that it too bears little or no relationship to any dish historically known, nor does its preparation bear a resemblance to the techniques of food preparation hallowed by time and the mastery of which can be so satisfying an experience as to have the right, as with any other mode of cultural expression, to be named imaginative and creative.

None of that is to say that people should stop doing these things. The damage wrought to the enjoyment of food by the likes of Truby King, who tried to force people to consume only what is wholesome and good for them, are much worse than taking pleasure in what has come to be dismissively described as junk food. A well-made hamburger with fries and a thickshake can be an enjoyable experience once in a while. That much is known to any child; children, who know what they like to eat and are without pretension in such matters, are often excellent deflators of that tedious band, the International Society of Food Snobs. None of this is to say that those who purvey highly processed and chemically treated food are the sorts of people one would wish to take home to meet one's mother. On the contrary.[1] But we should be much less concerned to read the hoi polloi a lesson in what is good for them than be aware of what people might have as better alternatives.

Eating food is one of the few human activities which we all do every day if we can. This happens from the moment we are born to the day we die. It is important to us, and what happens to the options we have in that regard, once we get beyond the questions of basic hunger and thirst, should be of the utmost importance to us. Progressively, and the café culture notwithstanding, those options are narrowing not expanding. Just as the internationalisation of the food production and distribution industries has been a major factor in undermining and eventually destroying the British immigrant cuisine of New Zealand, so it is forming and structuring its replacement. This is happening in ways which are not always for the best in the best of all possible worlds.

That the way we produce and sell what we eat internationally can have dire consequences is well known. There is a whole school of historical economic thought, for instance, which traces the origins of the First World War to imbalances in the international food production and distribution systems of the late nineteenth century. One of these historians declares bluntly:

> The distant causes of Germany's collapse in 1918 may be found in the new frontiers of farming which opened up in the last third of the nineteenth century. In the 1870s the United States emerged as a great food power. Its grainfields and stockyards threatened to overwhelm European rural economies.[2]

European countries, self-sufficient in food for centuries, ceased to be so in a very few years and became mass net importers of food. In a very real sense the First World War subsequently became a race to see who could starve whose civilian population first, and this determined the outcome. Other historical writers have found the origins of the international depression of the 1930s in the trade gaps created by over-supplies of food in relation to the capacity of the European net food importers to purchase at levels which allowed the supplying economies to function. We should not be surprised to discover that this phenomenon did not disappear with the prosperity of the 1950s and 1960s. On the contrary, the seeds of the problems which now imperil our food are inherent in that prosperity itself, and in the means which were developed to create it.

More specifically, the changes wrought in our eating habits have been to do with the relationship between the Codex Alimentarius, the

General Agreement on Tariffs and Trade (GATT), the incorporation of agricultural products in this, and the role played by the World Trade Organisation in ensuring that barriers to international commodity trading in such areas are minimised or dispensed with. But before focusing on the outcomes which this configuration has created, it is probably helpful to explain where these bodies stand in relation to food and to one another.

The Codex Alimentarius (or Codex as it is usually called) was set up in 1963 as an international intergovernmental body under the auspices of the World Health Organisation and the Food and Agriculture Organisation (both United Nations bodies). It has over 100 members, and its brief is to establish food standards in respect of pesticide residues, additives and labelling. It meets usually only every two years. Between times its work is carried out in a multiplicity of committees, the outcomes of which Codex then ratifies. On the face of it, this looks like an innocuous international body doing a necessary job without unnecessary fanfare. And at one level that is exactly what it is.

But it is also important to be aware that although it is theoretically a government body, it has always invited participation from those who have an interest in the matter of food standards. By and large, those which have taken up this opportunity have been large transnational corporations in the agribusiness and agrichemical fields. Over 140 of these regularly attend Codex committees, deploying over 600 representatives. By comparison, public-interest bodies field a meagre 26. Transnational corporations account for 41 percent of the participants in Codex committees. Most of the governments represented on these committees are from the wealthy industrial OECD. The Codex is, practically speaking, a rich industrial nations' club dominated by the international food and chemical business.[3]

This should be a matter for some concern, but there always used to be a safeguard because the standards the Codex set were guidelines. Ultimately, the responsibility for setting food standards rested with the national sovereign states of the world. This is no longer the case. Since the most recent round of the GATT, which brought both agricultural and pastoral products within its net for the first time and which created the World Trade Organisation, the standards set by the Codex have served a new purpose. They are now the standards used to determine the right of access by importers to the domestic markets of specific countries. This means that whereas previously a national government could for its own reasons set standards higher than those imposed by the Codex, those governments which choose to do so can now be prosecuted by the World Trade Organisation.

This situation is exacerbated in New Zealand by the peculiar way we have chosen to set our food standards. In 1995 New Zealand signed an agreement with Australia which effectively established a joint system for common food standard development. This was to ensure the growth of a free market in foodstuffs between the two countries. These arrangements are enshrined in a 1996 amendment to the 1981 New Zealand Food Act. This is not an equal agreement. Effectively New Zealand has the status within it of an Australian state, and it is Australia which sets the standards for both countries. The Australian New Zealand Food Standards Authority (ANZFA), like its international counterpart, the Codex, is in practice dominated by the representatives of international agribusiness and those who command the chemical industry, particularly in the field of food additives and pesticides.

A process which began in the middle of the nineteenth century as a means of feeding the workers in the industrial cities of Europe by the application of industrial techniques to food production and transportation in other parts of the world has come to dominate the world food industry in ways which ensure that we no longer have much say over what we will eat. It is one of the ironies of history that the New Zealand economy, created in the interests of a pilgrim dream to serve the social ambitions of Britain's surplus population, is now in thrall to a production and marketing system which imposes its own rules on what New Zealanders may eat. The irony lies in the motivation of those who fled Victorian Britain in the first place; they were seeking a new land where they might eat what they liked and this has been turned on its head.

A sudden chasm separates the food tradition described in this book from what now passes for our culture in food. But culture has meaning only when it is clearly related to the experience of the people to whom it belongs, and they have command of the process of determining those meanings. Any other approach alienates and commodifies the lives of those who are constrained by it. Something unique and of ourselves has been abandoned. We can only hope to restore our culture in this, as in many other fields, if we know where we have been. It is to be hoped that this narrative has been a contribution to that process of discovery.

REFERENCES

Abbreviations
AJHR *Appendices to the Journals of the House of Representatives*
ATL   Alexander Turnbull Library
NZJH *New Zealand Journal of History*

INTRODUCTION

1. For a thoroughly entertaining account of this period in English food history, see Christopher Driver, *The English at Table* 1940–1980 (London 1983).
2. Now published by *Which?*, the principal British consumer rights organisation, and running to nearly 600 pages of information not only on restaurants of Britain and Ireland and the more readily accessible of those of Northern France and the Low Countries, but also on wine, and including specialist essays on aspects of British food and eating.
3. The former by a friend and colleague, Dr. Michael Volkerling, and continuously in print since its first publication in 1974, and the latter a New Zealand institution, one of the most successful New Zealand books of all time, printed in numbers running into millions. It should also be recorded that the iconic 'Sure to Rise' building in Ferry Road, Christchurch, which graces its cover, was demolished in the 1980s on instruction of its owners, the asset-stripping Brierley investments, in an astonishing and inexplicable act of cultural vandalism.
4. The product of Prospect Books, the British publishers who have perhaps done the most in recent years to recover the rich English historical food publishing tradition not only through learned journal articles but also through the publication of facsimile editions of famous past books about food and cooking.
5. David Riesman, *The Lonely Crowd: A Study of the Changing American Character* (Yale 1950), p.143 (1961 edition).
6. The literature on this subject alone is vast, and includes the proceedings of two entire Oxford symposia, *National and Regional Styles of Cooking* (1981) and *Food in Motion* (1983), as well as those of a similar symposium in Melbourne in 1987 (*The Third Symposium of Australian Gastronomy: A Multiculinary Society*). The subject crops up whenever people meet to discuss food.
7. A typical and both readable and scholarly publication of this genre is Jane Carson, *Colonial Virginia Cookery* (Williamsburg 1985).
8. One of the most interesting of these has been the work of a New Zealander. See David Burton, *The Raj at Table* (London 1993).
9. M. Symons, *One Continuous Picnic: A History of Eating in Australia* (Ringwood, Victoria 1984).
10. See, for example, Suzy Benghiat, 'The Migration of Food and Cookery Methods', and Lionel Stone, 'Australia's Food Culture Originated in England', both in *Food in Motion: The Migration of Foodstuffs and Cookery Techniques*, Oxford Symposium 1983, proceedings published by Prospect Books.
11. Much of this scholarship is summarised in 'The Impact on Food of Colonialism and Migration' in S. Mennell, A. Murcott and A. van Otterloo, *The Sociology of Food: Eating, Diet and Culture* (London 1992).
12. J. Goody, *Cooking, Cuisine and Class: A Study in Comparative Sociology* (Cambridge 1982).
13. For an exploration of this theme, see the discussion paper, *Keeping It Out of Your Mouth*, prepared for the Alliance group in the New Zealand Parliament, October 1997.
14. B. Borda, 'Food as a Medium for Preserving Culture' in A. Riddervold and A. Ropeid (eds), *Food Conservation: Ethnological Studies* (London 1988), p.102.

15. The outcome was subsequently published in book form as *The Immigrants: The Great Migration from Britain to New Zealand, 1830–1890* (Auckland 1997).

16. Particularly by Mary Browne, Helen Leach and Nancy Tichborne in *The New Zealand Bread Book* (Wellington 1981; republished Auckland 1996), and *More from the Cook's Garden* (Auckland 1987).

17. David Burton, *Two Hundred Years of New Zealand Food and Cookery* (Wellington 1982).

CHAPTER ONE

1. Athenaeus (c.170–c.230), a Greek of Naucratis in Egypt, put together a work he entitled *The Deipnosophists (The Philosophers at Dinner)*. He has done us all a service. It contains over 2500 quotations from 800 writers of classical antiquity, many of whom are otherwise unknown or who are know but quoted from lost works. This quotation is from line 282 of the Loeb edition (Cambridge 1927).
As for *anthias*, the only enlightenment we get from antiquity is that it was also known as 'beauty fish'. There is a long passage about this in J. Wilkins and S. Hill, in 'The Sources and Sauces of Athenaeus' in *Food in Antiquity* (Exeter 1995), but it doesn't get us any closer to a meaningful identification.

2. C.B. Robinson (ed), *Rural Economy in Yorkshire in 1641, Being the Farming and Account Books of Henry Best* (London 1857), pp.134–35.

3. Quoted by C.A. Wilson in *Food and Drink in England* (London 1973), p.73.

4. K. Thomas, *Religion and the Decline of Magic* (London 1971), pp.618, 649.

5. Hunter Davies, *A Walk Along the Wall* (London 1974), and A.K. Bowman, *Life and Letters on the Roman Frontier* (London 1994).

6. ibid., p.126.

7. Wilson, op. cit., p.67.

8. A. Birley, *Life in Roman Britain* (London 1964), p.108.

9. See Patience Gray, *Honey from a Weed* (London 1986), pp.25–28.

10. For this and much of the material which follows, see J. Gimpel, *The Medieval Machine* (London 1977).

11. ibid., p.52.

12. L. Stouff, *Ravitaillement et alimentation en Provence aux XIVe et Xve siècles* (Paris 1970), p.220.

13. Both of these sumptuous repasts are detailed in M.P. Cosman, *Fabulous Feasts: Medieval Cookery and Ceremony* (New York 1976), pp.20–24.

14. There are many descriptions of it. One of the more recent and thorough is M. Shaida, *The Legendary Cuisine of Persia* (London 1992). It is also comprehensively described in Claudia Roden, *Book of Middle Eastern Food* (London 1968).

15. Published as *To the King's Taste*, L.J. Sass (ed) (New York 1975).

16. Salt is a crucial commodity in any culture, and has long formed the basis of regional trade. The standard work is S.A.M. Adshead, *Salt and Civilisation* (Christchurch 1992). See pp.85–98 for salt in medieval Europe.

17. E. Power (trans.), *The Goodman of Paris* (London 1928), p.250.

18. Wilson, op. cit, p.44.

19. Dame Alice's household accounts make fascinating reading. They have been published as *The Household Book of Dame Alice de Bryene of Acton Hall Suffolk, September 1412–September 1413* (Ipswich 1931).

20. For more on this, see B.K. Wheaton, *Savouring the Past: The French Kitchen and Table from 1300 to 1789* (London 1983), pp.18–26.

21. For a fascinating insight into this world and its food, see *The Merchant of Prato*, an account of the domestic life of Francesco Datini, based on his surviving voluminous correspondence. There are many editions of this work, the most handsome of which is the Folio Society imprint.

22. Quoted unsourced in Wilson, op. cit, p.303.

23. On Evelyn, see Jane Grigson, *Food with the Famous* (London 1979), pp.13–34.

24. *Narrative of Some Things of New Spain and of the Great City of Temestitan* (Boston 1972), p.37.
25. For a compelling account of the fundamental effect of not only the potato but also a range of basic introduced foodstuffs on European culture, see Henry Hobhouse, *Seeds of Change* (London 1985).
26. See L. Bareham, *In Praise of the Potato* (London 1988).
27. Grigson, op. cit., p.394.
28. Wilson, op. cit, p.198.
29. Quoted in Sophie Coe, 'Aztec Cuisine', an article in three parts published in *Petits Propos Culinaires* Nos. 19, 20, 21, 1985. Sahagun's account, entitled *A General History of the Things of New Spain*, was written in both Spanish and the native language Nahuatl, and was published some time in the 1530s. It was not translated into English until 1955.
30. *Memoirs of François Misson* (translated by J. Ozell in 1719), cited by Wilson, op. cit., p89.
31. ibid., p.90.
32. There are many accounts of Jane Austen's life. Most of this material is drawn from M. Black and D. le Fay, *The Jane Austen Cookbook* (London 1995).
33. As Parson Woodforde records in the diary he kept for many years, and where he recorded many of the meals he ate. Cited by Grigson, op. cit., p.45.
34. First referred to, as far as can be ascertained, in F. Massialot, *The Court and Country Cook* (1702).
35. Quoted by Wilson, op. cit., p.202.
36. Piero Camporesi, *Exotic Brew: The Art of Living in the Age of Enlightenment* (London 1994), p.7.
37. Black and le Fay, op. cit., p.31.
38. For a prime example, see Edward Thompson, *Customs in Common* (London 1991).

CHAPTER TWO
1. With apologies to John Burnett for borrowing his title of one of the best standard works on the period: *Plenty and Want: A Social History of Diet in England from 1815* (London 1979).
2. Massimo Montanari, *The Culture of Food* (Oxford 1994).
3. ibid., p.129.
4. For accounts of the effects of this, see G. Rudé, *The Crowd in the French Revolution* (Oxford 1959), and more recently S. Schama, *Citizens* (London 1989), pp.371–73.
5. For the considerable detail available, see C. Petersen, *Bread and the British Economy 1770–1870* (Aldershot 1995), chapter 6.
6. For data on these prices and their fluctuations, see Burnett, op. cit.; Petersen, op. cit.; J.C. Drummond and A. Wilbraham, *The Englishman's Food* (revised edition London 1991).
7. David Fischer, *The Long Wave* (Oxford 1996).
8. For an exploration of the endemic nature of disease in human culture, see H. Zinsser, *Rats, Lice and History* (New York 1971).
9. Brilliantly evoked by Barbara Tuchman in *A Distant Mirror* (London 1979).
10. According to Jane Grigson in *The Vegetable Book* (London 1978), p.393, although she does not give a source.
11. Montanari, op. cit., pp.133–44.
12. The best account of this remains C. Woodham-Smith, *The Great Hunger* (London 1962).
13. F. Braudel, *Capitalism and Material Life 1400–1800* (New York 1973), p.82.
14. See E.P. Thompson, *Whigs and Hunters: The Origin of the Black Act* (New York 1975) and Woodham-Smith, op. cit. This process had been proceeding for centuries but accelerated greatly in the eighteenth century. For the background, see M. Beresford, *The Lost Villages of England* (Gloucester 1954) and, more recently,

Christopher Hill, *Liberty Against the Law* (London 1997).

15. One of the most interesting of these was the Luddite uprising of 1812 which, among other things, contributed a word to the language, and has often been misunderstood as an irrational response to change. It was anything but. See R. Reid, *The Land of Lost Content* (London 1986).

16. Cited by R. Tannahill in *Food in History* (revised edition London 1988), p.285.

17. There are numerous accounts. Burnett, Drummond and Wilbraham, both op. cit., provide excellent overall summaries and bibliographies.

18. See E. Howe (ed), *The London Compositor, Documents Relating to Wages, Working Condition, and Customs of the London Printing Trade* (London 1947).

19. ibid.

20. op. cit., p.289.

21. See, for example, Engels' *The Condition of the Working Class in England in 1844*, widely republished since and still in print, or Cobbett's *Political Register*, a periodical published more or less continuously between 1802 and 1835.

22. Such as a fascinating study in 1841 under the auspices of William Neild, the mayor of Manchester and published in the *Journal of the Statistical Society of London* Vol. IV 1841, p.322.

23. Henry Mayhew's famous *London Labour and the London Poor* Vol. 1 1861, and subsequent volumes, maps working-class diet into the sixth decade of the century. His work is supplemented for the period further into the century by bodies such as the Association for the Advancement of Science, which produced a comprehensive report on British diet in 1881 (cited by Burnett, op. cit., p.130).

24. From *The Family Oracle of Health* Vol.2 (London 1824).

25. Cited by Burnett, op. cit., p.84.

26. Quoted in Paul Johnson (ed), *The Oxford Book of Political Anecdotes* (Oxford 1986), p.123.

27. From his *Modern Housewife* 1849, also cited by Burnett, op. cit., p.91.

28. 'Mrs Beeton and Mrs Dickens' in Cyril Ray (ed), *The New Complete Imbiber* (London 1986), p.36.

29. ibid., p.35.

30. Cited by Richard Douthwaite in *The Growth Illusion* (Dublin 1992), p.261.

31. The detail of this is set out in my book *The Immigrants: The Great Migration from Britain to New Zealand 1830–1890* (Auckland 1997).

32. The considerable controversy over where New Zealand's nineteenth-century immigrants came from will never be resolved because the vital records were destroyed in the 1970s. See D.H. Akenson, *Half the World from Home: Perspectives on the Irish in New Zealand 1860–1950* (Wellington 1990).

33. Paul Hirst and Grahame Thompson, *Globalisation in Question* (Cambridge 1996).

34. Much of this debate is canvassed in A. Offer, *The First World War: An Agrarian Interpretation* (Oxford 1991).

35. There is a large literature on this subject. For the economic background, see F. Crouzot, *The Victorian Economy* (London 1982), pp.147–84. The social consequences are widely canvassed in G.E. Mingay, *The Victorian Countryside* (2 vols, London 1981).

36. The detailed background to this is comprehensively explored in R. Arnold, *The Farthest Promised Land* (Wellington 1981).

37. Writing in the *Political Register*, 2 October 1813.

38. *Rural Rides*, 27 November 1821, cited by Drummond and Wilbraham, op. cit., p.279.

39. Cited by Ian Dyck in *William Cobbett and Rural Popular Culture* (Cambridge 1992), p.156.

40. First published Oxford 1939, and never since out of print.

41. All of these are quoted in Burnett, op. cit. and *passim*.

42. Charles Dickens, *The Pickwick Papers*.

43. Henry Mayhew, *London Labour and the London Poor* (London 1851).

44. See S. Freeman, *Mutton and Oysters: The Victorians and their Food* (London 1989), p.47.

45. Drummond and Wilbraham, op. cit.

46. Op. cit. 1851, p.194.

47. Noted by Tannahill, op. cit., p.326.

48. Passages from the *Notebook of Nathaniel Hawthorne* Vol.1, p.236, cited by Freeman, op. cit.

49. Freeman, op. cit., p.198.

50. Mayhew, op. cit., p.62.

51. Claudia Roden, *The Book of Jewish Food* (London 1997), p.100.

52. John Walton, *Fish and Chips and the British Working Class* (Leicester 1992).

53. For an astonishing account of the nineteenth-century game laws, see E.S. Turner, 'Spring guns set here', in *Roads to Ruin* (London 1950).

CHAPTER THREE

1. These figures from the *Official Handbook* of 1883 and the *Yearbook* for 1908.

2. The detail of this astonishing piece of official vandalism, along with a very interesting examination of the available statistical material and the problems of definition that the words 'British' and 'English' pose, is covered in D.H. Akenson, *Half the World from Home: Perspectives on the Irish in New Zealand 1860–1950* (Wellington 1990), from p.15.

3. These figures also from the *Official Handbook* (1883), pp.112–13.

4. This subject has been very amply explored by Rollo Arnold in *The Farthest Promised Land* (Wellington 1981).

5. Two books by Raewyn Dalziel cover aspects of this period: *The Origins of New Zealand Diplomacy* (Wellington 1975); and *Julius Vogel: Business Politician* (Auckland 1986).

6. See his entry in Jane Grigson, *Food with the Famous* (London 1979), p.13.

7. See John Brewer, *The Pleasures of the Imagination: English Culture in the Eighteenth Century* (London 1997), p.87.

8. ibid., p.621. Simon Schama explores some of the same themes towards the end of his monumental *Landscape and Memory* (London 1996), particularly in the sections dealing with the gardens at Fontainebleau from p.546.

9. This subject is well covered in Helen Leach, *1000 Years of Gardening in New Zealand* (Wellington 1984), from p.73.

10. One of the most interesting detailed explorations of these enclosures is to be found in E.P. Thompson, *Whigs and Hunters* (New York 1975), and more broadly in his classic work *The Making of the English Working Class* (London 1963) and the later *Customs in Common* (London 1991).

11. op. cit., 1980 edition, p.79.

12. There are many references to this. See, for example, H. Newby, *Country Life: A Social History of Rural England* (London 1987), pp.33, and Thompson, op. cit. 1991, *passim*.

13. D.H. Morgan, *Harvesters and Harvesting 1840–1900* (London 1982), p.61.

14. ibid., pp.169–73.

15. G.E. Mingay (ed), *The Victorian Countryside* Vol.2 (London 1981), p.607.

16. ibid., p.610.

17. M. Norvak, *The Farmhouse Kitchen* (London 1979), p.33.

18. This and similar horrors are to be found in T. Coleman, *Passage to America* (London 1992), chapter 7.

19. Quoted by D. Charlwood in *The Long Farewell* (Sydney 1981), p.172.

20. ibid., p.173.

21. ibid., p.174.

22. Cited in A. Hassam, *Sailing to Australia: Shipboard Diaries by Nineteenth Century British Immigrants* (Manchester 1994), p.126.

23. ibid.

24. A number of passengers died on this journey and there was a coroner's inquest which reveals many incidental details on travel in steerage in the period. See *Wellington Independent* of 1 April 1857, p.2. These details kindly supplied by L.J. Dangerfield who had an ancestor on board.

25. ATL MS ADA.

26. Fauchery subsequently published his experiences as *Letters from a Miner in Australia* (1857), translated and published in Melbourne, 1865. This is from p.9.

27. ATL MS Paper 1192.

28. ATL MS ADA.

29. Personal communication from a descendant of another passenger who has investigated the circumstances of this voyage (see note 24 above).

30. The complete schedule is set out in John Ward, *Information Relative to New Zealand Compiled for the Use of Colonists* (London 1840), p.162. Ward was secretary to the Company.

31. Alexander Majoribanks, *Travels in New Zealand* (Edinburgh 1845), p.14.

32. Helen Simpson quotes this in the centennial history, *The Women of New Zealand* (Wellington 1940), p.38, which in its turn is cited by M. Turnbull and I. McLaren, *The Land of New Zealand* (Aberdeen 1964), p.51.

33. ATL MS ADA.

34. Alfred Fell, *Journal of a Voyage from London to New Zealand*, p.31. This journal was kept on the way to Nelson in 1841, but was not published until 1926.

35. C. Warren Adams, *A Spring in the Canterbury Settlement* (London 1853), p.10.

36. ATL MA Papers 1353.

37. There are many available explorations and explications of this. See, for example, C. Shaw and M. Chase (eds), *The Imagined Past, History and Nostalgia* (Manchester 1989); I. Dyck, *William Cobbett and Rural Popular Culture* (Cambridge 1992); D. Thompson, *The Chartists* (London 1984); G. Stedman Jones, *Languages of Class* (Cambridge 1983); P. Joyce, *Visions of the People* (Cambridge 1991).

38. See Thompson, ibid., pp.299–306.

39. Edmund Wilson has quite a lot to say about this in his classic *To the Finland Station* (London 1940).

40. Arnold, op. cit., and M. Fairburn, *The Ideal Society and its Enemies* (Auckland 1989). See also T. Brooking, 'Use it or Lose it: Unravelling the Land Debate in Late Nineteenth-century New Zealand', *NZJH* Vol.30 No.2, from p.141.

41. This and following citations from Fairburn, op. cit., p.42.

42. *AJHR* 1890 B-15.

43. op. cit., p.100.

44. 'Return of Expenditure by Working Men', from the Official Census 1891.

45. For a study of this market, see John E. Martin, 'Unemployment, Government and the Labour Market in New Zealand 1860–1890', *NZJH* Vol.29 No.2, from p.170.

46. See my *The Sugarbag Years* (Wellington 1974).

47. From his *New Zealand Journal*, cited by Leach, op. cit., p.118.

48. By Winsome Shepherd for the Colonial Cottage Society.

49. E.J. Wakefield, *Adventure in New Zealand* (1845, reprinted Auckland 1975).

50. Charlotte Godley, *Letters from Early New Zealand* (Christchurch 1951), p.19.

51. A. and L.R. Drummond, *At Home in New Zealand* (Auckland 1967), p.33.

52. ibid., p.58.

53. Lady Barker, *Station Life in New Zealand* (London 1883; facsimile edition Auckland, c.1972), p.108.

54. F. Porter and C. Macdonald, *My Hand Will Write What My Heart Dictates* (Auckland 1996), p.165.

55. Arnold, op. cit., p.60.

56. ibid., p.154.

57. ibid., p.155.

58. ibid.

59. *Labourers' Union Chronicle* 26 June 1875. Many of the farm labourers who wrote of their experiences had these letters published in their union journals as an encouragement to others to follow their lead.
60. Arnold, op. cit., p.63.
61. ibid.
62. 'Hopeful', *Taken In, A Sketch of New Zealand Life* (London 1887), p.110.
63. Personal communication with the author.

CHAPTER FOUR
1. Alfred Saunders, *Tales of a Pioneer* (Christchurch 1927), p.31.
2. F. Hunt, *Twenty-five Years' Experience in New Zealand* (Wellington 1866), p.9.
3. James Belich, *Making Peoples: A History of the New Zealanders* (Auckland 1996), chapter 2, pp.37–66.
4. Where in eastern Polynesia, and when, remains conjectural. A point of entry to the debate is contained in D.G. Sutton, *The Origins of the First New Zealanders* (Auckland 1994).
5. The food habits of the Lapita and successor cultures are detailed in Helen Leach, *1000 Years of Gardening in New Zealand* (Wellington 1984), chapter 2, and in J. Davidson, *The Prehistory of New Zealand* (Auckland 1984).
6. J.C. Beaglehole (ed), *The Journals of Captain James Cook* (Cambridge 1968), p.583.
7. There is a list of the edible properties of these in David Burton, *Two Hundred Years of New Zealand Food and Cookery* (Wellington 1982), pp.4–12.
8. Belich, op. cit., p.68, citing Leach and others.
9. Davidson, op. cit., p.147.
10. Cited by J. Druett, *Exotic Intruders: The Introduction of Plants and Animals into New Zealand* (Auckland 1983), p.12.
11. G.F. Angas, *Savage Life and Scenes in Australia and New Zealand* (London 1847).
12. Journal entry for 21 November 1773.
13. Edward Markham, *New Zealand or Recollections of It* (ed E.H. McCormick, Wellington 1962), p.48.
14. G. Bayley, *Sea-life Sixty Years Ago* (London 1885), p.127, in H.M. Wright, *New Zealand 1769–1840* (Harvard 1959), p.76.
15. Angas, op. cit. Vol.2, p.28.
16. From Ormond Wilson, *From Hongi Hika to Hone Heke* (Dunedin 1985), p.114.
17. John Gorst, *The Maori King* (London 1864, reprinted Auckland 1959).
18. Markham, op. cit., p.49.
19. J. Polack, *New Zealand Being a Narrative of Travels and Adventures* Vol.1 (London 1838, reprinted 1974), p.229.
20. ibid. Vol.1, p.49.
21. Raymond Firth, *The Economics of the New Zealand Maori* (Wellington 1959), p.309.
22. G.B. Earp, *Handbook for Intending Emigrants to the Southern Settlements of New Zealand* (London 1849).
23. Eliza Stack (née Jones) kept a remarkable diary between 1857 and 1860. This was subsequently published as part of one of three books under her husband's name, *Further Maoriland Adventures* (Wellington 1938). See p.203.
24. From his Auckland Journal, quoted by A. and L.R. Drummond in *At Home in New Zealand* (Auckland 1967), p.52.
25. William Shakespeare alludes to this practice in *The Merry Wives of Windsor*.
26. Cited by N. Taylor, *Early Travellers in New Zealand* (Wellington 1959), p.265.
27. Samuel Butler, *A First Year in Canterbury Settlement* (London 1863).
28. Druett, op. cit., p.45.
29. *New Zealand Official Yearbook* 1893.
30. Cited by Druett, op. cit., p.11.
31. Both these quotes from ibid., pp.68 and 70.
32. Lady Barker, *Station Life in New Zealand* (London 1883; facsimile edition Auckland

c.1872), p.147.

33. In *Following the Equator* (New York 1897) and quoted by D. Stone in *Verdict on New Zealand* (Wellington 1959), p.61.

34. Druett, op. cit., pp.128–49.

35. 'Hopeful', *Taken In, A Sketch of New Zealand Life* (London 1887), p.113.

36. Stack, op. cit., p.86.

37. Lady Barker, *Station Amusements in New Zealand* (London 1873), p.45.

38. It must have been early on. My father recalled them as a child before the First World War, and they were a feature of the landscape long before then, as my grandmother (born in Central Otago in 1876) was wont to remark.

39. Stack, op. cit., p.140.

40. Adela Stewart, *My Simple Life in New Zealand* (London 1908), p.56.

41. For the background to Davidson and his activities, see M. Palmer, 'William Soltau Davidson, a Pioneer of New Zealand Estate Management' in *NZJH* Vol.7 No.2, October 1973.

42. See R.C.J. Stone, *Makers of Fortune* (Auckland 1973).

43. These figures from *New Zealand Official Yearbooks* cited by M.F. Lloyd Pritchard in *An Economic History of New Zealand* (Auckland 1970), p.204 and Appendix table 14.

CHAPTER FIVE

1. Seigfried Geidion in *Mechanisation Takes Command* (New York 1969), p.527.

2. For a description of the reflecting oven (and a modern photograph of its use), see C. Fennelly (ed), *Food, Drink and Recipes of Early New England* (Old Sturbridge, Mass. 1963), p.11.

3. Caroline Davidson, 'Historic Kitchen Restoration: The Example of Ham House' in *Petits Propos Culinaires* No.12, November 1982.

4. ibid.

5. Elizabeth Ray (ed), *The Best of Eliza Acton* (Harmondsworth 1974), p.102.

6. ibid., p.100.

7. Hannah Glasse, *The Art of Cookery Made Plain and Easy* (London 1847). This book has been almost continuously in print since, most recently in a handsome 1983 facsimile edition from Prospect Books, London.

8. E.J. Wakefield, *Adventure in New Zealand* (1845, reprinted Auckland 1975), p.140.

9. op. cit., p.395.

10. This was subsequently corrupted to 'girdle' scones, a curious and meaningless expression. The iron griddle was much more common in eighteenth-century America than in New Zealand. See Jane Carson, *Colonial Virginia Cookery* (Williamsburg 1985), p.86, for some discussion of this and some contemporary recipes.

11. M. Symons, *One Continuous Picnic: A History of Eating in Australia* (Melbourne 1984), p.63.

12. Eileen Soper, *The Otago of Our Mothers* (Dunedin 1948), p.45.

13. May Brown (McDermott), *Early Days on the Northern Wairoa River*, unpublished reminiscence, ATL MS papers 2517.

14. Soper, op. cit.

15. The writer can attest to this. Between 1969 and 1972 he lived in an old Wellington house with a coal range which doubled as water heater. From cold, and using the right coal and combination of chimney dampers, it was possible to use the stove to heat sufficient water for a deep bath within half an hour.

16. For the role of Shacklock in the Dunedin industrial scene of the times, see E. Olssen, *Building the New World: Work, Politics and Society in Caversham 1880s–1920s* (Auckland 1995), pp.62–65.

17. J. Botero, 'The Most Ancient Recipes of All' in J. Wilkins, D. Harvey and M. Dobson (eds), *Food in Antiquity* (Exeter 1995), p.248.

18. There are many editions of Apicius. One of particular interest is that published in

London in 1984 as *The Roman Cookery of Apicius*, with an introduction by John Edwards and many of the recipes are adapted for the modern palate and available ingredients.

19. See Andrew Dalby, *Siren Feast* (London 1996), from p.160.

20. Lady Barker, *Station Amusements in New Zealand* (London 1847), p.193.

21. J. Burnett, *Plenty and Want* (London 1979), p.185.

22. There was a lush undergrowth of these tracts during the period. For the background, see Muriel Jaegar, *Before Victoria* (London 1956).

23. A whole tract on this subject with recipes, *The Cottage Cook or Mrs Jones's Cheap Dishes*, was published in its entirety in *Petits Propos Culinaires* No. 12, November 1982.

24. For the detail on the early science of nutrition, see S. Freeman, *Mutton and Oysters: The Victorians and their Food* (London 1989), chapter 11.

25. I. Dyck, *William Cobbett and Rural Popular Culture* (Cambridge 1992), pp.107–24.

26. To track this line, see C. Shaw and M. Chase (eds), *The Imagined Past: History and Nostalgia* (Manchester 1989).

27. For this and other detail, see Freeman, op. cit., pp.169–76.

28. For an account of this episode, see C. Hibbert, *The Destruction of Lord Raglan* (London 1963), p.308. Soyer wrote his own account of the business, *Soyer's Culinary Campaign* (1857).

29. Editions and edited extracts continue to appear. The most recent seems to be Elspeth Davies (ed), *Dr Kitchener and the Cook's Oracle* (Durham 1992).

30. Joyce Toomre, 'Soyer's Soups' in *Petits Propos Culinaires* No.13, March 1983.

31. There were dozens of these helpful works. The only one still generally available, and that as an antiquarian curiosity, is *Brett's Colonists' Guide and Cyclopaedia of Useful Knowledge*, originally published in Auckland in 1883, and republished as a facsimile edition by the Capper Press in 1980.

32. Acton's cookery book remained continuously in print until 1914, long after her death in 1859, and there have been numerous reprints since. References here are to a cheap edition edited by Elizabeth Ray and published in 1968 with an introduction by Elizabeth David.

33. Many of the subsequent editions (including that of 1906, regarded as the definitive) bear virtually no relationship to the first. A large number of the works published in her name have no connection with her books at all, or are so loosely based upon them as to constitute entirely new works. 'Mrs Beeton' has become a generic token for Victorian household management in all its manifestations. In this book the edition used is *The Concise Mrs Beeton's Book of Cookery*, which is actually a book of the recipes which appeared in the edition of 1861, but updated and revised for current tastes.

34. For a detailed account of these traditional techniques in use, see D. Hartley, *Food in England* (London 1954), pp.319–47, and Carson op. cit., from p.113.

35. A. Riddervold, 'Gravlaks, the Buried Salmon: The Old Tradition of Burying Fish in the Ground for Preparation and Preservation in Circumpolar Areas', in *Proceedings of the Oxford Symposium on Food and Cookery 1984 and 1985*. See also W.W. Weaver, 'When Shad Comes In: Shad Cookery in Old Philadelphia', in *Petits Propos Culinaires* No.11, June 1982.

36. C.A. Wilson, *Food and Drink in Britain* (London 1973), p.315.

37. See J.C. Drummond and A. Wilbraham, *The Englishman's Food* (London 1991), pp.317–22.

38. ibid., p.318.

39. Quoted unsourced, ibid., p.322.

40. J. Gimpel, *The Medieval Machine* (London 1976).

41. For a fascinating glimpse of the Assize of Bread at work, see M.P. Cosman, *Fabulous Feasts: Medieval Cookery and Ceremony* (New York 1976), pp.67–73.

42. For the detail of this and of the transformation of bread production, see Geidion, op. cit., pp.188–98.

43. These are set out in C. Petersen, *Bread and the British Economy 1770–1870* (Aldershot 1995), p.53.

44. For some idea of the scope and range of ready-made food items available, see M. Black, *Food and Cooking in Nineteenth Century Britain* (London 1985), pp.8–10, and Freeman, op. cit., pp.11–29.

45. It is set out in detail in Drummond and Wilbraham, op. cit., pp.288–312, and in Burnett, op. cit., pp.99–122. This summary is based on J.M. Strang, 'Caveat Emptor: Food Adulteration in Nineteenth Century England' in *The Oxford Symposium on Food and Cookery 1986*, pp.129–33.

46. Her warning is quoted in D. and R. Mabey, *Jams, Pickles and Chutneys* (London 1975), p.58.

47. A.A. Hassall, *Narrative of a Busy Life* (London 1893), p.47.

48. The doctrine of humours and its application to food has its own large literature. It is fairly comprehensively summarised in J.T. Benham, 'Is that Hippocrates in the Kitchen?' in *The Oxford Symposium for 1984 and 1985*.

49. For the detail of how this growing body of nutritional knowledge developed, see Freeman, op. cit., chapter 11.

50. Burnett, op. cit., p.186.

51. Symons, op. cit., p.65.

CHAPTER SIX

1. From *A Year in Space* (London 1953), and quoted by Desmond Stone in *Verdict on New Zealand* (Wellington 1959), p.218.

2. British Census of Population 1891.

3. Eliza White, writing her *Journal* at the Mangungu Mission Station on the Hokianga on 20 February 1832, quoted by F. Porter and C. Macdonald, *My Hand Shall Write What My Heart Dictates* (Auckland 1996), p.77.

4. See, for example, M. Chaytor, 'Household and Kinship: Ryton in the Late 16th and Early 17th Centuries' and K. Wrightson, 'Household and Kinship in Sixteenth Century England' in respectively *History Workshop Journal* No.10, Autumn 1980, and No.12, Autumn 1981.

5. M.P. Cosman, *Fabulous Feasts* (New York 1976), pp.26–31.

6. See, for example, Elizabeth Longford, *Your Most Obedient Servant* (London 1985), an account of the activities of James Thornton, cook to the Duke of Wellington.

7. These figures are cited in C. Davidson, *A Woman's Work is Never Done, A History of Housework in the British Isles 1650–1950* (London 1982), chapter 8.

8. In *Lark Rise to Candleford* (Oxford 1939), Martha, the sister of the narrator, Flora Thompson, goes into service, and there is considerable detail of what this involved at pp.155–72.

9. Davidson, op. cit., p.181.

10. See K. Schlegel, 'Mistress and Servant in Nineteenth Century Hamburg', and D. A. Kent, 'Ubiquitous but Invisible: Female Domestic Servants Mid-Eighteenth Century London' in *History Workshop Journal* No.15, Spring 1983, and No.28, Autumn 1989.

11. This figure cited by C. Macdonald in *A Woman of Good Character* (Wellington 1990), p.26.

12. Porter and Macdonald, op. cit., p.159.

13. ATL qMS–0369.

14. Lady Barker, *Station Life in New Zealand* (London 1883, facsimile edition Auckland c.1972), pp.42 and 71.

15. Cited by Porter and Macdonald, op. cit., p.160.

16. ATL MS Papers 1279.

17. Anthony Trollope, *Australia and New Zealand* (London 1873), cited in D. Stone (ed), *Verdict on New Zealand* (Wellington 1959), p.46.

18. Stevan Eldred-Grigg, *A Southern Gentry* (Wellington 1980), p.89.

19. These figures are given in M.F. Lloyd Pritchard, *An Economic History of New Zealand* (London 1970), p.100.
20. *New Zealand Official Yearbook* 1899, p.308.
21. C.L. Money, *Knocking About in New Zealand* (Melbourne 1871), pp.58–59.
22. E.J. Wakefield, *Adventure in New Zealand* (1845, reprinted Auckland 1975), p.140.
23. C.W. Adams, *A Spring in the Canterbury Settlement* (London 1853), p.46.
24. Lady Barker, *Station Amusements in New Zealand* (London 1873), p.170.
25. Mrs Robert Wilson, *In the Land of the Tui* (London 1894), p.249.
26. Adela Stewart, *My Simple Life in New Zealand* (London 1908), p.133.
27. Cited by Porter and Macdonald, op. cit., p.184.
28. Mary Hobhouse kept a fascinating diary between 1859 and 1866, passages of which have been variously reproduced, in this case in A. Drummond and L.R. Drummond, *At Home in New Zealand* (Auckland 1967), p.159.
29. Stewart, op. cit., p.57.
30. Barker, op. cit., 1883, p.99.
31. From Porter and Macdonald, op. cit., p.184.
32. E. Stack (née Jones), *Further Maoriland Adventures* (Wellington 1938), p.114.
33. Barker, op. cit., 1883, p.103.
34. Quoted by Drummond and Drummond, op. cit., p.141.
35. P.R. May, *The West Coast Gold Rushes* (Christchurch 1962), p.311.
36. Stewart, op. cit., p.65.
37. Op. cit., p.573.
38. Julie Park (ed), *Ladies a Plate* (Auckland 1991), from the chapter 'Women and Food'.
39. ibid., p.145.
40. Adams, op. cit., p.74.
41. Porter and Macdonald, op. cit., p.157.
42. Drummond and Drummond, op. cit., p.155.
43. Porter and Macdonald, op. cit., p.171.
44. ibid., p.176.
45. ibid., p.181.
46. *Letters from Early New Zealand* (Christchurch 1951), p.309.
47. L.E. Ward, *Early Wellington* (reprinted Christchurch 1975), p.159.
48. ATL Ephemera A Dining 1860s.
49. The menu for this sumptuous repast is to be found in the W. Light Collection, ATL MS papers 1362. A Nesselrode pudding was a common ice-cream dessert in the nineteenth century. It involves an egg custard into which is beaten chestnut puree, raisins, sultanas, chopped peel and Madeira. This is then frozen for serving.
50. Also from the W. Light Collection, ATL.
51. Eldred-Grigg, op. cit., p.93. His contrast with the poor fare of shepherds seems a little overdrawn. The latter ate quite well, if not as genteelly.
52. R. Galbreath, *Walter Buller: The Reluctant Conservationist* (Wellington 1989), p.206.
53. ATL Ephemera A Dining 1883.
54. H. Roth, *George Hogben: A Biography* (Wellington 1952), p.134.
55. For a much fuller account, see G.E. Thompson, *A History of the University of Otago 1869–1919* (Dunedin 1919).
56. ibid., p.247.

CHAPTER SEVEN

1. A. Bell, *Sydney Smith* (Oxford 1980), p.149.
2. J. Burnett, *Plenty and Want* (London 1979), p.246.
3. E.S. Turner, *Roads to Ruin* (London 1966), p.206.
4. Burnett, op. cit., p.247.
5. R. Trench and E. Hillman, *London Under London* (London 1993), p.88.
6. C.A. Wilson, *Food and Drink in England* (London 1973), p.357. For a fuller history

of rum, see H.W. Allen, *Rum, The Englishman's Spirit* (London 1931).

7. This curious circular trade is described in S.E. Morrison, *The Maritime History of Massachusetts* (Boston 1979), pp.8–26.

8. R.G. Albion, W.A. Baker and B.W. Laboree, *New England and the Sea* (Connecticut 1972), p.109.

9. For the background to this, see D.C. North, *The Economic Growth of the United States 1790–1860* (New York 1961).

10. See G. Carson, *Rum and Reform in Old New England* (Sturbridge 1966).

11. R. Hughes, *The Fatal Shore* (London 1987), from p.110 has much of interest on this subject.

12. ibid., p.290.

13. Cited by A.G.L. Shaw in *Convicts and Colonies* (London 1971), p.72.

14. R. McNab, *The Old Whaling Days* (reprinted Auckland 1975), p.98.

15. N. Colquhon (ed), *Song of a Young Country* (Wellington 1972), p.10.

16. Edward Markham, *New Zealand or Recollections of It* (ed E.H. McCormick Wellington 1962), p.40.

17. W. Colenso, *The Authentic and Genuine History of the Signing of the Treaty of Waitangi* (Wellington 1890), p.20.

18. From his *Philosopher Dick* (London 1891). This and the following passage cited by J.O.C. Phillips in *A Man's Country?* (Auckland 1987), p.56. Phillips has much of interest to say on the widespread habit of social drinking.

19. Kennedy's *Colonial Travel* (Edinburgh 1876), p.195.

20. Cited by D. Stone, *Verdict on New Zealand* (Wellington 1959), p.35.

21. Brad Patterson, 'Early Colonial Society Through a Prism: Reflections on Wellington's First Anniversary Day', Wellington Historical and Early Settlers' Association annual lecture, April 1994.

22. Nancy Taylor (ed), *The Journal of Ensign Best 1837–1843* (Wellington 1966), p.275.

23. Charles Mundy, quoted by John Miller in *Early Victorian New Zealand* (Wellington 1974), p.167.

24. Cited by R. Stone in 'Auckland Party Politics in the Early Years of the Provincial system 1853–1858', *NZJH* Vol.14 No.2 (1980), p.160.

25. The matter is set out in some detail, including a transcript of the evidence, in *AJHR* 1876 1–2.

26. C. Macdonald, 'Crime and Punishment in New Zealand 1840–1913: A Gendered History', *NZJH* Vol.23 No.1, April 1989, pp5–21.

27. From the *AJHR* reports for that year.

28. P.R. May, *The West Coast Gold Rushes* (Christchurch 1967), p.289.

29. E. Stack, *Further Adventures in Maoriland* (Wellington 1938), p.133.

30. Quoted without attribution in S. Eldred-Grigg, *A Southern Gentry* (Wellington 1980), p.45.

31. *Taken In, A Sketch of New Zealand Life* (London 1887), p.161.

32. These figures are given unsourced by S. Eldred-Grigg in *Pleasures of the Flesh* (Wellington 1984), p.210, and are also available in the *New Zealand Official Yearbook* 1899, p.173.

33. Eldred-Grigg, op. cit. 1984, p.77.

34. Included in Harvey McQueen (ed), *The New Place, The Poetry of Settlement in New Zealand 1852–1914* (Wellington 1993), p.23.

35. The most entertaining account of the rake's progress of our licensing laws remains Conrad Bollinger's *Grog's Own Country* (Auckland 1959, reprinted 1967).

36. All of these figures from the *New Zealand Official Yearbooks*.

37. Adela Stewart, *My Simple Life in New Zealand* (London 1908), p.85.

38. J. Druett, *Exotic Intruders: The Introduction of Plants and Animals into New Zealand* (Auckland 1983), p.42.

39. M.R. Lloyd Pritchard, *An Economic History of New Zealand* (Auckland 1970), p.60.

40. See R. Bailey and H. Roth, *Shanties by the Way* (Christchurch 1967), p.14.

41. For a background to the nineteenth-century international tea trade, see H.

Hobhouse, *Seeds of Change* (London 1985), pp.95–140.

42. For the background to this, see C.A. Wilson, *Food and Drink in England* (London 1973), p.367.

43. From J.B. Botsford, *English Society in the Eighteenth Century as Influenced from Overseas* (London 1924), p.66.

44. J. Beresford (ed), *James Woodforde: The Diary of a Country Parson 1758–1802* (reprinted London 1997).

45. For a variety of these dietaries covering both urban and rural workers throughout the century, see J. Burnett, *Plenty and Want* (London 1979), pp.44, 62, 65, 194 and 210.

46. I. Dyck, *William Cobbett and Rural Popular Culture* (Cambridge 1992), p.120.

47. For much incidental information on tea and its adulteration, see J. Drummond and A. Wilbraham, *The Englishman's Food* (London 1991), pp.204–05 and 329.

48. Lady Barker, *Station Amusements in New Zealand* (London 1873), p.21.

49. Cited by Eldred-Grigg, op. cit.1984, p.228. Unfortunately, he does not give his source.

50. For the detail of the use of caffeine in New Zealand, see Eldred-Grigg, op. cit. 1984, pp.228–34.

51. A. Drummond and L.R. Drummond, *At Home in New Zealand* (Auckland 1967), p.59.

CONCLUSION

1. The sorts of people they are has been very adequately explored by John Vidal in *McLibel, Burger Culture on Trial* (London 1997).

2. Avner Offer, *The First World War: An Agrarian Interpretation* (Oxford 1989).

3. For a critique of the activities of the Codex, see T. Lang and C. Hines, *The New Protectionism: Protecting the Future Against Free Trade* (London 1993), pp.100–03.

INDEX OF RECIPES

INDEX